THE CLASSICS OF WESTERN SPIRITUALITY
A Library of the Great Spiritual Masters

Teresa of Avila
THE INTERIOR CASTLE

TRANSLATION
BY
KIERAN KAVANAUGH, O.C.D.
and OTILIO RODRIGUEZ, O.C.D.

INTRODUCTION
BY
KIERAN KAVANAUGH, O.C.D.

PREFACE
BY
RAIMUNDO PANIKKAR

PAULIST PRESS
NEW YORK • RAMSEY • TORONTO

Cover Art
The artist CAROLE KOWALCHUK ODELL studied at the Ontario College of Art in Toronto, Canada from 1966 to 1971 and has since been working as an illustrator in the United States and Canada. She is presently living and working in New York City. Of her cover art she says, "I wanted to illustrate as simply as possible the feeling of transcendence that St. Teresa was able to achieve in her meditation."

Design: Barbini Pesce & Noble, Inc.

Library of Congress
Catalog Card Number: 79-66484

ISBN: 0-8091-0303-6 (cloth)
0-8091-2254-5 (paper)

Published by Paulist Press
Editorial office: 1865 Broadway, New York, N. Y. 10023
Business office: 545 Island Road, Ramsey, N. J. 07446

Printed and bound in the
United States of America

CONTENTS

The Author of the Preface

RAIMUNDO PANIKKAR a Roman Catholic priest, was born in Spain 60 years ago. He is presently Professor of Comparative Philosophy of Religion and History of Religions at the University of California, Santa Barbara. He holds three doctoral degrees. From the University of Madrid he received his degrees in Chemical Science and Philosophy and from the Lateran University his degree in Theology. A past winner of the Spanish National Prize for Literature for his book *La India: Gente. Cultura. Creencias*, he has been guest lecturer at more than ninety universities around the world. Dr. Panikkar has authored more than twenty-five books in many languages including *The Unknown Christ of Hinduism, Worship and Secular Man, The Trinity and the Religious Experience of Man, The Vedic Experience, The Intra-Religious Dialogue* and *Myth, Faith and Hermeneutics*.

The Editors of this Volume

KIERAN KAVANAUGH, O. C. D. was born in Milwaukee, Wisconsin in 1928. A priest of the Discalced Carmelite Order, he is presently prior of the Carmelite Monastery in Brookline, Massachusetts. Father Kavanaugh is past President of The Institute of Carmelite Studies and the co-translator with Father Otilio Rodriguez, O. C. D. of *The Collected Works of St. John of the Cross*, and *The Collected Works of St. Teresa of Avila*. His articles have appeared in many publications including *Spiritual Life*, *The New Catholic Encyclopedia*, and *The Catholic Historical Review*.

OTILIO RODRIGUEZ, O. C. D. was born in Mantinos Palencia, Spain in 1910. Also a priest of the Discalced Carmelites he lives and works at the Carmelite Historical Institute in Rome, Italy.

Acknowledgments

We are happy to acknowledge our indebtedness to all those who have urged us on in the preparation of this work. The Institute of Carmelite Studies has given us support and provided us with necessary materials otherwise unobtainable in libraries in the United States. A special expression of gratitude must go to Fr. Tomás Alvarez for his Spanish edition of the complete works of St. Teresa. His punctuation of the text and many footnotes were an important help to us in working with difficult passages. Many of our own notes, with his kind consent, are based on or taken exactly from his edition. We are grateful as well to Fr. Adrian J. Cooney and Sr. Mary Elizabeth Stanton for their suggestions and assistance and to our typist Jean Mallon.

PREFACE

I. INTRODUCTION—WHAT IS HOLINESS?

In our anthropocentric (humanistic) times it is common to hear too much of an anthropomorphic concept of sanctity, considered as the summit of human perfection. A person is said to be a saint, in this humanistic climate, when he is perfect. That is not altogether wrong, but depends on the meaning we give to the concept of "human perfection". Beauty, for instance, is undoubtedly a human perfection, but does it strictly belong to sanctity? Perfection means fullness, completion, and a being is perfect when it does not lack anything that is due to it, (when it has no holes). If that being is composite it is required further that all its parts are blended in a harmonic unity (so that again it has no gaps). But what is the *human* being, so that we may know its perfection? When does a person reach his fullness? Is there or can there be real sanctity here on earth?

To follow these philosophical *ascending* considerations we would come to the conclusion that only God is perfect and that consequently holiness is His exclusive attribute, so far as we can speak of attributes in the Godhead. We could, further, from here develop some theological—*descending* reflexions, of some importance for our subject.

Only God is holy. Strictly speaking only God is good and beautiful and true, and even only He *is*, only He is being. Nevertheless, there is a participation, an analogy, a communication of all this in the creatures. Our human being—for example—only "is" and, in consequence, only is good and beautiful and true insofar as it participates and receives all this from God.

But there is something peculiar with sanctity. Every being by the very fact that it "is", is good and beautiful and true, but is not holy. It may be sacred, each existence being a participation in God, but as such it is not holy.

What is, then, sanctity? It is God Himself, it is His very Life, His Existence, the proper Structure of His Being, if we may speak so. God bestows and communicates along with being all the constitutive attributes of being to the creatures. But He does not communicate Sanctity, because it cannot properly be created or given along with being, for it is the very Essence of God Himself.

And yet, there are saints on earth, because the Almighty can still do one thing, namely, communicate and give Himself. He can descend and dwell in the person of the saint. He can simply take possession of His creatures in a personal and intimate way. Here lies the role of Christ as an ontic Mediator between God and Creation.

So, sanctity is on the one hand an absolute perfection, viz. God, and on the other hand it is the Life of this very God in some of His creatures. It is not, in consequence, primarily a moral concept, but an ontological reality; the divine reality communicating His intimate and proper Life to some of His children. The saint is thus not primarily the *humanly* perfect Man, but the divinised human person. Of course, that divinisation implies a very peculiar transformation of the saint and an ontological—and in consequence also moral—purity, but it does not require a *humanistic* perfect man.

The saint—"santus"—is, thus, the man God has taken specially for Himself, the man He has "reserved" and "segregated". God calls everybody to be divinely perfect, i.e., holy. Each person receives his personal vocation to sanctity. But only the saint answers fully to that divine call and freely accepts, wills, loves to be this living Temple of the Holy. Each saint is, in consequence, a kind of Revelation of God, he has a message to deliver, though not always with words, he is an instrument of the Divine, he is the Man (and Woman) in whom God, who is Love, finds not only His resting but also His acting place. True sanctity is not so much God-realisation on Man's part, as Man-realisation on God's part. The saint is the ontological full human personality in spite of our rational concepts about human perfection, and notwithstanding the *objective* shortcomings in his pilgrimage towards God. We cannot forget that sanctity is a concept-limit, only attainable here on earth as far as the everlasting life of Union has already shattered all human limitations.

II. Teresa of Avila

Some saints reflect the perfections of God by their hidden and silent lives; some others are leaders, some are heroes of sacrifice and some victims of love; some have a rather weak human nature and some are real *genii* if we look at them from a human point of view. Sanctity is as manifold as Man and his nature.

There is, however, not a little difficulty in classifying Teresa of Avila. If we class her as contemplative because she reached the highest degree of fruition of God and union with Him, we forget that she led an extremely active life. If we rank her among the teachers, we overlook the fact that she was also a reformer in the active field as well as a poet.

1. *The example of her life.*

It is almost a foolish presumption to attempt to summarise the spiritual climate, the political problems and the cultural crisis of that turning-point in European history which took place in Spain during the 16th Century.* The destiny of the world, not simply in a political sense or in a superficially cultural interpretation, but in an ontologically real and spiritual meaning, was, shall we say, not precisely in the hands, but in the life, hearts and minds of a relatively small number of persons, inhabiting one of the most peculiar corners of Europe. There was taking place at the time not only the birth of "modern" Europe, or the end of the "medieval" age, but also the big conflict and one of the few and most decisive encounters among cultures, worlds, religions. The seeds were sown and the problems of a world-culture began to be dealt with in a very conscious and serious way.

---

*Cf. the masterly chapter by Friedrich Heer, *Europaische Geiteschichte*, Stuttgart (W. Kohlhammer) 1953. pp. 280-331.

about the relation of Men to God and with the Universe, the relation of Christianity and the Christian culture with other religions and cultures, not simply under a theological, but under a vital, existential point of view. Everything was in ferment and Spain was the battleground of such a historical moment, though, of course, not all the factors and ideas were Spanish.

During that time, Teresa de Cepeda y Ahumada (1515-1582) was born in Castilia, Central Spain.

Teresa was twenty-one when she entered religious life and became a Carmelite nun in Avila, her native town. The aim of the Carmelite Order is to enable its members to lead a life of contemplation through a long practice of prayer (in its highest sense), preceded by detachment and penance. And, of course, this centered on a loving and not merely speculative contemplation. Two years after she entered the Convent of the Incarnation (1538), she writes: "The Lord began to be so gracious to me on this way of prayer of Quiet, and occasionally even to the Union". Aware, as she was, of her interior life we may rely on her own terminology and affirm that she began a life of habitual and steady contemplation only 12 years afterwards. She followed this highest life of the spirit for 33 years. She was of an extreme sensitiveness and also of intense awareness in things spiritual; thus, this her second period may be divided into two different stages: cne of simple prayer of quiet, transcending all conceptual understanding and with partial consciousness of her union with God (12 years), and the other of habitual union with God in a life of identification of will (11 years) and of spiritual marriage (10 years).

It was in her fortieth year, having attained habitual union with God, that she realised her apostolic mission of raising the spiritual climate and observance of her Order, and instead of enjoying, relishing her own spiritual perfection she started the colossal adventure of reforming the Carmel with no other means than her great love and confidence in God. She had to overcome all sorts of difficulties and misunderstandings from all sides. In spite of her continuous ill health, and without losing the intensity of her contemplative life and habitual union with God, she undertook the most astonishing active life of founding convents of "discalced" Carmelites all over Spain.

Perhaps one of the most striking features was her thoroughness, her wholeness. Her holiness brought her to such close union with God as a person can have in this world and such union really divinised her being. All the same she remained a full human personality with a sense for all little human business on earth, even with a very exquisite sense of humour. Her union with God did not separate her from her fellowmen and she remained throughout a woman with all the complexity of a feminine soul. The secret of her positive attitude towards life and nature was her christocentric spirituality. Her awareness of God and her God-like life was due of her discovery and experience of God *in* and *through* Christ, not excluding His Humanity. It is an essential feature of the Carmelite spirituality to consider Christ as the bridegroom of the soul and to find in that living union (spiritual marriage) the most perfect transformation into God, for we should bear in mind that Christ realises in Himself the highest unity of God and creature.

St. John of the Cross (1542-1591), like St. Teresa, also born in Castilia, Central Spain, entered the Order of the "calced" Carmelites friars at 21, and when 26 he met Teresa, who was already 53. Instead of passing over to the Carthusian Order to live a more austere life of penance and contemplation as he first intended to do, he joined St. Teresa in the noble work of reforming the Carmel among men, as Teresa had already begun among the women. For the realisation of that project he had to endure calumnies and persecution of the most cruel sort. Unlike Teresa he never became the juridical Founder, but he was the inspiring soul of Carmel. He was a well trained theologian (student of Alcala and Salamanca) and became one of the greatest mystics of all times. He wrote several books, all published after his death. He is also one of the best poets in the whole of Spanish literature.

2. The Mystical Doctrine

Only a mystic can teach a mystic doctrine, and this teaching is a vital communication. If they, by chance, should write something, that is only a substitute and a reminder. If we try to summarise again what they have written at length, and yet as shortly as possible, for they do not use superfluous words, we surely misrepresent their doctrine and only give a shadow of it. How can we dare suggest an outline of their message and point out aspects under which they tried to express the ineffable? We may however make an attempt to investigate the philosophical implications of their doctrine by pointing out their metaphysical structure.

The aim and end of human life is Union with God, it is the transformation of our being and its divinisation. But the creature of itself is no-thing, or, as our saint repeats constantly, a *nonada*, a not-nothingness, i.e. the creature is a pure negation of its "not-yet-being". It exists, because somehow it subsists outside nothingness—"extra nihilum" being suspended over the abyss of pure nothingness by the creative power of God. Thus, the creature, in order to reach God and be united with Him, must abandon and forsake its own way of being, i.e., its "not-yet-being", its negativity and negate its own *no*-thingness. Being cannot be destroyed. All that we annihilate is the inherent negative element of our temporal existence. In other words, this union with God is not simply one of mere knowledge, but an ontological incorporation, though our intellect is also a part of our being. It is not simply by "knowing" God that we shall be transformed into Him, but by being fully united with Him (and our being is something more than intellect.) It is by being one with Him, that we reach our ultimate destiny.

Now, strictly speaking, between the "creature" as such, and God as such, there is nothing in common. If the former has to be united with God, i.e., it has to be divinised, its character has to be stripped off. Not only can I not reach God, but my being cannot be united with Him as long as it remains "creature". Not because "nature" is bad, but because it is not of the order of the Divinity. But I have, of myself, nothing of this order; my nature does not possess anything homogeneous with God so that it could be utilised in my union with Him.

That leads us to the famous way of absolute nothingness of our mystic. I cannot trust my senses, nor my feelings, nor my intellect with *its* intuitions, nor my will, nor even my very being. I cannot rely upon any created thing. If I see God, if I feel Him, even if I love Him, so far as it is my love, *that* which I see, feel, love or experience is not Him, for He is beyond all *my* modes of apprehension and of possession.

I can be transformed and united with Him, I can be God, only if I leave absolutely everything that I feel, like, think and experience and even what I "imagine" to be, and it is He who takes possession of me and takes me and "remakes" me. And only thus is our real personality realised. This is the action of Grace within me. Here the importance of the creature is replaced by the absolute power of God. The naked way of pure faith is neither a blind belief, nor a desperate effort in saving myself, but it is the divine and gratuitous gift bestowed upon me which calls me and transforms me. I do not rely anymore upon myself, but on God alone.

"God has only spoken One Word which is His Son and He has spoken It in eternal silence," says St. John of the Cross, repeating a common statement of the Fathers of the Church. In order to be incorporated in Him we must enter into that Silence, not only reducing to stillness all voices, images and thoughts about everything and even about God Himself, but reducing our very being into an ontological silence. "In order to have the All you must leave the all," including ourselves.

The real, the royal path to God taught by this great contemplative is not that of mere contemplation of God as an object, is not the purified and high contemplative gaze on or experience of God; our gaze has to transcend all our powers and faculties and even our own being. In Christian terms it is the naked and supernatural way of pure faith as a participation of God's own knowledge and Light, as an introduction to the divine Life in us, which is supported, so to say, in us through His gifts of Faith, Hope and Charity. The progress of a spiritual person towards God is rather the progress of God in him or her. The ascent to the mountain on a person's part corresponds to the more real descent of God into his/her being.

Once, St. Teresa was amorously complaining to God in prayer about her sufferings and trials. She heard the Lord telling her: "Teresa, so do I treat My friends!" making her thereby understand the purificatory character of suffering. But Teresa, who knew it already, answered boldly: "That's why you have so few (friends)." Some have pointed out the difficulty and the impossibility of following the doctrine of our Carmelite saint, erroneously taken to be an inhuman self-denial. If we think in terms of human courage, it is true that the thorough spoilation of one's self exacted by her for the purpose of reaching the Simple One is above human strength, and so if such spoilation is undertaken out of a selfish spiritual greediness, it would be not only impossible but also antinatural. No human force can perform that work and walk along the path of absolute denial, by the very reason, that if there is no God sustaining us, even from below, nothing remains under our feet. It is quite true that no one by mere human force can climb up to the top of the mountain where God dwells. It is God and God alone who calls and gives the gifts and necessary graces to such an ascent.

3. The Sanctity of the Carmelite Saint

Manifold and wonderful is God in His saints. Some sparks of His perfection shine forth in these selected ones. Simplicity, love, obedience, spiritual power, personality, and so many other values are reflected in the lives of the saints. Which is the special feature of this mystic?

I would dare to say that her characteristic feature, which at the same time constitutes an urgent and important message for our times, is simply that of sanctity itself. And perhaps this is also the feature of the other great saint of the Carmel of our days, St. Thérèse of Lisieux, the Little Flower.

Obviously, by the very fact that one is a saint he or she reflects the sanctity of God, but the colour of the divine light may be the red colour of love, or the green of hope, or the violet of penance, or the infra-red of an unsophisticated surrender, or the ultra-violet of mysticism and so on.

In spite of her rich personality and the high mystical gifts with which she was endowed, she does not insist on or preach only contemplation and mysticism, she does not want everybody to deny the world, nor does she make self-denial her central doctrine. She simply preaches and lives a holy life: that is to say, sanctity, pure and unalloyed. The rest is ultimately irrelevant and all are means for the "only one thing necessary." Her writings were written under obedience. And yet her books are truly universal and the example of her life, in spite of the particular scope of her activities, constitutes a lesson for every religious soul.

What ultimately matters is not our ideas, or our experiences or our denying this or doing that; what "matters" is not a method of prayer or a peculiar way of life. The all-important thing, the unique and the ultimate end of man is sanctity, union with God, transformation in God, divinisation of our full being.

Throughout the whole of the 16th century Europe was suffering from a world crisis in all aspects. Everywhere problems and solutions were planned and enforced in the horizontal line. The answer of the Carmelite nun has only a single tune: sanctity. But not a sanctity of the nature of a selfish self-reform, not an individualistic saintliness in order to arrange the world and solve its problems, or to save oneself, i.e., as means for something else, or as first condition, but a true sanctity as an end in itself, because the ontological weight of a divinised person is greater than anything else, because the meaning of life on earth—this "bad night in a bad inn"—is not to organise heaven on earth, but to move earth into heaven. And yet, as a consequence, as something that comes from itself, it is the only real approach to the world. According to its deep nature, will life on earth be truly human and happy and beautiful. "Is it not somehow amazing that a poor nun of St. Joseph's Cloister can reign over the whole earth and elements?"* It is the least world-denying attitude imaginable, because it sees the whole creation as an outburst of divine Love. Only then will humankind be the king of creation and transform everything into the real everlasting Kingdom, which is much more than a mere temporal world.

The reason is clear: I am not more mine, but it is God that is in me and I in Him. That is the Christian mystery of Christ!

*St. Teresa, *Life*, VI, 104.

INTRODUCTION

The Second Vatican Council pointed out that by penetrating the revealed message the Christian mystics enrich our comprehension of it and thereby contribute to the Church's living tradition.[1] Among the mystics, Saint Teresa of Avila holds a unique position as a witness to divine realities. Her common sense, humor, and penchant for everyday images liven her writings; but she is above all remarkable for her analytical abilities in probing the mystery of God's workings in the soul. On September 27, 1970, Pope Paul VI proclaimed Teresa a Doctor of the Church. During the ceremony the pope spoke of her as a teacher of "marvelous profundity."[2]

TERESA'S LIFE

Teresa was born in Avila, Spain, on March 28, 1515, and lived at a time in which her country had become the greatest power on earth. Her deeply religious father, Don Alonso Sanchez de Cepeda, after the death of his first wife and with two children from that marriage, wed Doña Beatriz de Ahumada, who was only fifteen at the time. Doña Beatriz died at the age of thirty-three and left behind her ten children among whom was Teresa. Twelve years old when her mother died, Teresa, a couple of years later, was placed by her father in a school (under the charge of the Augustinian nuns) for girls from the nobility. As her father had hoped, Teresa benefitted by the pious Christian atmosphere of the school; but, as he had not expected, she began to feel the first attraction to the religious life. After reading the *Letters* of St. Jerome, she decided that she must follow the call to enter religion. But her father, strongly attached to this favorite daughter, was unwilling to allow her to leave. On November 2, 1535, she fled home and entered the Carmelite Monastery of the Incarnation in Avila itself. This separation from her father, although accomplished by stealth, did not come easily, and she later recalled that it felt like every bone in her body was being sundered.[3] Once the deed was done, Don Alonso acquiesced, and his daughter entered into her new life enthusiastically. She made her profession two years later. In autumn 1538 she became seriously ill, and when doctors were unable to determine the cause or find a remedy, she had to leave the cloister to undergo experimentation with some more drastic methods of cure used by a woman in the town of Becedas who had acquired a fame for them. The result was nearly death for Teresa. After being in a coma for three days, without any signs of life—indeed, believed to be dead—Teresa somehow revived. Yet she was left so paralyzed that three years later she was still unable to walk. Her acute sufferings remained in part for the rest of her life.

The events surrounding the saint's illness led to her reading Saint Gregory the Great's *Morals*, and through this classic Teresa discovered the riches of biblical thought and the drama of Job. She read, too, the Franciscan friar De Osuna's *Third Spiritual Alphabet*. This work became a guide for her life of prayer. Her initial efforts at mental prayer were favored with the first experiences of mystical prayer. After regaining a good measure of her health (she attributes her cure to Saint Joseph and recommends him as an advocate),[4] she passed through in the following years a tedious and long period of difficulty in her spiritual life and describes her prayer of that time as unpleasant: "I don't know what heavy penance could have come to mind that frequently I would not have gladly undertaken rather than recollect myself in the practice of prayer."[5] These struggles for some kind of recollection lasted until she was thirty-nine. Those years represent a time in which she was unable to integrate her relationships with the world and with God: "I was living an extremely burdensome life, because in prayer I understood more clearly my faults. On the one hand God was calling me; on the other hand I was following the world."[6] At one point in her pain over the whole situation she decided that the more humble thing to do would be to give up the practice of prayer. Although she gave it up for only a short time, she was forever lamenting that mistaken humility. She regarded this error as the worst of her life and recognized that it could have had dire consequences.[7]

On two occasions in 1554, the first by means of a statue and then through a spiritual book, she experienced a new conversion and the liberating power of Christ. At the sight of a statue of her Lord in His sufferings she was stirred deeply, and with many tears begged Him to strengthen her, at last coming to put her trust fully in Him. In the other instance, she was reading the *Confessions* of St. Augustine. When she read of how Augustine heard the voice calling him in the garden, it seemed that she was hearing the Lord from deep within calling her, and Teresa felt a new strength.[8] She was left renewed after these experiences. From this time on, she says, a new life began for her.

In this new life the experience of passive quiet, and often of union, became her habitual manner of prayer.[9] This supernatural prayer, as she calls it because of its passive character, drew her further into a labyrinth of extraordinary experiences difficult to understand and impossible for her to describe in a satisfactory way to those from whom she sought guidance. Since some of the spiritual directors she consulted refused to suppose that such graces could be received by someone with her weaknesses, they suspected the devil as the culprit.[10] Both the hardship Teresa met with in trying to make herself understood to her directors and confessors and their suspicions about what she was trying to describe afflicted her gravely but resulted in her preliminary attempts to explain her spiritual state on paper in what has become one of the classics of Christian spirituality, *The Book of Her Life*. This work was composed in its first form in 1562. As a result of her efforts to describe her experiences and receive the proper guidance, a group of people came to know Teresa and were fascinated by both her personality and her writings. Among these were theologians and teachers of spirituality, Dominicans, Jesuits, secular priests, lay men and women, and even the bishop of Avila.

After many extraordinary mystical experiences of rapture, locutions, and intellectual and imaginative visions, Teresa received her terrifying vision of hell,[11] the result of which was her determination to live the Carmelite rule with greater perfection, which in turn led to another mission: the founding of a new manner of contemplative life within the Church. Her new way of life began with the first monastery of Saint Joseph in Avila in 1562. She tells the story of this foundation in chapters 32–36 of the final draft of her *Life*.

The nuns who joined Teresa in this new Carmel soon began to feel keenly their need for more doctrine and practical instruction about the life of prayer. In response to this need, Teresa began another work in 1565; this later became known as *The Way of Perfection*.

In establishing her new foundation, Teresa's goals were modest: a small community with eleven nuns (in contrast to the 180 living in the Incarnation), who would dedicate themselves seriously to the contemplative life according to the Carmelite rule, observing in particular its spirit of unceasing prayer.

In the years following this first foundation, Teresa became aware of a new meaning and purpose in what she had begun, and, consequently, she felt the growing desire to found other similar Carmels. News of the conflicts tearing the Church in Northern Europe and of the millions of souls living in the Indies as yet to be evangelized set the fires of love and zeal that were already a spiritual torment to her burning even more intensely.[12] Teresa felt that since Christ has so few friends, these must be good ones. Through their intimacy with Him, they can be of service to the Church in the mission of defending and spreading the faith of Jesus Christ, to whom she referred throughout her writings as "His Majesty."[13] A visit to Spain in 1567 from Father Rubeo, the general of the Carmelite order, provided an answer to Teresa's deepest longings. A spiritual man with high goals for the order, the general was impressed both by Teresa and by what he saw at Saint Joseph's. He gave her orders to found as many of these contemplative monasteries as she could, and he also gave her permission to found monasteries of the same kind of life for the friars. In response to this latter permission, she arranged to meet Saint John of the Cross and convinced him to join her in this work.

INTRODUCTION

A number of new Carmels were founded in the following years, and Teresa describes their beginnings in *The Book of Foundations*. By the time of her death in 1582, she had founded fourteen monasteries. But these foundations were not made easily. All along the way she met with incredible problems and misunderstandings that gave scope to her marvelous human qualities and talents by which she attracted many to God, and this not only in her own age but through the years and even centuries into the present time. She once wrote in regard to those who think that to be perfect they must live rigidly that such constraint "will not bring many souls to God, because they will see so much repression and tenseness. Our nature is such that this constraint is frightening and oppressive to others, and they flee from following the road that you are taking, even though they know clearly that it is the more virtuous path."14

Her new mission meant travel throughout Spain, to large cities and small towns; it meant acquaintanceship with the poor and unlettered as well as with the nobility, with those who walk in high society, anxious for their social positions and honor. The list of those she had to deal with is a long one: the king (Philip II), the apostolic nuncios, bishops, the general, provincials, university professors, inquisitors of the Spanish Inquisition, missionaries and country priests, princes and princesses, dukes and duchesses, counts and countesses, merchants and bankers, builders and carpenters, mule drivers and innkeepers. In Spain's golden age, a time during which that once remote peninsula had become ruler of the largest empire the world had yet seen, she found herself involved in the most varied affairs: differences between the king and the family of the Duke of Alba; threats of war between Spain and Portugal; litigations in her own family; clashes between the Castilian and Andalusian temperament, and between conflicting commands from the royal government and Rome.

Her enormous correspondence kept her up at times until two or three in the morning despite the obligation of rising again at five to be in choir with her community. In a letter to her brother Lorenzo, she wrote: "On that day I had so much correspondence and business to attend to that I was writing till two in the morning, and this gave me a dreadful headache. But I think it happened for the best since the doctor has told me I must never write after midnight and I am not always to do the writing myself."[15]

Amid all the tangled complexities into which she was hurled by her mission, Teresa demonstrated a unique quality of ardor, a capacity to win others to her cause through human warmth and motherly charm, openness and joy in readiness to suffer for God what must be suffered: the wretched health with its severe fevers, the terrible roads and traveling conditions, the disappointments of unfulfilled promises, harsh contradictions, serious misunderstandings, and hostile opposition to her monasteries. Through letters or, whenever possible, through personal contact, she tried to explain her work in love and humility to whoever she heard was opposed. In the end, worn out from the fatigue caused by her last foundation at Burgos in 1582, she nonetheless forced herself to obey a difficult order given by Fr. Antonio de Jesus to undertake a journey that had no spiritual purpose save merely to satisfy the desires of the Duchess of Alba. Arriving in the little city of Alba and emptied of all strength, she died in her small Carmelite cell, October 4, 1582, repeating some verses from The Song of Songs and thanking God that she had been a daughter of the Church.

TERESA'S MYSTICAL EXPERIENCE

In the midst of the fascinating and unusual exterior events surrounding her work of establishing new Carmels, there was taking place within Teresa an event even more fascinating and unusual: a mystical journey into a more intimate understanding of the Christian mysteries. Throughout her various writings, Teresa traces both her outward travels and, even more explicitly, her inward journey.

Her mystical experience began with a feeling of the presence of God that "would come upon me unexpectedly so that I could in no way doubt He was within me or I totally immersed in Him."[16] This presence of God so manifested itself to Teresa as she went on that the doctrine of God's omnipresence became an essential element of her teaching on the spiritual life. The seemingly obvious truth that God is in things and, above all, in human persons was strangely enough denied by some of the priests Teresa consulted, and their denial troubled her until a Dominican theologian, Fr. Vicente Barrón, explained that God is indeed present even when a soul is not in His grace.

Some books Teresa had read induced her to think that because of the passive prayer she experienced, the time had come for a more abstract manner of procedure and that attention to the human Christ would impede her absorption in union, but she soon discovered her error and later in her teaching insisted that to turn aside from Christ in one's spiritual journey would end in failure to arrive at the highest stages of that journey, the final rooms of the interior castle.[17]

Some time after she had corrected this error, a new mode of experiencing Christ's presence came into her life.[18] In 1556, in her first experience of rapture, Teresa heard, not through her bodily ears but in her soul, Christ speaking to her. About two years later, in addition to the locutions that were now occurring, she knew through what she calls an intellectual vision, that is, one without external or internal image, that Jesus Christ was at her side. This vision did not pass but formed a part of her everyday life.[19] Then, though of a less spiritual quality but still beneficial to Teresa's growth, came the imaginative but transitory visions of Christ. In this latter form, the Lord showed Himself to her in His glorious risen body. Yet this was done not all at once: first His hands, then, a few days later, His face, then, "this most sacred humanity in its risen form was represented to me completely ... with wonderful beauty and majesty."[20] Human weakness could not have borne such shining beauty and glory all together and at once. As for the presence of Christ in the intellectual and more sublime vision, Teresa writes: "In the prayer of union or quiet some impressions of the Divinity are bestowed; in the vision, along with the impressions, you see that also the most sacred humanity accompanies us and desires to grant us favors."[21]

The last stage in Teresa's journey was marked by a series of experiences of the mystery of the Trinity. Deep within her spirit she perceived an area reserved for communion with the persons of the Blessed Trinity. In 1571, after she had expounded much of her doctrine on prayer in both the *Life* and the *Way of Perfection*, yet a further inner depth was revealed; and Teresa insists repeatedly on the profundity of the area in which her experience now takes place. Here was shown to her, in the fullness of light through an intellectual vision, the presence of the three Persons of the Blessed Trinity. Though this presence was not afterward always felt in such light and intensity, she did enjoy habitually the company of these three Persons.[22] Now, mystically, she understood the words in John's gospel about the indwelling of the divine Persons.[23] Shortly afterward she experienced, on the other hand, that she herself was dwelling in God: "It seemed to me there came the thought of how a sponge absorbs and is saturated with water; so, I thought, was my soul, which was overflowing with that divinity and in a certain way rejoicing within itself and possessing the three Persons. I also heard the words: 'Don't try to hold Me within yourself, but try to hold yourself within Me.' "[24]

This new companionship of the three Persons did not impede her intellectual vision of Christ's humanity. On November 18, 1572, she received the grace of the spiritual marriage through an imaginative vision of the humanity of Christ in which He told her that from then on she should consider as her own all that belonged to Him and that He would take care of what was hers.[25] Among the fruits of these awesome favors was fortitude, the strength necessary for a life in imitation of Christ and for the service and good works that are the fruit of spiritual marriage. The fruit in Teresa's case was, among others, both the new Carmels and her writings.

SOURCES

The books that influenced Teresa at one or another phase of her life were for the most part writings of recognized value. *The Letters* of St. Jerome, *The Morals* of St. Gregory the Great, and *The Confessions* of St. Augustine represented the Church Fathers. In this category there were also selections from the *Vitae Patrum*, the *Collationes* of Cassian, and the pseudo-Augustinian *Soliloquys* and *Meditations*. The medieval classics that she read were the *Flos Sanctorum*, probably by De Voragine; *The Life of Christ* by Ludolph of Saxony; and *The Imitation of Christ*. Among contemporary Spanish authors she read Luis de Granada,

Saint Peter of Alcántara, Francisco de Osuna, Bernardino de Laredo, Alonso de Madrid, and Bernabé de Palma.

Whether or not Teresa received any spiritual instruction during her novitiate training, it is difficult to discern. Certainly on the occasion of her first foundation she did make a study of the Carmelite rule, *The Rule of St. Albert.* When the Inquisitor General, Don Fernando Valdés, published the notorious Index of forbidden books in 1559, Teresa complied and parted with a number of her cherished books. Afterward she heard these words from the Lord: "Don't be sad, for I shall give you a living book."[26] From then on Teresa felt little need for books; the Lord Himself became a living book from whom she drew the clear water of divine wisdom. More than ever before, the words of the gospels spoke to her with splendid eloquence, and she attests to the particular power they possessed to bring recollection to her soul.[27]

Finally, the inquisitive mind of Teresa discovered another source of learning and spirituality in theologians, such as the Dominicans Pedro Ibáñez and Domingo Báñez, and in saints, such as Peter of Alcántara, Francis Borgia, and John of the Cross (who also, like Teresa, was proclaimed a Doctor of the Church in this twentieth century).

HER STYLE

In the Bible we read both the great and the small stories of salvation in a synthesis of episodes and doctrine. So, too, in Teresa's testimony, there is a continual interplay between experience and doctrine. The weft of her theoretical and practical teaching is skillfully carried through the warp of her concrete experience. But despite her gifts, writing for this sixteenth-century woman was a dreaded chore. Her health and energy were often not up to it. At the beginning, especially, of this call and even command to write, she felt powerless, unable to communicate what was of another world; and there was always that repugnance toward narrating graces of which she believed firmly she was unworthy. How much she would rather spend her time spinning, she protests. But once a work was undertaken, she came to know often the forcefulness of inspiration and was not embarrassed to admit her pleasure at how a work had turned out. From time to time, in chapter headings, she goes so far as to praise her own work and admire the way she dealt with the matter.[28]

Unlike other great Spanish authors, Teresa had no training as a writer. Her style is thoroughly spontaneous and unsophisticated. Since she wrote the way she spoke, her writings reflect the language of the Castilian people of her time. It is natural, direct, colorful, and incisive. With a mind always quick to see the thousand aspects of a subject, she is lured into sentences that become hopelessly involved, parentheses and digressions piling one on the other, but she never bothers to disentangle them. She takes little care about grammar. There are no paragraphs or punctuation of any kind. The sense must often be gathered from the context. Yet despite all the shortcomings, there remains a basic logic, a colorful spontaneity, and a colloquial simplicity and wit that more than compensate for the defects. Teresa's writings are a treasure and a delight to read. Those who had the privilege of observing her write have testified that she could do so as rapidly as any public notary. She never paused to reflect, or correct a word, or cross one out. She once summed it all up herself when she said she wished she could write with both hands so that all the ideas pouring into her head could be gotten on paper.

None of Teresa's writings fails to have a spiritual character. Even her business letters have a way of linking the profane to the spiritual.

WORKS

Teresa's literary production took place during the final twenty years of her life and in submission for the most part to directors and confessors who believed it to be a means of better understanding both this unusual person and God's ways of communing with His creatures. Even in the year before her death, Teresa was still called on to write an account of her spiritual state for the bishop of Osma, a former confessor of hers.[29] She finished the *Foundations* only a few months before her death.

INTRODUCTION

The major works and many of the shorter ones and letters have been preserved complete in their autographs and are in good condition. This obviates a number of critical problems and complications that are met with in the presentation of some other spiritual classics.

Her *Life*, which has come to us in its final version completed in 1565 and written for the scrutiny of her confessors, tells of her early years, of God's graces and her failures, and about her vocation, her severe illnesses and spiritual struggles. After a small treatise on prayer inserted in the middle of her story, she takes up again the account of her experiences, feeling assured that the reader may now grasp more easily the unusual mystical path along which she was led and which worked a striking change in her. In the final part of this book, she tells the story of her first foundation and, in addition, the further favors, the knowledge of which, she thinks, will be beneficial to the reader. As a result of her personal experience she is able to protest vigorously against those who belittle the favors bestowed lavishly by God in the mystical life and, on the other hand, against those who think these favors can be evoked through various clever skills and techniques.

The Way of Perfection, existing in two redactions, was written in its first and less inhibited form sometime between 1562 and 1566. After comments from the censors, it was completed in its revised form at the latest by 1569. In this book of basic teaching destined for her Sisters, Teresa begins by expounding her reasons for the new Carmel, reflecting on how the life of prayer must be for the service of the Church. But to live this life of unceasing prayer, as the Carmelite rule prescribes, Teresa insists that peace of soul is necessary. Peace of soul, as a disposition for growth in prayer, is fostered by the practice of detachment (evangelical poverty of spirit), love of neighbor, and humility. After these preliminary but essential teachings, she takes up the topic of mental prayer. She explains how vocal prayer requires mental prayer and how this vocal prayer does not impede even pure contemplation. All these reflections lead to her masterful commentary on the Our Father, Christ's prayer in which she discovers the entire spiritual journey from the beginning stages to the point where God engulfs the soul in union and gives it to drink from the fount of living water.

Another work Teresa wrote at Saint Joseph's in Avila and finished in its first form there, perhaps in 1567, is the small but doctrinally rich *Meditations on the Song of Songs*. This treatise begins with an analysis of the various kinds of false peace and goes on to examine true peace; in this work she speaks once more of the prayer of quiet and of union.

The *Foundations*, begun in August 1573, tells the history, with its many vicissitudes, of the establishment of the other Carmels founded after Saint Joseph's. She carries the reader into the practical problems of everyday life and combines materials from the sacred and the profane, the active and the contemplative life; and she forms with these the brilliant patterns of her spirituality. This is the case as well with the 440 *Letters* that have come down to us, most of them from the last six years of her life.

But if asked to single out one work as her masterpiece, most of those acquainted with the Teresian writings would probably choose *The Interior Castle*. Since it is this contribution that is chosen for this series, the work will be discussed with greater detail later in this introduction.

Other works by Teresa are: the *Spiritual Testimonies* (some brief accounts of favors she received and also some accounts of her interior state written for her spiritual directors, one of these for the consultants of the Inquisition), the *Soliloquies*, her *Constitutions* and *Manner of Visiting Monasteries*, *Poetry*, and a few other miscellaneous works.

BASIC DOCTRINE

Teresa did not elaborate a system of thought or attempt a theoretical framework. Her preference is clearly for direct testimony, which she uses in turn for teaching purposes. Her terminology is inconsistent. She takes no care to remain faithful to the steps she worked out in her previous books. The four degrees of prayer, for example, described in the *Life*, do not coincide with those explained in *The Interior Castle*. What is true is that her story has universal application. The exceptional favors she receives are an indication of God's overflowing mercy and goodness. No one is precluded. Whoever does not follow this call to intimacy with God and allow grace to act in his life will not come to know the meaning of life or bring it to its fulfillment.

The experience of personal misery and divine mercy causes Teresa to feel special affinity with biblical figures who converted to God: King David, Peter, Paul, Mary Magdalene, and the Samaritan woman. From conversion to union, the story is not untypical. God descends to man, and man rises up and returns to God.

The asceticism as well as the concept of prayer in her doctrine is based on friendship. All comes to center on the divine Friend. Consequently, the attention and the powers of the human person turn to Him and are directed in His service. The goal is viewed not in terms of the ordering and perfecting of human passions and instincts but rather in terms of loving communion with His Majesty and of good works done in His service.

Her definition of prayer, quoted variously in thousands of books, articles, spiritual conferences, and sermons over the years, has friendship as its fundamental notion: "Mental prayer in my opinion is nothing else than an intimate sharing between friends; it means taking time frequently to be alone with Him who we know loves us."[30]

The way to this divine friendship is Christ. He "is the one through whom all blessings come to us."[31] Different forms of friendship can be realized in one's relationship with Christ, Teresa reflects: He is our Brother who enables us to call God our Father; He is a companion, especially in times of tribulation; He is a teacher and master who teaches us how to approach God—particularly in the Our Father; He is, notably in spiritual union, our Bridegroom or Spouse; He is our Lord, the Lord of the world, our King, His Majesty.[32] In Jesus Christ, God offers souls human friendship as well as divine. "It is for you to look at Him," she says; "He never takes His eyes off you."[33]

As with any friendship, prayer develops from the initial attempts at mutual knowledge to the final simplified and intense relationship of complete union.

Her intimacy with God is communicated to the reader on almost every page. Indeed, it is sufficient to read her to be carried into her own communion with God and swept up in all the common forms of Christian prayer. Going directly to the person of Christ, she brings Him to her consciousness as within her or beside her. Speaking to Christ came easily to this woman gifted with such a wonderful capacity for friendship and conversation. She asks: "Since you speak with other persons, why must words fail you when you speak with God?"[34]

Should we want to discuss a method in Teresa's teaching on prayer, we would have to begin with her own words: "Draw near, then, to this good Master . . . . "[35] She calls this practice "recollection," and insists that an important aspect of prayer is the fundamental truth that God is close, very near. "All the harm comes from not understanding that He is near."[36] Drawing near to God is called recollection because "the soul collects its faculties together and enters within itself to be with its God,"[37] to look at Him, to be present to Him (who is present to and looking at us), to center its attention on Him.

A method of prayer popular in sixteenth-century Spain was discursive meditation. Teresa admires the many books of meditation, and though she praises them, she elusively remarks that they are helpful for those who have methodical minds and good concentration.[38] When she actually teaches a method, she does not do so in view of those possessing the above talents. To them she says: ". . . it would be a mistake if you pay attention to what I say about prayer."[39] Instead, she addresses those with "souls and minds so scattered that they are like wild horses no one can stop."[40]

Along with the prayer of recollection, then, Teresa suggests for these persons the recitation of vocal prayer, especially the Our Father, the prayer Christ taught. For Teresa, vocal prayer without the accompanying prayer of recollection is unthinkable. She had little use for the cautious advice given to women at that time to avoid the complexities and dangers of mental prayer and to be satisfied with vocal prayer alone. The two, she argues, are inseparable. Thus while reciting vocal prayer, the gaze, that is, the attention, is fixed in a simple loving way on Christ, in whom the mystery of God is made known.

Teresa says that she "never knew what it was to pray with satisfaction until the Lord taught me this method."[41] The method, called so because it is something achievable through human effort, does not take long to get used to; and through it one will gradually experience gain through other deeper degrees of recollection.[42]

Vocal prayer together with presence to Christ, or recollection, was the best means Teresa knew for disposing one for mystical prayer. "The intellect is recollected much more quickly with this kind of prayer even though it may be vocal. . . . And its divine Master comes more quickly to teach it and give it the prayer of quiet than He would through any other method."[43]

Vocal prayer of this sort she learned could calm the wild horses, the restless faculties that were so much a problem to her: ". . . out of love for the Lord, get used to praying the Our Father with this recollection, and you will see the benefit before long. This is a manner of praying that the soul gets so quickly used to that it doesn't go astray, nor do the faculties become restless, as time will tell."[44] She then promises that those who use this method will not fail to drink from the fount of infused prayer.[45]

Having assured her readers in *The Way of Perfection* that the prayer of the Our Father leads to the fount of living waters, she refers them to her *Life*, the book in which she describes what the soul feels when it drinks this living water, how God satisfies and takes away thirst for earthly things.

THE INTERIOR CASTLE

Some ten years later, on May 28, 1577, for basically the same reasons, she was speaking again of what was contained in her *Life*, but this time the result was the command to write another book since the *Life* was then in the scrupulously cautious hands of the Inquisition. The scene of the fateful incident was Toledo at the Carmel newly founded by Teresa. Fr. Gratian, her confessor and also, as a Carmelite friar, an enthusiastic supporter in her reform, has left us his account of the event: "What took place with regard to the book of the *Dwelling Places* is that while I was superior and speaking with her once in Toledo of many things concerning her spirit, she said to me: 'Oh, how well this point was described in the book about my life, which is in the Inquisition!' I answered: 'Since we cannot have it, recall what you can and other things and write another book, but put down the doctrine in a general way without naming the one to whom the things you mentioned there happened.' And thus I ordered her to write this book of the *Dwelling Places*."[46]

Now sixty-two years old, Teresa had for five years been aware of the depth of spiritual life she describes as the ultimate stage of the mystical journey. She had come, then, to an experiential grasp of so much more than what she had written previously in her *Life*. In evidence of this, toward the outset of her *Interior Castle* she admits: "And although in other things I've written the Lord has given me some understanding, I know there were certain things I had not understood as I have come to understand them now, especially certain more difficult things."[47]

IMPEDIMENTS

If from the viewpoint of her own more evolved experience and understanding the command to undertake such a task again seemed well advised, from the standpoint of her physical sufferings and the external problems and trials that were being heaped on her at this time the mere thought of writing a new book was painful to her. The Prologue begins in complaint. Not many things that obedience had asked of her—and obedience had asked many difficult things—were as difficult as the chore of writing at this time yet another book. "I have been experiencing now for three months," she wearily reports, "such great noise and weakness in my head that I've found it a hardship even to write concerning necessary business matters."[48]

In addition to this miserable health, the year was a troublesome and discouraging one; what she had worked for zealously over the previous fifteen years could now be suppressed by the new authorities. Her work had become the center of a conflict that raged between Madrid and Rome. The jurisdictional complexities became so tangled and the misunderstandings, rivalries, and calumnies so much a part of everyday life that historians today find it difficult to judge objectively.[49]

INTRODUCTION

In 1576 Fr. Jerónimo Tostado arrived in Spain with the faculties of visitor, reformer, and commissary general of the Spanish provinces and with the responsibility of carrying out the decrees of the order's chapter at Piacenza, which had directed that the houses opened in Andalusia against the will of the general be abandoned. The "contemplative," or "primitive," fathers were forbidden to form a province or a congregation separate from the province of Castile. Mother Teresa was not to leave her monastery. The unpleasant rumor was that Tostado had come to quash Teresa's work, and his presence was the cause of considerable disquiet. But the papal nuncio in Spain, Nicolás Ormaneto, who favored Teresa and her foundations, advised Tostado to postpone his visit to Andalusia (where Gratian, under an assignment of the nuncio, was on a mission of reform among the Carmelites there) and instead to pass on to Portugal. In a letter dated September 7, 1576, Teresa thus wrote to María de San José: "But, as God has delivered us from Tostado, I hope His Majesty will help us in everything. You are not maligning him in describing how he has worked against the discalced fathers and against me, for he has given clear indications of having done so."

In June 1577 Ormaneto died, and without the nuncio's favor Teresa's followers now felt lost. With the death of Ormaneto, the mother foundress thought it would be better to return to her monastery of Saint Joseph in Avila and to remain there "as a kind of prisoner" in accordance with the order of the general definitory. To make matters worse, Ormaneto's successor, Felipe Sega, whose reference to Teresa as a "restless gadabout" at least demonstrated a lack of firsthand information, at once set out with his new authority to discard the plans of reform sponsored by Ormaneto.

About this time, as well, there appeared a scurrilous pamphlet denouncing Teresa and calumniating Gratian with a number of crimes, some too foolish and lurid to be believed but yet sufficient to arouse at least faint suspicions. In October 1577 Teresa was once more elected prioress of the Incarnation; she felt nothing but aversion toward taking up again such a responsibility. When this election became known, Tostado unwittingly came to Teresa's rescue and gave orders to annul the valid election. The nuns, persisting to vote for Teresa in a second election, were then duly excommunicated. Though happy to be left in peace, Teresa protested the injustice: "Learned men declare that they are not excommunicated at all and that the friars are going against the Council in declaring anyone elected prioress who has a minority of votes. . . . Everyone is shocked to see something like this, so offensive to everyone."[50]

It was while she was in the midst of all these unpleasant and disturbing events that Teresa was engaged in writing her sublime book on prayer. The work was begun, appropriately, on the feast of the Holy Trinity, June 2, 1577. Within little more than a month, she had proceeded as far as the fifth dwelling place. We may suppose this from the copy made in Toledo and ending with chapter 2 of the fifth dwelling place when Teresa departed for Avila in mid July. Already in chapter 2 of the fourth dwelling place she had alluded to the inconvenience of interruptions: "God help me with what I have undertaken! I've already forgot what I was dealing with, for business matters and poor health have forced me to set this work aside just when I was at my best; and since I have a poor memory everything will come out confused because I can't go back to read it over."[51]

Nothing more was done on the work until the beginning of November, as she asserts at the outset of chapter 4 of the fifth dwelling place: "About five months have passed since I began, and because my head is in no condition to read over what I've written, everything will have to continue without order, and perhaps some things will be said twice."[52] She completed the remaining large section, more than half the work, by November 29, within less than a month. Thus the actual time spent on this spiritual masterpiece was a mere two months.

INSPIRATION

Despite her trials and ill health, Teresa held firmly to her belief that "obedience usually lessens the difficulty of things that seem impossible."[53] She prayed when beginning: "May He, in whose mercy I trust and who has helped me in other more difficult things so as to favor me, do this work for me."[54] Her prayer was heard. By the time she had reached the epilogue, her mood was entirely changed: "Although when I began writing this book I am sending you I did so with the aversion I mentioned in the beginning, now that I am finished I admit the work has brought me much happiness, and I consider the labor, though I confess it was small, well spent."[55]

At times she seemed to feel special inspiration, and that a work of such brilliance was brought to a conclusion so quickly is itself extraordinary. In one instance she wrote: "If what I have said up to now about this prayer is worthwhile, I know clearly that I'm not the one who has said it."[56] When she turns to the topic of mystical prayer she prays: "In order to speak of the fourth dwelling places I really need to entrust myself, as I've already done, to the Holy Spirit and beg Him to speak for me from here on that I may say something about the remaining rooms in a way that you will understand."[57] Among those who actually saw Teresa writing this book was María del Nacimiento, who gave the following testimony: "When the said Mother Teresa of Jesus wrote the book called *The Dwelling Places*, she was in Toledo, and this witness saw that it was after Communion that she wrote this book, and when she wrote she did so very rapidly and with such great beauty in her countenance that this witness was in admiration, and she was so absorbed in what she was writing that even if some noise was made there, it did not hinder her; wherefore this witness understood that in all that which she wrote and during the time she was writing she was in prayer."[58]

THE IMAGE OF A CASTLE

The *Interior Castle* has come to be regarded as Teresa's best synthesis. In it the spiritual doctrine is presented through the unifying outline of seven dwelling places among which there is a division into two sections. The first three groups of dwelling places speak of what is achievable through human efforts and the ordinary help of grace. The remaining four groups deal with the passive, or mystical, elements of the spiritual life.

The question has been raised, as one would expect among academics, as to how Teresa conceived the notion of using the castle as a symbol for the interior life. What she reveals leaves room for interpretation: "Today while beseeching our Lord to

19

speak for me because I wasn't able to think of anything to say, nor did I know how to begin to carry out this obedience, there came to my mind what I shall now speak about, that which will provide us with a basis to begin with. It is that we consider our soul to be like a castle made entirely out of a diamond or of very clear crystal, in which there are many rooms, just as in heaven there are many dwelling places."[59] Previously, in *The Way of Perfection*, with similar thoughts, Teresa had advised: "Well, let us imagine that within us is an extremely rich palace, built entirely of gold and precious stones; in sum, built for a Lord such as this.... Imagine, also, that in this palace dwells this mighty King."[60]

In an interesting account, one of her early biographers, Fr. Diego de Yepes, testifies that Teresa told him that on the eve of Trinity Sunday, 1577, God showed her in a flash the whole book. There was "a most beautiful crystal globe like a castle in which she saw seven dwelling places, and in the seventh, which was in the center, the King of Glory dwelt in the greatest splendor. From there He beautified and illumined all those dwelling places to the outer wall. The inhabitants received more light the nearer they were to the center. Outside of the castle all was darkness, with toads, vipers, and other poisonous vermin. While she was admiring this beauty, which the grace of God communicates to souls, the light suddenly disappeared and, although the King of Glory did not leave the castle, the crystal was covered with darkness and was left as ugly as coal and with an unbearable stench, and the poisonous creatures outside the wall were able to get into the castle. Such was the state of a soul in sin."[61] This was told to Yepes, a former confessor of Teresa's, when she met him by chance one snowy day in an inn in Arevalo either in 1579 or 1580. Yepes also adds with a certain self-satisfaction that "although in the *Book of Her Life* and the *Dwelling Places* she mentions this, she doesn't in either of them communicate this vision as specifically as she did to me."[62] But if this vision came to Teresa in 1577, we are left wondering both how she could have referred to it in her *Life*, written in the 1560s, and about the value of Diego de Yepes' testimony. Nonetheless, Teresa's vague expression "there came to my mind" (*se me ofreció*) does not rule out the possibility of a vision as the basis of her symbol.

INTRODUCTION

As described in her *Life*, she once did receive a mystical vision of God's presence and what it is for a soul to be in mortal sin: "Once while I was reciting with all the Sisters the hours of the Divine Office, my soul suddenly became recollected; and it seemed to me to be like a brightly polished mirror, without any part on the back or sides or top or bottom that wasn't totally clear. In its center Christ, our Lord, was shown to me ... I was given understanding of what it is for a soul to be in mortal sin. It amounts to clouding this mirror with mist and leaving it black; and thus this Lord cannot be revealed or seen even though He is always present giving us being."[63] Later in the same chapter it seems from her reference that this experience influenced her thinking when she compares the Divinity to a very clear diamond in which everything is visible including sin with all its ugliness.[64]

Whatever the speculation on matters like the above, the point must be made that the *Interior Castle* is principally the fruit of her own experience, and though Teresa makes the effort to hide her identity by referring to this other person she knows, her talents for concealing the identity were abysmally poor.

THE SYNTHESIS

Although the outer wall of the castle (the body) is plain, it nonetheless may lure the soul's attention from the inner brilliant castle.[65] Inside the castle are many dwelling places, above, below, and to the sides. In other words, the spiritual life that goes on within the castle is a complex matter involving the individual's capacities, the diversity of ways, and spiritual depths. In speaking of the seven dwelling places, we must keep in mind that "in each of these are many others, below and above and to the sides, with lovely gardens and fountains and labyrinths, such delightful things that you would want to be dissolved in praises of the great God who created the soul in His own image and likeness."[66] At the center of the castle is God's dwelling place.

The gate of entry is prayer.[67] Prayer is a door that opens up into the mystery of God and at the same time a means of communing with Him. It actuates the personal relationship with the Lord present in the very depths of the spirit.

The first dwelling places. Setting aside those souls outside the castle, paralyzed and crippled, in need of special healing from the Lord Himself if they are to enter,[68] Teresa turns her attention to those who have entered the first area. Little of the glowing light from the King's royal chamber filters into these first dwelling places. Too many things entice and distract souls here and thus prevent them from taking the time to search for the true light. "So, I think, must be the condition of the soul. Even though it may not be in a bad state, it is so involved in worldly things and so absorbed with its possessions, honor, or business affairs, as I have said, that even though as a matter of fact it would want to see and enjoy its beauty these things do not allow it to; nor does it seem that it can slip free from so many impediments."[69] Such people do have some good desires, however; and they even pray on occasion. Their need, as is true of everyone, is for self-knowledge and for knowledge of the beauty of a soul in grace and of the ugliness of one in sin; in a word, for some insight into the Christian mystery of sin and grace. Self-knowledge and humility grow as the soul moves onward through the castle toward the center.

The second dwelling places. Here we have rooms set apart for those who have taken some first steps in the practice of prayer, who are more receptive to the promptings and invitations of Christ's grace, which comes especially through external means such as books, sermons, good friendships, and trials. The struggle with the forces of evil is now more keenly felt, and the time is ripe for the characteristically Teresian determination to persevere convinced that the spiritual life cannot be grounded on consolations. Conformity with God's will must be the goal of one's strivings.

The third dwelling places. To persevere in prayer and the struggle involved is to go forward.[70] Those who have come to this stage begin to long not to offend His Majesty; they guard against venial sin, are fond of both ascetical practices and periods of recollection, seek to use their time well, practice charity toward their neighbor, and maintain balance in the use of speech and dress and in the management of their household. They are good Christians, and the Lord will not deny these souls entrance into the final dwelling place if they so desire.[71]

Like the young man in the gospel, however, they could turn away on hearing the requirements for becoming perfect. Any threat to wealth or honor will quickly uncover their attachments to these, and they are excessively discreet about their health—to the point of fearing everything.[72] In addition to their reluctance to part with wealth and honor, they have a tendency to be too easily shocked by the faults of others and quickly distraught by a little dryness.[73] Though these persons find more consolation in the spiritual life than they do in material comforts and distractions, they seldom receive the deeper, more delectable peace and quiet of contemplation except occasionally as an invitation to prepare better for what lies ahead.[74] They need someone who is free of the world's illusions with whom they might speak.

Dealing less extensively with these first three dwelling places, Teresa says little about prayer; nor does she give advice about methods. The impression left on her reader is that she is anxious to advance quickly to the part that deals more immediately with what God does; and she complains that while we are admonished to pray, only what we can do ourselves is explained and little is said of what the Lord does, "I mean about the supernatural."[75] It is in response to this need that Teresa felt that she could contribute.

The question might be raised here: Is it not useless for people to read about mystical prayer and favors when they do not themselves, for whatever reason, experience the same things? In answer to this, Teresa replies that to learn about God's work will lead a receptive person to the prayer of praise. Characteristically she reasons that if she who was so wretched was led to this praise when she read of such things, how much more will good and humble souls praise Him upon learning of them. Also, she thinks that these favors superabound with love and fortitude, enabling a person to do more good and to journey with less toil; therefore there is the consequence of the reader's learning how much he may lose through his own fault.

The fourth dwelling places. The beginning of the supernatural or mystical marks off this section and presents Teresa with the problem of how to explain infused prayer.[76] She first seeks a solution through an analysis of the difference between consolations (*contentos*) and spiritual delight (*gustos*); she notes that the former have their beginning in our human nature and end in God while the latter has its beginning in God and overflows to human nature.[77] The consolations, then, result from our own efforts accompanied by God's grace; the spiritual delight is received not through human efforts but passively. In this dwelling place the first degrees of infused prayer are discussed. Though there are no rules about the length of time required to reach this point, "the important thing is not to think much but to love much, and so do that which best stirs you to love."[78] In Teresa's thinking, love "doesn't consist in great delight but in desiring with strong determination to please God in everything, in striving, insofar as possible, not to offend Him, and in asking Him for the advancement of the honor and glory of His Son."[79]

This contemplative prayer begins with a passive experience of recollection, a gentle drawing of the faculties inward; it is different from the recollection achieved at the cost of human effort.[80] This prayer of infused recollection is a less intense form of initial contemplation or, as called by Teresa, the prayer of quiet. While the will finds rest in the prayer of quiet, in the peace of God's presence, the intellect (in Teresa's terminology) continues to move about. One should let the intellect go and surrender oneself into the arms of love,[81] for distractions, the wandering mind, are a part of the human condition and can no more be avoided than can eating and sleeping.

In a further effort to explain the difference between acquired and infused prayer, she turns to another analogy: the different ways in which two water troughs are filled. One trough is filled with water channelled through aqueducts, by the exercise of a great deal of ingenuity, while the other is filled by a spring bubbling up from the very spot where the trough is. However, the worth of one's prayer is not judged by its passive character; rather "it is in the effects and deeds following afterward that one discerns the true value of prayer."[82]

Finally, in this dwelling place, since the passive prayer is in its beginning stages, the natural (active) and the supernatural (passive) are joined. It is not unusual for souls to enter here.

The fifth dwelling places. The prayer of union characterizes these rooms, an experience in which the faculties become completely silent, or, in Teresa's words, are suspended, and which leaves a certitude that the soul "was in God and God was in it."[83] Such certitude is not present when the union is merely partial as in the previous dwelling place.[84]

Here Teresa, never wanting in her attempts to find the best explanation, turns to another analogy. Leaving aside the castle and the troughs of water, she finds an unusual comparison as an example for explaining what is in her mind: the silkworm. Through the image of the silkworm she speaks ingeniously of death and of new life in Christ. In this prayer of union, God Himself becomes the dwelling place or cocoon in which a person dies. Once a soul is indeed dead to itself and its attachments, it breaks forth from the cocoon transformed as does a small white butterfly.[85]

Having made the point of the soul's death in Christ, Teresa introduces her final analogy, which serves to lead her readers through the remaining dwelling places to the center of the castle: marriage and its preparatory stages. In her day, before two people became engaged, they progressed through certain stages by which they sought to know first if there was any likeness between them and then whether there was any chance for love. If these were affirmatively established, they shared in additional meetings so as to deepen their knowledge of each other. In these experiences of union, then, His Majesty is desirous that the soul may get to know Him better.[86]

Teresa makes a final plea that love be not idle. One so intimate with His Majesty must walk with special care and attentiveness in the exercise of virtue and with particular emphasis on love of neighbor, humility (the desire to be considered the least), and the faithful performance of ordinary tasks.[87]

The sixth dwelling places. The longest section of the *Interior Castle* is devoted to this stage of the inward journey. Teresa deals here with many extraordinary mystical phenomena. Though the spiritual betrothal takes place in these rooms, the desires of the soul at a cost to itself must first increase.[88] Through both vehement desires for God and the sufferings these desires cause, the Lord enables the soul to have the courage to be joined with Him and take Him as its Spouse.[89] Aware that her readers will wonder why all this courage is necessary for something that should be looked on as an attractive opportunity, Teresa asserts strongly: "I tell you there is need for more courage than you think."[90] Without the courage, which must be given by God, such a union would be impossible. This fortitude comes through many trials both exterior and interior: opposition from others; praise (itself becoming a trial); severe illnesses; inner sufferings, fears, and misunderstanding on the part of the confessor and the consequent anxiety that God will allow one to be deceived; and a feeling of unbearable inner oppression and even of being rejected by God.[91]

Other preparations for the betrothal come in the form of certain spiritual awakenings and impulses deep within the soul. These are of many kinds and include the woundings of love that can cause at one and the same time both pain and delight.[92]

The betrothal itself takes place when His Majesty "gives the soul raptures that draw it out of its senses. For if it were to see itself so near this great majesty while in its senses, it would perhaps die."[93] Though the soul in ecstasy is without consciousness in its outward life, it was never before so awake to the things of God nor did it ever before have so deep an enlightenment and knowledge of God.[94]

Besides locutions from God with their beneficial effects, the soul may now also begin to receive, through intellectual and imaginative visions, understanding about the divine mysteries.[95] Accompanying the discussion of these diverse favors are also many sharp analyses and keenly perceptive rules for discerning authentic mystical experiences from pseudomystical phenomena. The effects the authentic favors leave in the soul are like the jewels the Spouse gives to the betrothed; they are knowledge of the grandeur of God, self-knowledge together with humility, and rejection of earthly things except of those that can be used in the Lord's service.[96] Finally, joy will reach such an excess that the soul will want to be a herald to the entire world that all might help it praise the Lord.[97]

When speaking of the intellectual and imaginative visions of Christ, Teresa pauses to make some firm assertions about the human and divine Christ present throughout one's spiritual pilgrimage. No state is so sublime that a person must always be occupied with divinity and thus obliged to empty the mind of all reference to the human Christ. The inability of contemplative souls to engage in discursive thought about the mysteries of the Passion and the life of Christ in their prayer is very common, Teresa holds. But contemplating these mysteries, "dwelling on them with a simple gaze," in Teresa's words, "will not impede the most sublime prayer."[98] On the contrary, an effort to forget Christ and live in continual absorption in the divinity will result in a failure to enter the last two dwelling places. Teresa is most insistent on this. The purification of the person is realized not merely through the sufferings inherent in the human condition but especially through contact with the person of Christ in his humanity and divinity.

Through these many favors and purifications, the desires of love are always increasing and the flight of the butterfly is ever more restless. These desires reach a point of extreme spiritual torment, causing the soul a final purification of the spirit before entering the seventh dwelling place, "just as those who will enter heaven must be cleansed in purgatory."[99] Not only can this intense spiritual torment cause ecstasy, as can intense spiritual joy, but it can also place one in danger of death.[100] Nonetheless, the soul is aware that this spiritual suffering is a precious favor.

The seventh dwelling places. On account of these moments of great illumination, Teresa is able to teach that there are no closed doors between the sixth and the seventh dwelling places. If she divides them, it is "because there are things in the last that are not revealed to those who have not yet reached it."[101] In the prayer of union explained in the fifth dwelling place and in the raptures of the sixth, the Lord makes the soul blind and deaf as was Saint Paul in his conversion. When God joins the soul to Himself, it does not understand anything of the nature and kind of favor enjoyed.[102] But in the seventh dwelling place the union is wrought differently: "Our good God now desires to remove the scales from the soul's eyes and let it see and understand, although in a strange way, something of the favor He grants it."[103] Now fortified, a person lifted up to these exalted mysteries no longer loses equilibrium or falls into ecstasy, but rather experiences them as a proper object, as connatural.

Entry into these last and most luminous dwelling places takes place through an amazing intellectual vision of the Most Blessed Trinity. Teresa places much emphasis on the depth at which this experience occurs, a spiritual profundity previously unrevealed, in "the extreme interior, in some place very deep within itself."[104] Though the presence of the Trinity remains and is felt habitually, it is not revealed in the fullness of light as at first or sometimes afterward when the Lord "desires that the window of the intellect be opened."[105] What seems awesome is that the habitual intellectual vision of the Trinity does not interfere with multiple and diverse daily duties carried out as acts of service.

The grace of spiritual marriage, of perfect union, is bestowed also in this center dwelling place and occurs through an imaginative vision of the Lord's most sacred humanity "so that the soul will understand and not be ignorant of receiving this sovereign gift."[106] The vision was so much at variance with previous ones that it left Teresa "stupefied," for as does the vision of the Trinity, this takes place in that most interior depth of the spirit. In successive experiences of this grace, which is repeatable, the vision is an intellectual one. Suggesting the trait of inseparability, the term marriage designates the union and the degree of His Majesty's love. It is so great and reaches such a point that the spirit is made one with God "just as those who are married cannot be separated."[107] With no allowance for division, as there is in spiritual betrothal (likened to the joining and separation of the two candles), the union of spiritual marriage makes Teresa think of the rain that has fallen into a river or of a stream that enters the sea or of the beams of light entering a room through different windows and becoming one.[108]

At this point the butterfly dies with the greatest joy because its new life is Christ. In Saint Paul's words: "He that is joined or united to the Lord becomes one spirit with him," and "for me to live is Christ."[109] The ultimate goal, then, of Teresa's journey, the spiritual marriage, is a union with Jesus incarnate, now no longer living as the divine Logos but as the Word incarnate, risen and connotated by the attributes of His earthly adventure, especially those of His resurrection. With the passing of time, the soul understands more clearly that its life is Christ.

Having examined the effects of this union, Teresa in the final chapter explains that the purpose of all these splendid favors is that one might live like Christ and that the fruit of the spiritual marriage must be good works. The interior calm fortifies these persons so that they may endure much less calm in the exterior events of their lives, that they might have the strength to serve.[110] The works of service may be outstanding ones, as in Teresa's case, but they need not be. One must concentrate on serving those who are in one's company. "The Lord doesn't look so much at the greatness of our works as at the love with which they are done." His Majesty will join our sacrifice with that which He offered for us. "Thus even though our works are small they will have the value our love for Him would have merited had they been great."[111]

THE AUTOGRAPH

The *Interior Castle* was not revised by Teresa, although the manuscript does contain the marks of censors and learned men. Some of these insertions of censors were later canceled by others who disagreed.

Teresa gave the new book to Fr. Gratian to guard, for the *Book of Her Life* was still at the Inquisition. Gratian brought the work to Seville in 1580 and entrusted it for safekeeping to María de San José. Sometime between 1582 and 1585, while he was still provincial, Gratian gave the work as a gift to Don Pedro Cerezo Pardo, who was a generous benefactor of the Discalced Carmelites. Between 1586 and 1588 the autograph was in the hands of Fray Luis de León, who was at the time preparing the first edition of Teresa's works; it was then returned to Don Pedro Cerezo. In 1618 Don Pedro's daughter, Doña Constancia de Ayala, made her profession of vows in the monastery of the Discalced Carmelite nuns in Seville. She had brought with her to the Carmel the autograph of the *Interior Castle*, and it has remained with the nuns in Seville ever since, with one exception. In 1961 it was brought to Rome for repair, and in the following year, beautifully restored, the spiritual masterpiece was returned to the Carmelites in Seville. The red-bound book, referred to by its author as a jewel, is now set like a ruby in a reliquary that has walls like those of Avila and in the shape of a castle surrounding and protecting it.[112]

Teresa of Avila
THE INTERIOR CASTLE

THE CLASSICS OF WESTERN SPIRITUALITY

The Interior Castle

JHS

[Prologue]

Teresa of Jesus, a nun of Our Lady of Mount Carmel, wrote this treatise for her Sisters and daughters, the Discalced Carmelite nuns.

1. Not many things that I have been ordered to do under obedience have been as difficult for me as is this present task of writing about prayer. First, it doesn't seem that the Lord is giving me either the spirit or the desire to undertake the work. Second, I have been experiencing now for three months such great noise and weakness in my head that I've found it a hardship even to write concerning necessary business matters. But, knowing that the strength given by obedience usually lessens the difficulty of things that seem impossible, I resolved to carry out the task very willingly, even though my human nature seems greatly distressed. For the Lord hasn't given me so much virtue that my nature in the midst of its struggle with continual sickness and duties of so many kinds doesn't feel strong aversion toward such a task. May He, in whose mercy I trust and who has helped me in other more difficult things so as to favor me, do this work for me.

2. Indeed, I don't think I have much more to say than what I've said in other things they have ordered me to write;[1] rather, I fear that the things I write about will be nearly all alike. I'm, literally, just like the parrots that are taught to speak; they know no more than what they hear or are shown, and they often repeat it. If the Lord wants me to say something new, His

Majesty will provide. Or, He will be pleased to make me remember what I have said at other times, for I would be happy even with this. My memory is so poor that I would be glad if I could repeat, in case they've been lost, some of the things that I was told were well said.[2] If the Lord doesn't make me remember, I will gain just by tiring myself and getting a worse headache for the sake of obedience—even though no benefit will be drawn from what I say.

3. And so I'm beginning to comply today, the feast of the most Blessed Trinity, in the year 1577, in this Carmelite monastery of Saint Joseph in Toledo where I am at present.[3] In all that I say I submit to the opinion of the ones who ordered me to write, for they are persons of great learning.[4] If I should say something that isn't in conformity with what the holy Roman Catholic Church holds, it will be through ignorance and not through malice. This can be held as certain, and also that through the goodness of God I always am, and will be, and have been subject to her. May He be always blessed and glorified, amen.

4. The one who ordered me to write told me that the nuns in these monasteries of our Lady of Mount Carmel need someone to answer their questions about prayer and that he thought they would better understand the language used between women, and that because of the love they bore me they would pay more attention to what I would tell them. I thus understood that it was important for me to manage to say something. So, I shall be speaking to them while I write; it's nonsense to think that what I say could matter to other persons. Our Lord will be granting me favor enough if some of these nuns benefit by praising Him a little more. His Majesty well knows that I don't aim for anything else. And it should be very clear that if I manage to say something well the Sisters will understand that this does not come from me since there would be no foundation for it, unless the Lord gave it to me; otherwise they would have as little intelligence as I ability for such things.

THE FIRST DWELLING PLACES

CONTAINS TWO CHAPTERS

CHAPTER ONE

Discusses the beauty and dignity of our souls. Draws a comparison in order to explain, and speaks of the benefit that comes from understanding this truth and knowing about the favors we receive from God and how the door to this castle is prayer.

1. Today while beseeching our Lord to speak for me because I wasn't able to think of anything to say nor did I know how to begin to carry out this obedience, there came to my mind what I shall now speak about, that which will provide us with a basis to begin with. It is that we consider our soul to be like a castle made entirely out of a diamond or of very clear crystal, in which there are many rooms, just as in heaven there are many dwelling places.[1] For in reflecting upon it carefully, Sisters, we realize that the soul of the just person is nothing else but a paradise where the Lord says He finds His delight.[2] So then, what do you think that abode will be like where a King so powerful, so wise, so pure, so full of all good things takes His delight? I don't find anything comparable to the magnificent beauty of a soul and its marvelous capacity. Indeed, our intellects, however keen, can hardly comprehend it, just as they cannot comprehend God; but He Himself says that He created us in His own image and likeness.[3]

Well if this is true, as it is, there is no reason to tire ourselves in trying to comprehend the beauty of this castle. Since this castle is a creature and the difference, therefore, between it and God is the same as that between the Creator and

35

His creature, His Majesty in saying that the soul is made in His own image makes it almost impossible for us to understand the sublime dignity and beauty of the soul.

2. It is a shame and unfortunate that through our own fault we don't understand ourselves or know who we are. Wouldn't it show great ignorance, my daughters, if someone when asked who he was didn't know, and didn't know his father or mother or from what country he came? Well now, if this would be so extremely stupid, we are incomparably more so when we do not strive to know who we are, but limit ourselves to considering only roughly these bodies. Because we have heard and because faith tells us so, we know we have souls. But we seldom consider the precious things that can be found in this soul, or who dwells within it, or its high value. Consequently, little effort is made to preserve its beauty. All our attention is taken up with the plainness of the diamond's setting or the outer wall of the castle; that is, with these bodies of ours.

3. Well, let us consider that this castle has, as I said,[4] many dwelling places: some up above, others down below, others to the sides; and in the center and middle is the main dwelling place where the very secret exchanges between God and the soul take place.

It's necessary that you keep this comparison in mind. Perhaps God will be pleased to let me use it to explain something to you about the favors He is happy to grant souls and the differences between these favors. I shall explain them according to what I have understood as possible. For it is impossible that anyone understand them all since there are many; how much more so for someone as wretched as I. It will be a great consolation when the Lord grants them to you if you know that they are possible; and for anyone to whom He doesn't, it will be a great consolation to praise His wonderful goodness. Just as it doesn't do us any harm to reflect on the things there are in heaven and what the blessed enjoy—but rather we rejoice and strive to attain what they enjoy—it doesn't do us any harm to see that it is possible in this exile for so great a God to commune with such foul-smelling worms; and, on seeing this, come to love a goodness so perfect and a mercy so immeasurable. I hold as certain that anyone who might be

36

harmed by knowing that God can grant this favor in this exile would be very much lacking in humility and love of neighbor. Otherwise, how could we fail to be happy that God grants these favors to our brother? His doing so is no impediment toward His granting them to us, and His Majesty can reveal His grandeurs to whomever He wants. Sometimes He does so merely to show forth His glory, as He said of the blind man whose sight He restored when His apostles asked Him if the blindness resulted from the man's sins or those of his parents.[5] Hence, He doesn't grant them because the sanctity of the recipients is greater than that of those who don't receive them but so that His glory may be known, as we see in Saint Paul and the Magdalene, and that we might praise Him for His work in creatures.

4. One could say that these favors seem to be impossible and that it is good not to scandalize the weak. Less is lost when the weak do not believe in them than when the favors fail to benefit those to whom God grants them; and these latter will be delighted and awakened through these favors to a greater love of Him who grants so many gifts and whose power and majesty are so great. Moreover, I know I am speaking to those for whom this danger does not exist, for they know and believe that God grants even greater signs of His love. I know that whoever does not believe in these favors will have no experience of them, for God doesn't like us to put a limit on His works. And so, Sisters, those of you whom the Lord doesn't lead by this path should never doubt His generosity.

5. Well, getting back to our beautiful and delightful castle we must see how we can enter it. It seems I'm saying something foolish. For if this castle is the soul, clearly one doesn't have to enter it since it is within oneself. How foolish it would seem were we to tell someone to enter a room he is already in. But you must understand that there is a great difference in the ways one may be inside the castle. For there are many souls who are in the outer courtyard—which is where the guards stay—and don't care at all about entering the castle, nor do they know what lies within that most precious place, nor who is within, nor even how many rooms it has. You have already heard in some books on prayer that the soul is advised to enter within itself;[6] well that's the very thing I'm advising.

6. Not long ago a very learned man told me that souls who do not practice prayer are like people with paralyzed or crippled bodies; even though they have hands and feet they cannot give orders to these hands and feet.[7] Thus there are souls so ill and so accustomed to being involved in external matters that there is no remedy, nor does it seem they can enter within themselves. They are now so used to dealing always with the insects and vermin that are in the wall surrounding the castle that they have become almost like them. And though they have so rich a nature and the power to converse with none other than God, there is no remedy. If these souls do not strive to understand and cure their great misery, they will be changed into statues of salt, unable to turn their heads to look at themselves, just as Lot's wife was changed for having turned her head.[8]

7. Insofar as I can understand, the gate of entry to this castle is prayer and reflection. I don't mean to refer to mental more than vocal prayer, for since vocal prayer is prayer it must be accompanied by reflection. A prayer in which a person is not aware of whom he is speaking to, what he is asking, who it is who is asking and of whom, I do not call prayer however much the lips may move. Sometimes it will be so without this reflection, provided that the soul has these reflections at other times. Nonetheless, anyone who has the habit of speaking before God's majesty as though he were speaking to a slave, without being careful to see how he is speaking, but saying whatever comes to his head and whatever he has learned from saying at other times, in my opinion is not praying. Please God, may no Christian pray in this way. Among yourselves, Sisters, I hope in His Majesty that you will not do so, for the custom you have of being occupied with interior things is quite a good safeguard against falling and carrying on in this way like brute beasts.

8. Well now, we are not speaking to these crippled souls, for if the Lord Himself doesn't come to order them to get up— as He did the man who waited at the side of the pool for thirty years[9]—they are quite unfortunate and in serious danger. But we are speaking to other souls that, in the end, enter the castle. For even though they are very involved in the world, they have good desires and sometimes, though only once in a while, they

entrust themselves to our Lord and reflect on who they are, although in a rather hurried fashion. During the period of a month they will sometimes pray, but their minds are then filled with business matters that ordinarily occupy them. They are so attached to these things that where their treasure lies their heart goes also.[10] Sometimes they do put all these things aside, and the self-knowledge and awareness that they are not proceeding correctly in order to get to the door is important. Finally, they enter the first, lower rooms. But so many reptiles get in with them that they are prevented from seeing the beauty of the castle and from calming down; they have done quite a bit just by having entered.

9. You may have been thinking, daughters, that this is irrelevant to you since by the Lord's goodness you are not among these people. You'll have to have patience, for I wouldn't know how to explain my understanding of some interior things about prayer if not in this way. And may it even please the Lord that I succeed in saying something, for what I want to explain to you is very difficult to understand without experience. If you have experience you will see that one cannot avoid touching upon things that—please God, through His mercy—do not pertain to us.

CHAPTER TWO

Treats of how ugly a soul is when in mortal sin and how God wanted to let a certain person know something about this. Discusses, also, some matters on the theme of self-knowledge. This chapter is beneficial, for there are noteworthy points. Explains what is meant by these dwelling places.

1. Before going on I want to say that you should consider what it would mean to this so brilliantly shining and beautiful castle, this pearl from the Orient, this tree of life planted in the very living waters of life[1]—that is, in God—to fall into mortal sin; there's no darker darkness nor anything more obscure and black. You shouldn't want to know anything else than the fact that, although the very sun that gave the soul so much brilliance and beauty is still in the center, the soul is as though it were not there to share in these things. Yet, it is as capable of enjoying His Majesty as is crystal capable of reflecting the sun's

brilliance. Nothing helps such a soul, and as a result all the good works it might do while in mortal sin are fruitless for the attainment of glory. Since these works do not proceed from that principle, which is God, who is the cause of our virtue's being really virtue, and are separated from Him, they cannot be pleasing in His sight. Since, after all, the intention of anyone who commits a mortal sin is to please the devil, not God, the poor soul becomes darkness itself because the devil is darkness itself.

2. I know a person to whom our Lord wanted to show what a soul in mortal sin was like.[2] That person says that in her opinion if this were understood it would be impossible to sin, even though a soul would have to undergo the greatest trials imaginable in order to flee the occasions. So the Lord gave her a strong desire that all might understand this. May He give you, daughters, the desire to beseech Him earnestly for those who are in this state, who have become total darkness, and whose works have become darkness also. For just as all the streams that flow from a crystal-clear fount are also clear, the works of a soul in grace, because they proceed from this fount of life in which the soul is planted like a tree, are most pleasing in the eyes of both God and man. There would be no freshness, no fruit, if it were not for this fount sustaining the tree, preventing it from drying up, and causing it to produce good fruit. Thus in the case of a soul that through its own fault withdraws from this fount and plants itself in a place where the water is black and foul smelling, everything that flows from it is equally wretched and filthy.

3. It should be kept in mind here that the fount, the shining sun that is in the center of the soul, does not lose its beauty and splendor; it is always present in the soul, and nothing can take away its loveliness. But if a black cloth is placed over a crystal that is in the sun, obviously the sun's brilliance will have no effect on the crystal even though the sun is shining on it.[3]

4. O souls redeemed by the blood of Jesus Christ! Understand and take pity on yourselves. How is it possible that in realizing these things you don't strive to remove the pitch from this crystal? See that if your life comes to an end you will never again enjoy this light. O Jesus, how sad a thing it is to see a soul

separated from this light! How miserable is the state of those poor rooms within the castle! How disturbed the senses are, that is, the people who live in these rooms! And in the faculties, that is, among the custodians, the stewards, and the chief waiters, what blindness, what bad management! In sum, since the tree is planted where the devil is, what fruit can it bear?

5. I once heard of a spiritual man who was not surprised at things done by a person in mortal sin, but at what was not done. May God in His mercy deliver us from so great an evil. There is nothing, while we are living, that deserves this name "evil" except mortal sin, for such sin carries in its wake everlasting evils. This, daughters, is what we must go about in fear of and what we must ask God in our prayers to protect us against. For if He doesn't guard the city, our labor will be in vain,[4] since we are vanity itself.

That person I mentioned[5] said she received two blessings from the favor God granted her: the first, an intense fear of offending Him, and so in seeing such terrible dangers she always went about begging Him not to let her fall; the second, a mirror for humility, in which she saw how none of our good deeds has its principle in ourselves but in this fount in which the tree, symbolizing our souls, is planted and in this sun that gives warmth to our works. She says that this truth was represented to her so clearly that in doing something good, or seeing it done, she gave heed to the source and understood how without this help we could do nothing. As a result she would begin immediately to praise God and usually not think of herself in any good thing that she did.

6. The time you spend in reading this, or I in writing it, Sisters, would not be lost if we were left with these two blessings. Learned and wise men know about these things very well, but everything is necessary for our womanly dullness of mind; and so perhaps the Lord wills that we get to know comparisons like these. May it please His goodness to give us grace to profit by them.

7. These interior matters are so obscure for our minds that anyone who knows as little as I will be forced to say many superfluous and even foolish things in order to say something that's right. Whoever reads this must have patience, for I have to have it in order to write about what I don't know. Indeed,

sometimes I take up the paper like a simpleton, for I don't know what to say or how to begin. I understand well that it's important for you that I explain some things about the interior life as best I can. We always hear about what a good thing prayer is, and our constitutions oblige us to spend so many hours in prayer.[6] Yet only what we ourselves can do in prayer is explained to us; little is explained about what the Lord does in a soul, I mean about the supernatural.[7] By speaking about this heavenly interior building and explaining and considering it in many ways we shall find great comfort. It is so little understood by mortals, even though many walk through it. And although in other things I've written the Lord has given me some understanding,[8] I know there were certain things I had not understood as I have come to understand them now, especially certain more difficult things. The trouble is that before discussing them, as I have said,[9] I will have to repeat matters that are well known; on account of my stupidity things can't be otherwise.

8. Well now let's get back to our castle with its many dwelling places. You mustn't think of these dwelling places in such a way that each one would follow in file after the other; but turn your eyes toward the center, which is the room or royal chamber where the King stays, and think of how a palmetto[10] has many leaves surrounding and covering the tasty part that can be eaten. So here, surrounding this center room are many other rooms; and the same holds true for those above. The things of the soul must always be considered as plentiful, spacious, and large; to do so is not an exaggeration. The soul is capable of much more than we can imagine, and the sun that is in this royal chamber shines in all parts. It is very important for any soul that practices prayer, whether little or much, not to hold itself back and stay in one corner. Let it walk through these dwelling places which are up above, down below, and to the sides, since God has given it such great dignity. Don't force it to stay a long time in one room alone. Oh, but if it is in the room of self-knowledge! How necessary this room is—see that you understand me—even for those whom the Lord has brought into the very dwelling place where He abides. For never, however exalted the soul may be, is anything else more fitting than self-knowledge; nor could it be even were the soul

to so desire. For humility, like the bee making honey in the bee-hive, is always at work. Without it, everything goes wrong. But let's remember that the bee doesn't fail to leave the beehive and fly about gathering nectar from the flowers. So it is with the soul in the room of self-knowledge; let it believe me and fly sometimes to ponder the grandeur and majesty of its God. Here it will discover its lowliness better than by thinking of itself, and be freer from the vermin that enter the first rooms, those of self-knowledge. For even though, as I say, it is by the mercy of God that a person practices self-knowledge, that which applies to what is less applies so much more to what is greater, as they say. And believe me, we shall practice much better virtue through God's help than by being tied down to our own misery.

9. I don't know if this has been explained well. Knowing ourselves is something so important that I wouldn't want any relaxation ever in this regard, however high you may have climbed into the heavens. While we are on this earth nothing is more important to us than humility. So I repeat that it is good, indeed very good, to try to enter first into the room where self-knowledge is dealt with rather than fly off to other rooms. This is the right road, and if we can journey along a safe and level path, why should we want wings to fly? Rather, let's strive to make more progress in self-knowledge, for in my opinion we shall never completely know ourselves if we don't strive to know God. By gazing at His grandeur, we get in touch with our own lowliness; by looking at His purity, we shall see our own filth; by pondering His humility, we shall see how far we are from being humble.

10. Two advantages come from such activity. First, it's clear that something white seems much whiter when next to something black, and vice versa with the black next to the white. The second is that our intellects and wills, dealing in turn now with self, now with God, become nobler and better prepared for every good. And it would be disadvantageous for us never to get out of the mire of our miseries. As we said of those who are in mortal sin, that their streams are black and foul smelling, so it is here; although not entirely—God deliver us—for we are just making a comparison. If we are always fixed on our earthly misery, the stream will never flow free

from the mud of fears, faintheartedness, and cowardice. I would be looking to see if I'm being watched or not; if by taking this path things will turn out badly for me; whether it might be pride to dare begin a certain work; whether it would be good for a person so miserable to engage in something so lofty as prayer; whether I might be judged better than others if I don't follow the path they all do. I'd be thinking that extremes are not good, even in the practice of virtue; that, since I am such a sinner, I might have a greater fall; that perhaps I would not advance and would do harm to good people; that someone like myself has no need of special things.

11. Oh, God help me, daughters, how many souls must have been made to suffer great loss in this way by the devil! These souls think that all such fears stem from humility. And there are other things I could mention. The fears come from not understanding ourselves completely. They distort self-knowledge; and I'm not surprised if we never get free from ourselves, for this lack of freedom from ourselves, and even more, is what can be feared. So I say, daughters, that we should set our eyes on Christ, our Good, and on His saints. There we shall learn true humility, the intellect will be enhanced, as I have said,[11] and self-knowledge will not make one base and cowardly. Even though this is the first dwelling place, it is very rich and so precious that if the soul slips away from the vermin within it, nothing will be left to do but advance. Terrible are the wiles and deceits used by the devil so that souls may not know themselves or understand their own paths.

12. I could give some very good proofs from experience of the wiles the devil uses in these first dwelling places. Thus I say that you should think not in terms of just a few rooms but in terms of a million;[12] for souls, all with good intentions, enter here in many ways. But since the devil always has such a bad intention, he must have in each room many legions of devils to fight souls off when they try to go from one room to the other. Since the poor soul doesn't know this, the devil plays tricks on it in a thousand ways. He's not so successful with those who have advanced closer to where the King dwells. But since in the first rooms souls are still absorbed in the world and engulfed in their pleasures and vanities, with their honors and pretenses, their vassals (which are these senses and faculties) don't have

the strength God gave human nature in the beginning. And these souls are easily conquered, even though they may go about with desires not to offend God and though they do perform good works. Those who see themselves in this state must approach His Majesty as often as possible. They must take His Blessed Mother and His saints as intercessors so that these intercessors may fight for them, for the soul's vassals have little strength to defend themselves. Truly, in all states it's necessary that strength come to us from God. May His Majesty through His mercy give it to us, amen.

13. How miserable the life in which we live! Because elsewhere I have said a great deal about the harm done to us by our failure to understand well this humility and self-knowledge,[13] I'll tell you no more about it here, even though this self-knowledge is the most important thing for us. Please God, I may have now said something beneficial for you.

14. You must note that hardly any of the light coming from the King's royal chamber reaches these first dwelling places. Even though they are not dark and black, as when the soul is in sin, they nevertheless are in some way darkened so that the soul cannot see the light. The darkness is not caused by a flaw in the room—for I don't know how to explain myself—but by so many bad things like snakes and vipers and poisonous creatures that enter with the soul and don't allow it to be aware of the light. It's as if a person were to enter a place where the sun is shining but be hardly able to open his eyes because of the mud in them. The room is bright but he doesn't enjoy it because of the impediment of things like these wild animals or beasts that make him close his eyes to everything but them. So, I think, must be the condition of the soul. Even though it may not be in a bad state, it is so involved in worldly things and so absorbed with its possessions, honor, or business affairs, as I have said,[14] that even though as a matter of fact it would want to see and enjoy its beauty these things do not allow it to; nor does it seem that it can slip free from so many impediments. If a person is to enter the second dwelling places, it is important that he strive to give up unnecessary things and business affairs. Each one should do this in conformity with his state in life. It is something so appropriate in order for him to reach the main dwelling place that if he doesn't begin doing this I hold that it

will be impossible for him to get there. And it will even be impossible for him to stay where he is without danger even though he has entered the castle, for in the midst of such poisonous creatures one cannot help but be bitten at one time or another.

15. Now then, what would happen, daughters, if we who are already free from these snares, as we are, and have entered much further into the castle to other secret dwelling places should turn back through our own fault and go out to this tumult? There are, because of our sins, many persons to whom God has granted favors who through their own fault have fallen back into this misery. In the monastery we are free with respect to exterior matters; in interior matters may it please the Lord that we also be free, and may He free us. Guard yourselves, my daughters, from extraneous cares. Remember that there are few dwelling places in this castle in which the devils do not wage battle. True, in some rooms the guards (which I believe I have said are the faculties)[15] have the strength to fight; but it is very necessary that we don't grow careless in recognizing the wiles of the devil, and that we not be deceived by his changing himself into an angel of light.[16] There's a host of things he can do to cause us harm; he enters little by little, and until he's done the harm we don't recognize him.

16. I've already told you elsewhere[17] that he's like a noiseless file, that we need to recognize him at the outset. Let me say something that will explain this better for you.

He gives a Sister various impulses toward penance, for it seems to her she has no rest except when she is tormenting herself. This may be a good beginning; but if the prioress has ordered that no penance be done without permission, and the devil makes the Sister think that in a practice that's so good one can be rightly daring, and she secretly gives herself up to such a penitential life that she loses her health and doesn't even observe what the rule commands, you can see clearly where all this good will end up.

He imbues another with a very great zeal for perfection. Such zeal is in itself good. But it could follow that every little fault the Sisters commit will seem to her a serious breach; and she is careful to observe whether they commit them, and then informs the prioress. It could even happen at times that she doesn't see her own faults because of her intense zeal for the religious observance. Since the other Sisters don't understand what's going on within her and see all this concern, they might not accept her zeal so well.

17. What the devil is hereby aiming after is no small thing: the cooling of the charity and love the Sisters have for one another. This would cause serious harm. Let us understand, my daughters, that true perfection consists in love of God and neighbor; the more perfectly we keep these two commandments, the more perfect we will be. All that is in our rule and constitutions serves for nothing else than to be a means toward keeping these commandments with greater perfection. Let's forget about indiscreet zeal; it can do us a lot of harm. Let each one look to herself. Because I have said enough about this elsewhere,[18] I'll not enlarge on the matter.

18. This mutual love is so important that I would never want it to be forgotten. The soul could lose its peace and even disturb the peace of others by going about looking at trifling things in people that at times are not even imperfections, but since we know little we see these things in the worst light; look how costly this kind of perfection would be. Likewise, the devil could tempt the prioress in this way; and such a thing would be more dangerous. As a result much discretion is necessary. If things are done against the rule and constitutions, the matter need not always be seen in a good light. The prioress should be cautioned, and if she doesn't amend, the superior informed. This is charity. And the same with the Sisters if there is something serious. And to fail to do these things for fear of a temptation would itself be a temptation. But it should be carefully noted—so that the devil doesn't deceive us—that we must not talk about these things to one another. The devil could thereby gain greatly and manage to get the custom of gossiping started. The matter should be discussed with the one who will benefit, as I have said. In this house, glory to God, there's not much occasion for gossip since such continual silence is kept; but it is good that we be on guard.

THE SECOND DWELLING PLACES

CHAPTER ONE

Discusses the importance of perseverance if one is to reach the final dwelling places; the great war the devil wages; and the importance of taking the right road from the beginning. Offers a remedy that has proved very efficacious.

1. Now let us speak about the type of soul that enters the second dwelling places and what such a soul does in them. I'd like to say only a little, for I have spoken at length on this subject elsewhere.[1] And it would be impossible to avoid repeating much of it, for I don't remember a thing of what I said. If I could present the matter for you in a variety of ways, I know well that you wouldn't be annoyed since we never tire of books—as many as there are—that deal with it.

2. This stage pertains to those who have already begun to practice prayer and have understood how important it is not to stay in the first dwelling places. But they still don't have the determination to remain in this second stage without turning back, for they don't avoid the occasions of sin. This failure to avoid these occasions is quite dangerous. But these persons have received a good deal of mercy in that they sometimes do strive to escape from snakes and poisonous creatures, and they understand that it is good to avoid them.

These rooms, in part, involve much more effort than do the first, even though there is not as much danger, for it now seems that souls in them recognize the dangers, and there is great hope they will enter further into the castle. I say that

48

these rooms involve more effort because those who are in the first dwelling places are like deaf-mutes and thus the difficulty of not speaking is more easily endured by them than it is by those who hear but cannot speak. Yet, not for this reason does one have greater desire to be deaf, for after all it is a wonderful thing to hear what is being said to us. So these persons are able to hear the Lord's callings. Since they are getting closer to where His Majesty dwells, He is a very good neighbor. His mercy and goodness are so bountiful, whereas we are occupied in our pastimes, business affairs, pleasures, and worldly buying and selling, and still falling into sin and rising again. These beasts are so poisonous and their presence so dangerous and noisy that it would be a wonder if we kept from stumbling and falling over them. Yet this Lord desires intensely that we love Him and seek His company, so much so that from time to time He calls us to draw near Him. And His voice is so sweet the poor soul dissolves at not doing immediately what He commands. Thus, as I say, hearing His voice is a greater trial than not hearing it.

3. I don't mean that these appeals and calls are like the ones I shall speak of later on.[2] But they come through words spoken by other good people, or through sermons, or through what is read in good books, or through the many things that are heard and by which God calls, or through illnesses and trials, or also through a truth that He teaches during the brief moments we spend in prayer; however lukewarm these moments may be, God esteems them highly. And you, Sisters, don't underestimate this first favor, nor should you become disconsolate if you don't respond at once to the Lord. His Majesty knows well how to wait many days and years, especially when He sees perseverance and good desires. This perseverance is most necessary here. One always gains much through perseverance. But the attacks made by devils in a thousand ways afflict the soul more in these rooms than in the previous ones. In the previous ones the soul was deaf and dumb—at least it heard very little and resisted less, as one who has partly lost hope of conquering. Here the intellect is more alive and the faculties more skilled. The blows from the artillery strike in such a way that the soul cannot fail to hear. It is in this stage that the devils represent these snakes (worldly things) and the temporal plea-

sures of the present as though almost eternal. They bring to mind the esteem one has in the world, one's friends and relatives, one's health (when there's thought of penitential practices, for the soul that enters this dwelling place always begins wanting to practice some penance) and a thousand other obstacles.

4. O Jesus, what an uproar the devils instigate here! And the afflictions of the poor soul: It doesn't know whether to continue or to return to the first room. Reason, for its part, shows the soul that it is mistaken in thinking that these things of the world are not worth anything when compared to what it is aiming after. Faith, however, teaches it about where it will find fulfillment. The memory shows it where all these things end, holding before it the death of those who found great joy in them. Through the memory it sees how some have suffered sudden death, how quickly they are forgotten by all. Some whom it had known in great prosperity are under the ground, and their graves are walked on. This soul itself has often passed by these graves. It reflects that many worms are swarming over the corpses, and thinks about numerous other things. The will is inclined to love after seeing such countless signs of love; it would want to repay something; it especially keeps in mind how this true Lover never leaves it, accompanying it and giving it life and being. Then the intellect helps it realize that it couldn't find a better friend, even were it to live for many years; that the whole world is filled with falsehood; and that so too these joys the devil gives it are filled with trials, cares, and contradictions. The intellect tells the soul of its certainty that outside this castle neither security nor peace will be found, that it should avoid going about to strange houses since its own is so filled with blessings to be enjoyed if it wants. The intellect will ask who it is that finds everything he needs in his own house and, especially, has a guest who will make him lord over all goods provided that he wills to avoid going astray like the prodigal son and eating the husks of swine.[3]

5. These are reasons for conquering the devils. But, oh, my Lord and my God, how the whole world's habit of getting involved in vanities vitiates everything! Our faith is so dead that we desire what we see more than what faith tells us. And, indeed, we see only a lot of misfortune in those who go after

these visible vanities. But these poisonous things we are dealing with are the cause of this misfortune, for just as all is poisoned if a viper bites someone and the wound swells, so we will be poisoned if we do not watch ourselves. Clearly many remedies are necessary to cure us, and God is favoring us a good deal if we do not die from the wound. Certainly the soul undergoes great trials here; and, especially, if the devil realizes that it has all it needs in its temperament and habits to advance far, he will gather all hell together to make the soul go back outside.

6. Oh my Lord! Your help is necessary here; without it one can do nothing.[4] In Your mercy do not consent to allow this soul to suffer deception and give up what was begun. Enlighten it that it may see how all its good is within this castle and that it may turn away from bad companions. It's a wonderful thing for a person to talk to those who speak about this interior castle, to draw near not only to those seen to be in these rooms where he is but to those known to have entered the ones closer to the center. Conversation with these latter will be a great help to him, and he can converse so much with them that they will bring him to where they are. Let the soul always heed the warning not to be conquered. If the devil sees that it has the strong determination to lose its life and repose and all that he offers it rather than return to the first room, he will abandon it much more quickly. Let the soul be manly and not like those soldiers who knelt down to drink before going into battle (I don't remember with whom),[5] but be determined to fight with all the devils and realize that there are no better weapons than those of the cross.

7. Even though I've said this at other times,[6] it's so important that I repeat it here: It is that souls shouldn't be thinking about consolations at this beginning stage. It would be a very poor way to start building so precious and great an edifice. If the foundation is on sand, the whole building will fall to the ground. They'll never finish being dissatisfied and tempted. These are not the dwelling places where it rains manna; those lie further ahead, where a soul finds in the manna every taste it desires;[7] for it wants only what God wants. It's an amusing thing that even though we still have a thousand impediments and imperfections and our virtues have hardly begun to grow—and please God they may have begun—we are yet not

ashamed to seek spiritual delights in prayer or to complain about dryness. May this never happen to you, Sisters. Embrace the cross your Spouse has carried and understand that this must be your task. Let the one who can do so suffer more for Him, and she will be rewarded that much more. As for other favors, if the Lord should grant you one, thank Him for it as you would for something freely added on.

8. It will seem to you that you are truly determined to undergo exterior trials, provided that God favors you interiorly. His Majesty knows best what is suitable for us. There's no need for us to be advising Him about what He should give us, for He can rightly tell us that we don't know what we're asking for.[8] The whole aim of any person who is beginning prayer—and don't forget this, because it's very important—should be that he work and prepare himself with determination and every possible effort to bring his will into conformity with God's will. Be certain that, as I shall say later,[9] the greatest perfection attainable along the spiritual path lies in this conformity. It is the person who lives in more perfect conformity who will receive more from the Lord and be more advanced on this road. Don't think that in what concerns perfection there is some mystery or things unknown or still to be understood, for in perfect conformity to God's will lies all our good. Now then, if we err in the beginning, desiring that the Lord do our will at once and lead us according to what we imagine, what kind of stability will this edifice have? Let us strive to do what lies in our power and guard ourselves against these poisonous little reptiles, for the Lord often desires that dryness and bad thoughts afflict and pursue us without our being able to get rid of them. Sometimes He even permits these reptiles to bite us so that afterward we may know how to guard ourselves better and that He may prove whether we are greatly grieved by having offended Him.

9. Thus, if you should at times fall, don't become discouraged and stop striving to advance. For even from this fall God will draw out good, as does the seller of an antidote who drinks some poison in order to test whether his antidote is effective. Even if we didn't see our misery—or the great harm that a dissipated life does to us—through any other means than through this assault that we endure for the sake of being

brought back to recollection, that would be enough. Can there be an evil greater than that of being ill at ease in our own house? What hope can we have of finding rest outside of ourselves if we cannot be at rest within? We have so many great and true friends and relatives (which are our faculties) with whom we must always live, even though we may not want to. But from what we feel, these seem to be warring against us because of what our vices have done to them. Peace, peace, the Lord said, my Sisters; and He urged His apostle so many times.[10] Well, believe me, if we don't obtain and have peace in our own house we'll not find it outside. Let this war be ended. Through the blood He shed for us I ask those who have not begun to enter within themselves to do so; and those who have begun not to let the war make them turn back. Let these latter reflect that a relapse is worse than a fall; they already see their loss. Let them trust in the mercy of God and not at all in themselves, and they will see how His Majesty brings them from the dwelling places of one stage to those of another and settles them in a land where these wild animals cannot touch or tire them, but where they themselves will bring all these animals into subjection and scoff at them. And they shall enjoy many more blessings than one can desire—blessings even in this life, I mean.

10. Since, as I've said in the beginning,[11] I've written to you about how you should conduct yourselves in these disturbances set up here by the devil and how you cannot begin to recollect yourselves by force but only by gentleness, if your recollection is going to be more continual, I will not say anything else here than that in my opinion it is very important to consult persons with experience; for you will be thinking that you are seriously failing to do some necessary thing. Provided that we don't give up, the Lord will guide everything for our benefit, even though we may not find someone to teach us. There is no other remedy for this evil of giving up prayer than to begin again; otherwise the soul will gradually lose more each day—and please God that it will understand this fact.

11. Someone could think that if turning back is so bad it would be better never to begin but to remain outside the castle. I have already told you at the beginning—and the Lord Himself tells you—that anyone who walks in danger perishes in it[12]

and that the door of entry to this castle is prayer. Well now, it is foolish to think that we will enter heaven without entering into ourselves, coming to know ourselves, reflecting on our misery and what we owe God, and begging Him often for mercy. The Lord Himself says: *No one will ascend to My Father but through Me*[13] (I don't know if He says it this way—I think He does) and *whoever sees Me sees My Father.*[14] Well, if we never look at Him or reflect on what we owe Him and the death He suffered for us, I don't know how we'll be able to know Him or do works in His service. And what value can faith have without works and without joining them to the merits of Jesus Christ, our Good? Or who will awaken us to love this Lord?

May it please His Majesty to give us understanding of how much we cost Him, of how the servant is no greater than his master,[15] and that we must work in order to enjoy His glory. And we need to pray for this understanding so that we aren't always entering into temptation.[16]

The Third Dwelling Places

Chapter One

Treats of what little security we can have while living in this exile, even though we may have reached a high state, and of how we should walk with fear. This chapter has some good points.

1. What shall we say to those who through perseverance and the mercy of God have won these battles and have entered the rooms of the third stage, if not: *Blessed is the man who fears the Lord?*[1] His Majesty has done no small thing in giving me understanding right now of what this verse means in the vernacular, for I am ignorant in matters like this. Certainly we are right in calling such a man blessed, since if he doesn't turn back he is, from what we can understand, on the secure path to his salvation.[2] Here you will see, Sisters, how important it was to win the previous battles. I am certain the Lord never fails to give a person like this security of conscience, which is no small blessing. I said "security" and I was wrong, for there is no security in this life; so always understand that I mean "if he doesn't abandon the path he began on."

2. It is a great misery to have to live a life in which we must always walk like those whose enemies are at their doorstep; they can neither sleep nor eat without weapons and without being always frightened lest somewhere these enemies might be able to break through this fortress. O my Lord and my Good, how is it that You want us to desire so miserable a life, for it isn't possible to stop wanting and asking You to take us out of it unless there is hope of losing it for You or of

spending it very earnestly in Your service or, above all, of understanding what Your will is? If it is Your will, my God, may we die with You, as Saint Thomas said;[3] for living without You and with these fears of the possibility of losing You forever is nothing else than dying often. That's why, daughters, I say that the blessedness we must ask for is that of being already secure with the blessed. For with these fears, what happiness can anyone have whose whole happiness is to please God? Consider that this happiness was had—and in much greater degree—by some saints who fell into serious sins and that we are not sure that God will help us to get free from these sins and to do penance for them.

3. Certainly, my daughters, I am so fearful as I write this that I don't know how I'm writing it or how I live when I think about it, which is very often. Pray, my daughters, that His Majesty may live in me always. If He doesn't, what security can a life as badly spent as mine have? And do not become sad in knowing that this life has been badly spent, as I have sometimes observed you become when I tell this to you; you continue to desire that I might have lived a very holy life—and you are right. I too would want to have so lived, but what can I do if I have lost holiness through my own fault! I will not complain about God who gave me enough help to carry out your desires. I cannot say this without tears and without being very ashamed that I am writing something for those who can teach me. Doing so has been a hard command to obey! May it please the Lord that since it is being done for Him it may be of some benefit to you so that You may ask Him to pardon this miserable and bold creature. But His Majesty well knows that I can boast only of His mercy, and since I cannot cease being what I have been, I have no other remedy than to approach His mercy and to trust in the merits of His Son and of the Virgin, His Mother, whose habit I wear so unworthily, and you wear. Praise Him, my daughters, for you truly belong to our Lady. Thus you have no reason to be ashamed of my misery since you have such a good Mother. Imitate her and reflect that the grandeur of our Lady and the good of having her for your patroness must be indeed great since my sins and my being what I am have not been enough to tarnish in any way this sacred order.

4. But one thing I advise you: not because you have such a Mother or patroness should you feel secure, for David was very holy, and you already know who Solomon was. Don't pay any attention to the enclosure and the penance in which you live, or feel safe in the fact that you are always conversing with God and practicing such continual prayer and being so withdrawn from the world of things and, in your opinion, holding them in abhorrence. These practices are all good, but not a sufficient reason, as I have said,[4] for us to stop fearing. So, continue to say this verse and often bear it in mind: *Beatus vir qui timet Dominum.*[5]

5. I don't remember what I was speaking about, for I have digressed a great deal and in thinking of myself I feel helpless, as a bird with broken wings, when it comes to saying anything good. So I want to leave this matter aside for now. Let me get back to what I began telling you[6] concerning souls that have entered the third dwelling places, for the Lord has done them no small favor, but a very great one, in letting them get through the first difficulties. I believe that through the goodness of God there are many of these souls in the world. They long not to offend His Majesty, even guarding themselves against venial sins; they are fond of doing penance and setting aside periods for recollection; they spend their time well, practicing works of charity toward their neighbors, and are very balanced in their use of speech and dress and in the governing of their households—those who have them. Certainly, this is a state to be desired. And, in my opinion, there is no reason why entrance even into the final dwelling place should be denied these souls, nor will the Lord deny them this entrance if they desire it; for such a desire is an excellent way to prepare oneself so that every favor may be granted.

6. O Jesus, and who will say that he doesn't want a good so wonderful, especially after having passed through the most difficult trial? No, nobody will. We all say that we want this good. But since there is need of still more in order that the soul possess the Lord completely, it is not enough to say we want it, just as this was not enough for the young man whom the Lord told what one must do in order to be perfect.[7] From the time I began to speak of these dwelling places I have had this young man in mind. For we are literally like him, and ordinarily the

great dryness in prayer comes from this, although it also has other causes. And I'm leaving aside mention of some interior trials that many good souls undergo (unbearable trials and not at all due to their own fault), from which the Lord always frees them to their own great benefit, and mention of those who suffer from melancholy and other illnesses. Briefly, in all things we have to let God be the judge. What I've said, I believe, is what usually happens; for since these souls realize that they wouldn't commit a sin for anything—many wouldn't even advertently commit a venial sin—and that they conduct their lives and households well, they cannot accept patiently that the door of entry to the place where our King dwells be closed to them who consider themselves His vassals. But even though a king here on earth has many vassals, not all enter his chamber. Enter, enter, my daughters, into the interior rooms; pass on from your little works. By the mere fact that you are Christians you must do all these things and much more. It is enough for you to be God's vassals; don't let your desire be for so much that as a result you will be left with nothing. Behold the saints who entered this King's chamber, and you will see the difference between them and us. Don't ask for what you have not deserved, nor should it enter our minds that we have merited this favor however much we may have served—we who have offended God.

7. O humility, humility! I don't know what kind of temptation I'm undergoing in this matter that I cannot help but think that anyone who makes such an issue of this dryness is a little lacking in humility. I said that I've omitted mention of those great interior trials I've referred to,[8] for those involve much more than just a lack of devotion. Let us prove ourselves, my Sisters, or let the Lord prove us, for He knows well how to do this even though we often don't want to understand it. Let us speak now of those souls whose lives are so well ordered; let us recognize what they do for God, and we shall at once see how we have no reason for complaining of His Majesty. If, like the young man in the gospel, we turn our backs and go away sad[9] when the Lord tells us what we must do to be perfect, what do you want His Majesty to do? For He must give the reward in conformity with the love we have for Him. And this love, daughters, must not be fabricated in our imaginations but

proved by deeds. And don't think He needs our works; He needs the determination of our wills.

8. We seem to think that everything is done when we willingly take and wear the religious habit and abandon all worldly things and possessions for Him—even though these possessions may amount to no more than the nets Saint Peter possessed[10]—for he who gives what he has thinks he gives enough. This renunciation is a good enough preparation if one perseveres in it and doesn't turn back and become involved with the vermin in the first rooms, even if it be only in desire. There is no doubt that if a person perseveres in this nakedness and detachment from all worldly things he will reach his goal. But this perseverance includes the condition—and behold that I am advising you of this—that you consider yourselves useless servants, as Saint Paul, or Christ, says;[11] and believe that you have not put our Lord under any obligation to grant you these kinds of favors. Rather, as one who has received more, you are more indebted.[12] What can we do for a God so generous that He died for us, created us, and gives us being? Shouldn't we consider ourselves lucky to be able to repay something of what we owe Him for His service toward us? I say these words "His service toward us" unwillingly; but the fact is that He did nothing else but serve us all the time He lived in this world. And yet we ask Him again for favors and gifts.

9. Reflect a great deal, daughters, on some of the things that are here pointed out, even though in a jumbled way, for I don't know how to explain them further. The Lord will give you understanding of them so that out of dryness you may draw humility—and not disquiet, which is what the devil aims for. Be convinced that where humility is truly present God will give a peace and conformity—even though He may never give consolations—by which one will walk with greater contentment than will others with their consolations. For often, as you have read,[13] the divine Majesty gives these consolations to the weaker souls, although I think we would not exchange these consolations for the fortitude of those who walk in dryness. We are fonder of consolations than we are of the cross. Test us, Lord—for You know the truth—so that we may know ourselves.

CHAPTER TWO

Continues on the same topic; deals with dryness in prayer; with what, in her opinion, might take place at this stage; how it is necessary to test ourselves; and with the fact that the Lord does try those who are in these dwelling places.

1. I have known some souls and even many—I believe I can say—who have reached this state and have lived many years in this righteous and well ordered way both in body and soul, insofar as can be known. After these years, when it seems they have become lords of the world, at least clearly disillusioned in its regard, His Majesty will try them in some minor matters, and they will go about so disturbed and afflicted that it puzzles me and even makes me fearful. It's useless to give them advice, for since they have engaged so long in the practice of virtue they think that they can teach others and that they are more than justified in feeling disturbed.

2. In sum, I have found neither a way of consoling nor a cure for such persons other than to show them compassion in their affliction—and, indeed, compassion is felt on seeing them subject to so much misery—and not contradict their reasoning. For everything in their minds leads them to think they are suffering these things for God, and so they don't come to realize that their disturbance is an imperfection. This is another mistake of persons so advanced. There is no reason for us to be surprised at what they experience, although I do think the feeling stirred by such things should pass quickly. For God often desires that His chosen ones feel their wretchedness, and He withdraws His favor a little. No more is necessary, for I would wager that we'd then soon get to know ourselves. The nature of this trial is immediately understood, for they recognize their fault very clearly. Sometimes, seeing their fault distresses them more than the thing that disturbs them, for unable to help themselves they are affected by earthly happenings even though these may not be very burdensome. This distress, I think, is a great mercy from God; and although it is a defect, it is very beneficial for humility.

3. As for the persons I am speaking about, this is not so. But, as I have said, they canonize these feelings in their minds and would like others to do so. I want to mention some of these

feelings so that we may understand and test ourselves before the Lord tests us. It is very important to be prepared and to have understood ourselves beforehand.

4. A rich person without children or anyone for whom he might want his possessions happens to lose his wealth, but not to such an extent that he lacks necessities for himself and for the management of his household; he even has a surplus. If he should go about as worried and disturbed as he would be if not even a piece of bread were left, how can our Lord ask him to leave all for Him?[1] Here the person makes the excuse that he feels the way he does because he wants these things for the poor. But I believe that God has a greater desire that such a person conform to the divine will and that, though this person may try to procure such wealth, he keep his soul at rest rather than worry about charity of such a kind. And if the person doesn't do this, because the Lord has not brought him so far, well and good; but he should understand that he lacks this freedom of spirit. And because the Lord will ask him for it, he should prepare himself so that the Lord may give it to him; he will be asking His Majesty for it.

A person has plenty to eat and even a surplus; the opportunity presents itself for him to acquire more wealth; all right, let him do so if it is offered to him. But if he strives for wealth and after possessing it strives for more and more, however good the intention may be (for he should have it because, as I have said,[2] these are virtuous persons of prayer), he need have no fear of ascending to the dwelling places closest to the King.

5. There is a similar occurrence when an opportunity presents itself for these persons to be despised or to lose a little honor. God often grants them the favor of enduring such a thing, for He is very fond of favoring virtue publicly so that virtue itself will not undergo a loss of esteem. Or He will also do so because they have served Him, for this Beloved of ours is very good. But now they are left in such disquiet that they cannot help themselves, nor can they quickly get rid of this disturbance. God help me! Aren't these the ones who for a long while now have considered how the Lord suffered and how good suffering is, and who have desired it? They would like everyone to live a life as well ordered as they do; and please God they will not think their grief is for the faults of others

and in their minds turn it into something meritorious.

6. It must seem to you, Sisters, that I'm not staying on the subject or not speaking to you, for these things don't take place here. Neither do we have wealth nor do we desire or strive for it, nor does anyone do injury to us. As a result the examples are not relevant to us. But from these examples many lessons can be learned about things it would not be good to single out, nor would there be reason to do so. Through the above examples you will understand whether or not you are truly stripped of what you have left behind. For little things happen, even though not of this kind, in which you can very well test and know whether or not you are the rulers of your passions. And believe me the whole affair lies not in whether we wear the religious habit but in striving to practice the virtues, in surrendering our will to God in everything, in bringing our life into accordance with what His Majesty ordains for it, and in desiring that His will not ours be done.[3] Since we may not have reached this stage—humility, as I have said![4] Humility is the ointment for our wounds because if we indeed have humility, even though there may be a time of delay, the surgeon, who is our Lord, will come to heal us.

7. The penance these souls do is well balanced, like their lives. They desire penance a great deal so as to serve our Lord by it. Nothing of this is wrong, and thus they are very discreet in doing it in a way so as not to harm their health. Have no fear that they will kill themselves, for their reason is still very much in control. Love has not yet reached the point of overwhelming reason. But I should like us to use our reason to make ourselves dissatisfied with this way of serving God, always going step by step, for we'll never finish this journey. And since, in our opinion, we are continually walking and are tired (for, believe me, it is a wearisome journey), we will be doing quite well if we don't go astray. But does it seem to you, daughters, that if we could go from one land to another in eight days, it would be good to take a year through wind, snow, rain, and bad roads? Wouldn't it be better to make the journey all at once? For all these obstacles are present, as well as danger from snakes. Oh, what good proofs I could give of these things. And please God I may have passed beyond this stage, for often enough it seems to me I haven't.

8. Since we are so circumspect, everything offends us because we fear everything; so we don't dare go further—as if we could reach these dwelling places while leaving to other persons the trouble of treading the path for us. Since this is not possible, let us exert ourselves, my Sisters, for the love of the Lord; let's abandon our reason and our fears into His hands; let's forget this natural weakness that can take up our attention so much. Let the prelates take care of our bodily needs; that's their business. As for ourselves, we should care only about moving quickly so as to see this Lord. Even though the comfort you have is little or none at all, we could be deceived by worry about our health. Furthermore, worry over our health will not increase our health. This I know. And I also know that the whole affair doesn't lie in what pertains to the body, for this is what is the least important. The journey I am speaking of must be taken with great humility. For if you have understood, it is in relation to humility, I believe, that there is an obstacle for those who do not go forward. It should seem to us that we have gone but a few steps, and we should believe this to be so, and that those our Sisters have taken are rapid ones; and not only should we desire but we should strive that they consider us the most miserable of all.

9. With humility present, this stage is a most excellent one. If humility is lacking, we will remain here our whole life—and with a thousand afflictions and miseries. For since we will not have abandoned ourselves, this state will be very laborious and burdensome. We shall be walking while weighed down with this mud of our human misery, which is not so with those who ascend to the remaining rooms. But in these rooms we're speaking of the Lord, as one who is just or even merciful, does not fail to pay; for He always gives much more than we deserve by giving us consolations far greater than those we find in the comforts and distractions of life. But I don't think He gives much spiritual delight unless sometimes in order to invite souls by the sight of what takes place in the remaining dwelling places and so that they will prepare themselves to enter them.

10. It will seem to you that consolations and spiritual delights are the same, so why should I make this distinction? To me it seems there is a very great difference between the two. Now I can be wrong. I'll say what I understand about this

when I speak of the fourth dwelling places, which come after these. For since something will have to be explained about the spiritual delights the Lord gives there, the discussion will be more appropriate at that time. And although the explanation may seem to be useless it might help somewhat so that in understanding the nature of each thing you will be able to strive for what is best. Great solace comes to souls God brings there, and confusion to those who think they have everything. If souls are humble they will be moved to give thanks. If there is some lack in humility, they will feel an inner distaste for which they will find no reason. For perfection as well as its reward does not consist in spiritual delights but in greater love and in deeds done with greater justice and truth.

11. You will wonder, if this is true—as it is—what use it serves to explain and treat of these interior favors. I don't know. Ask him who ordered me to write, for I am not obliged to dispute with superiors but to obey—nor would disputing with them be right. What I can truthfully say to you is that at one time I didn't have or even know about these favors through experience or think that I would ever in my life know about them in this way—and rightly so, for it was happiness enough for me to know, or by conjecture understand, that I was pleasing God in something. But when I read in books about these delights and favors the Lord grants souls that serve Him, I was very much consoled and moved to give great praise to God. Well, if my soul, which was so wretched, did this, those souls that are good and humble will praise Him much more. And if one alone is led to praise Him even once, it is in my opinion very good that the subject be mentioned so that we know about the happiness and delight we lose through our own fault. Moreover, if these favors are from God they come brimming over with love and fortitude by which you can journey with less labor and grow in the practice of works and virtues. Don't think that it matters little to lose such favors through our own fault; when it isn't our fault, the Lord is just.[5] His Majesty will give you through other paths what He keeps from you on this one because of what He knows, for His secrets are very hidden; at least what He does will without any doubt be what is most suitable for us.

12. What it seems to me would be highly beneficial for those who through the goodness of the Lord are in this state (for, as I have said,[6] He grants them no small mercy because they are very close to ascending higher) is that they study diligently how to be prompt in obedience. And even if they are not members of a religious order, it would be a great thing for them to have—as do many persons—someone whom they could consult so as not to do their own will in anything. Doing our own will is usually what harms us. And they shouldn't seek another of their own making, as they say—one who is so circumspect about everything; but seek out someone who is very free from illusion about the things of the world. For in order to know ourselves, it helps a great deal to speak with someone who already knows the world for what it is. And it helps also because when we see some things done by others that seem so impossible for us and the ease with which they do them, it is very encouraging and seems that through their flight we also will make bold to fly, as do the bird's fledglings when they are taught; for even though they do not begin to soar immediately, little by little they imitate the parent. Receiving this help is most beneficial; I know. These persons will be right, however determined they are to keep from offending the Lord, not to place themselves in the occasion of offending Him. Since they are close to the first dwelling places, they could easily return to them. Their fortitude is not founded on solid ground, as is the case with those who are tried in suffering, for these latter know about the storms of the world and what little reason there is to fear them or desire the world's consolations. But it would be possible for the former in a great persecution to return to these consolations. The devil knows well how to stir up tempests so as to do us harm, and these persons would be unable to bear the trials that would come from their zeal to prevent others from committing sin.

13. Let us look at our own faults and leave aside those of others, for it is very characteristic of persons with such well-ordered lives to be shocked by everything. Perhaps we could truly learn from the one who shocks us what is most important even though we may surpass him in external composure and our way of dealing with others. Although good, these latter

things are not what is most important; nor is there any reason to desire that everyone follow at once our own path, or to set about teaching the way of the spirit to someone who perhaps doesn't know what such a thing is. For with these desires that God gives us, Sisters, about the good of souls, we can make many mistakes. So it is better to carry out what our rule says, to strive to live always in silence and hope,[7] for the Lord will take care of these souls. If we ourselves are not negligent in beseeching His Majesty to do so, we shall, with His favor, do much good. May He be blessed forever.

THE FOURTH DWELLING PLACES

CONTAINS THREE CHAPTERS

CHAPTER ONE

Discusses the difference between consolations (or feelings of tenderness) in prayer and spiritual delights.[1] Tells of her happiness on learning the difference between the mind and the intellect. This knowledge is very beneficial for anyone who is greatly distracted in prayer.

1. In order to begin to speak of the fourth dwelling places I really need to entrust myself, as I've already done, to the Holy Spirit and beg Him to speak for me from here on that I may say something about the remaining rooms in a way that you will understand. For supernatural experiences begin here. These are something most difficult to explain, if His Majesty doesn't do so, as was said in another book I wrote fourteen years ago, more or less, in which I dealt with these experiences to the extent of my knowledge of them at that time. Although I think I now have a little more light about these favors the Lord grants to some souls, knowing how to explain them is a different matter.[2] May His Majesty help me to do so if it will be of some benefit; and if not, then no.

2. Since these dwelling places now are closer to where the King is, their beauty is great. There are things to see and understand so delicate that the intellect is incapable of devising a way to explain them, although something might turn out to be well put and not at all obscure to the unexperienced; and anyone who has experience, especially when there is a lot of it, will understand very well.

It will seem that to reach these dwelling places one will

have had to live in the others a long while. Although it is usual that a person will have to have stayed in those already spoken about, there is no certain rule, as you will have often heard. For the Lord gives when He desires, as He desires, and to whom He desires. Since these blessings belong to Him, He does no injustice to anyone.[3]

3. Poisonous creatures rarely enter these dwelling places. If they enter they do no harm; rather, they are the occasion of gain. I hold that the situation is much better in this stage of prayer when these creatures do enter and wage war, for the devil could deceive one with respect to the spiritual delights given by God if there were no temptations, and do much more harm than when temptations are felt. The soul would not gain so much; at least all the things contributing to its merit would be removed, and it would be left in a habitual absorption. For when a soul is in one continual state, I don't consider it safe, nor do I think it is possible for the spirit of the Lord to be in one fixed state during this exile.

4. Well now, in speaking about what I said I'd mention here[4] concerning the difference in prayer between consolations and spiritual delights, the term "consolations," I think, can be given to those experiences we ourselves acquire through our own meditation and petitions to the Lord, those that proceed from our own nature—although God in the end does have a hand in them; for it must be understood, in whatever I say, that without Him we can do nothing.[5] But these consolations arise from the virtuous work itself that we perform, and it seems that we have earned them through our own effort and are rightly consoled for having engaged in such deeds. But if we reflect on this, we see that we experience the same joyful consolations in many of the things that can happen to us on earth, for example: when someone suddenly inherits a great fortune; when we suddenly see a person we love very much; when we succeed in a large and important business matter and of which all speak well; when you see your husband or brother or son alive after someone has told you he is dead. I have seen the flow of tears from great consolations, and this has even happened to me at times. I think that just as these joyful consolations are natural so are those afforded us by the things of God, but these latter are of a nobler kind, although the

others are not bad. In sum, joyful consolations in prayer have their beginning in our own human nature and their end in God.

The spiritual delights begin in God, but human nature feels and enjoys them as much as it does those I mentioned—and much more. O Jesus, how I long to know how to explain this! For I discern, I think, a very recognizable difference, but I don't have the knowledge to be able to explain myself. May the Lord do so.

5. Now I remember a line that we say at Prime, in the latter part of the verse at the end of the last psalm: *Cum dilatasti cor meum.*[6] For anyone who has had much experience these words are sufficient to see the difference between consolations and spiritual delights; for anyone who has not, more words are needed. The consolations that were mentioned do not expand the heart; rather, they usually seem to constrain it a little—although there is the greatest consolation at seeing what is done for God. But some anxious tears come that in a way, it seems, are brought on by the passions. I don't know much about these passions of the soul—knowledge of them might perhaps have enabled me to explain—and what proceeds from sensuality and from our human nature, for I am very dull. If only I knew how to explain myself, for since I have undergone this I understand it. Knowledge and learning are a great help in everything.

6. My experience of this state (I mean of this joy and consolation that comes during meditation) is that if I began to weep over the Passion I didn't know how to stop until I got a severe headache; if I did so over my sins, the same thing happened. Our Lord granted me quite a favor. Yet I don't want to examine now whether the one or the other is better, but I would like to know how to explain the difference there is between the one and the other. It is for these reasons sometimes that these tears flow and desires come, and they are furthered by human nature and one's temperament; but finally, as I have said,[7] they end in God regardless of their nature. They are to be esteemed if there is the humility to understand that one is no better because of experiencing them, for it cannot be known whether they are all effects of love. When they are, the gift is God's.

For the most part, the souls in the previous dwelling places are the ones who have these devout feelings, for these souls work almost continually with the intellect, engaging in discursive thought and meditation. And they do well because nothing further has been given them, although they would be right if they engaged for a while in making acts of love, praising God, rejoicing in His goodness, that He is who He is, and in desiring His honor and glory. These acts should be made insofar as possible, for they are great awakeners of the will. Such souls would be well advised when the Lord gives them these acts not to abandon them so as to finish the usual meditation.

7. Because I have spoken at length on this subject elsewhere,[8] I will say nothing about it here. I only wish to inform you that in order to profit by this path and ascend to the dwelling places we desire, the important thing is not to think much but to love much;[9] and so do that which best stirs you to love. Perhaps we don't know what love is. I wouldn't be very much surprised, because it doesn't consist in great delight but in desiring with strong determination to please God in everything, in striving, insofar as possible, not to offend Him, and in asking Him for the advancement of the honor and glory of His Son and the increase of the Catholic Church. These are the signs of love. Don't think the matter lies in thinking of nothing else, and that if you become a little distracted all is lost.

8. I have been very afflicted at times in the midst of this turmoil of mind. A little more than four years ago I came to understand through experience that the mind (or imagination, to put it more clearly) is not the intellect. I asked a learned man and he told me that this was so; which brought me no small consolation.[10] For since the intellect is one of the soul's faculties, it was an arduous thing for me that it should be so restless at times. Ordinarily the mind flies about quickly, for only God can hold it fast in such a way as to make it seem that we are somehow loosed from this body. I have seen, I think, that the faculties of my soul were occupied and recollected in God while my mind on the other hand was distracted. This distraction puzzled me.[11]

9. O Lord, take into account the many things we suffer on this path for lack of knowledge! The trouble is that since we do not think there is anything to know other than that we must think of You, we do not even know how to ask those who know nor do we understand what there is to ask. Terrible trials are

suffered because we don't understand ourselves, and that which isn't bad at all but good we think is a serious fault. This lack of knowledge causes the afflictions of many people who engage in prayer: complaints about interior trials, at least to a great extent, by people who have no learning; melancholy and loss of health; and even the complete abandonment of prayer. For such persons don't reflect that there is an interior world here within us. Just as we cannot stop the movement of the heavens, but they proceed in rapid motion, so neither can we stop our mind; and then the faculties of the soul go with it, and we think we are lost and have wasted the time spent before God. But the soul is perhaps completely joined with Him in the dwelling places very close to the center while the mind is on the outskirts of the castle suffering from a thousand wild and poisonous beasts, and meriting by this suffering. As a result we should not be disturbed; nor should we abandon prayer, which is what the devil wants us to do. For the most part all the trials and disturbances come from our not understanding ourselves.

10. While writing this, I'm thinking about what's going on in my head with the great noise there that I mentioned in the beginning.[12] It makes it almost impossible for me to write what I was ordered to. It seems as if there are in my head many rushing rivers and that these waters are hurtling downward, and that there are many little birds and whistling sounds, not in the ears but in the upper part of the head where, they say, the higher part of the soul is. And I was in that superior part for a long time for it seems this powerful movement of the spirit is a swift upward one. Please God I'll remember to mention the cause of this in discussing the dwelling places that come further on, for this is not a fitting place to do so, and I wouldn't be surprised if the Lord gave me this headache so that I could understand these things better. For all this turmoil in my head doesn't hinder prayer or what I am saying, but the soul is completely taken up in its quiet, love, desires, and clear knowledge.

11. Now then if the superior part of the soul is in the superior part of the head, why isn't the soul disturbed? This I don't know. But I do know that what I say is true. The pain is felt when suspension does not accompany the prayer. When suspension does accompany prayer, no pain is felt until the

suspension passes. But it would be very bad if I were to abandon everything on account of this obstacle. And so it isn't good for us to be disturbed by our thoughts, nor should we be concerned. If the devil causes them, they will cease with this suspension. If they come, as they do, from the misery, among many other miseries, inherited through the sin of Adam, let us be patient and endure them for the love of God since we are likewise subject to eating and sleeping without being able to avoid it, which is quite a trial.

12. Let us recognize our misery and desire to go where no one will taunt us, for sometimes I recall having heard these words the bride says in the Canticle.[13] And indeed I don't find in all of life anything about which they can be more rightly said. It sems to me that all the contempt and trials one can endure in life cannot be compared to these interior battles. Any disquiet and war can be suffered if we find peace where we live, as I have already said.[14] But that we desire to rest from the thousand trials there are in the world and that the Lord wants to prepare us for tranquillity and that within ourselves lies the obstacle to such rest and tranquillity cannot fail to be very painful and almost unbearable. So, Lord, bring us to the place where these miseries will not taunt us, for they seem sometimes to be making fun of the soul. Even in this life, the Lord frees the soul from these miseries when it reaches the last dwelling place, as we shall say later if God wills.[15]

13. These miseries will not afflict or assail everyone as much as they did me for many years because of my wretchedness. It seems that I myself wanted to take vengeance on myself. And since it was something so painful for me, I think perhaps that it will be so for you too. And I so often speak of it here and there that I might sometime succeed in explaining to you that it is an unavoidable thing and should not be a disturbance or affliction for you but that we must let the millclapper go clacking on, and must continue grinding our flour and not fail to work with the will and the intellect.

14. There is a more and a less to this obstacle in accordance with one's health and age. Let the poor soul suffer even though it has no fault in this; we have other faults, which makes it right for us to practice patience. And since our reading and the counsels we receive (that is, to pay no attention to

these thoughts) don't suffice, I don't think that the time spent in explaining these things for those of you with little knowledge and consoling you in this matter is time lost. But until the Lord wants to enlighten us, these counsels will be of little help. Yet, it is necessary and His Majesty wishes us to take the means and understand ourselves; and let's not blame the soul for what a weak imagination, nature, and the devil cause.

CHAPTER TWO

Continues on the same subject and explains through a comparison the nature of spiritual delight and how this is attained by not seeking it.

1. God help me with what I have undertaken! I've already forgot what I was dealing with, for business matters and poor health have forced me to set this work aside just when I was at my best; and since I have a poor memory everything will come out confused because I can't go back to read it over. And perhaps even everything else I say is confused; at least that's what I feel it is.

It seems to me I have explained the nature of consolations in the spiritual life.[1] Since they are sometimes mixed with our own passions, they are the occasion of loud sobbing; and I have heard some persons say they experience a tightening in the chest and even external bodily movements that they cannot restrain. The force of these passions can cause nosebleeds and other things just as painful. I don't know how to explain anything about these experiences because I haven't had any. But they must nonetheless be consoling, for, as I'm saying,[2] the whole experience ends in the desire to please God and enjoy His Majesty's company.

2. The experiences that I call spiritual delight in God, that I termed elsewhere the prayer of quiet,[3] are of a very different kind, as those of you who by the mercy of God have experienced them will know. Let's consider, for a better understanding, that we see two founts with two water troughs. (For I don't find anything more appropriate to explain some spiritual experiences than water; and this is because I know little and have no helpful cleverness of mind and am so fond of this element that I have observed it more attentively than other

things. In all the things that so great and wise a God has created there must be many beneficial secrets, and those who understand them do benefit, although I believe that in ᴖch little thing created by God there is more than what is understood, even if it is a little ant.)

3. These two troughs are filled with water in different ways; with one the water comes from far away through many aqueducts and the use of much ingenuity; with the other the source of the water is right there, and the trough fills without any noise. If the spring is abundant, as is this one we are speaking about, the water overflows once the trough is filled, forming a large stream. There is no need of any skill, nor does the building of aqueducts have to continue; but water is always flowing from the spring.

The water coming from the aqueducts is comparable, in my opinion, to the consolations I mentioned[4] that are drawn from meditation. For we obtain them through thoughts, assisting ourselves, using creatures to help our meditation, and tiring the intellect. Since, in the end, the consolation comes through our own efforts, noise is made when there has to be some replenishing of the benefits the consolation causes in the soul, as has been said.[5]

4. With this other fount, the water comes from its own source, which is God. And since His Majesty desires to do so— when He is pleased to grant some supernatural favor—He produces this delight with the greatest peace and quiet and sweetness in the very interior part of ourselves. I don't know from where or how, nor is that happiness and delight experienced as are earthly consolations in the heart. I mean there is no similarity at the beginning, for afterward the delight fills everything; this water overflows through all the dwelling places and faculties until reaching the body. That is why I said[6] that it begins in God and ends in ourselves. For, certainly, as anyone who may have experienced it will see, the whole exterior man enjoys this spiritual delight and sweetness.

5. I was now thinking, while writing this, that the verse mentioned above, *Dilatasti cor meum*,[7] says the heart was expanded. I don't think the experience is something, as I say, that rises from the heart, but from another part still more interior, as from something deep. I think this must be the center of the

soul, as I later came to understand and will mention at the end.[8] For certainly I see secrets within ourselves that have often caused me to marvel. And how many more there must be! O my Lord and my God, how great are Your grandeurs! We go about here below like foolish little shepherds, for while it seems that we are getting some knowledge of You it must amount to no more than nothing; for even in our own selves there are great secrets that we don't understand. I say "no more than nothing" because I'm comparing it to the many, many secrets that are in You, not because the grandeurs we see in You are not extraordinary; and that includes those we can attain knowledge of through Your works.

6. To return to the verse, what I think is helpful in it for explaining this matter is the idea of expansion. It seems that since that heavenly water begins to rise from this spring I'm mentioning that is deep within us, it swells and expands our whole interior being producing ineffable blessings; nor does the soul even understand what is given to it there. It perceives a fragrance, let us say for now, as though there were in that interior depth a brazier giving off sweet-smelling perfumes. No light is seen, nor is the place seen where the brazier is; but the warmth and the fragrant fumes spread through the entire soul and even often enough, as I have said,[9] the body shares in them. See now that you understand me; no heat is felt, nor is there the scent of any perfume, for the experience is more delicate than an experience of these things; but I use the examples only so as to explain it to you. And let persons who have not experienced these things understand that truthfully they do happen and are felt in this way, and the soul understands them in a manner clearer than is my explanation right now. This spiritual delight is not something that can be imagined, because however diligent our efforts we cannot acquire it. The very experience of it makes us realize that it is not of the same metal as we ourselves but fashioned from the purest gold of the divine wisdom. Here, in my opinion, the faculties are not united but absorbed and looking as though in wonder at what they see.

7. It's possible that in dealing with these interior matters I might contradict something of what I said elsewhere. That's no surprise, because in the almost fifteen years[10] since I wrote it

the Lord may perhaps have given me clearer understanding in these matters than I had before. Now, as then, I could be completely mistaken—but I would not lie, because by God's mercy I'd rather suffer a thousand deaths. I speak of what I understand.

8. It seems clear to me that the will must in some way be united with God's will. But it is in the effects and deeds following afterward that one discerns the true value of prayer; there is no better crucible for testing prayer. It is quite a great favor from our Lord if the person receiving the favor recognizes it, and a very great one if he doesn't turn back.

You will at once desire, my daughters, to obtain this prayer; and you are right, for, as I have said,[11] the soul will never understand the favors the Lord is granting there or the love with which He is drawing it nearer to Himself. It is good to try to understand how we can obtain such a favor; so I am going to tell you what I have understood about this.

9. Let's leave aside the times when our Lord is pleased to grant it because He wants to and for no other reason. He knows why; we don't have to meddle in this. After you have done what should be done by those in the previous dwelling places: humility! humility! By this means the Lord allows Himself to be conquered with regard to anything we want from Him. The first sign for seeing whether or not you have humility is that you do not think you deserve these favors and spiritual delights from the Lord or that you will receive them in your lifetime.

You will ask me how then one can obtain them without seeking them. I answer that for the following reasons there is no better way than the one I mentioned, of not striving for them. First, because the initial thing necessary for such favors is to love God without self-interest. Second, because there is a slight lack of humility in thinking that for our miserable services something so great can be obtained. Third, because the authentic preparation for these favors on the part of those of us who, after all, have offended Him is the desire to suffer and imitate the Lord rather than to have spiritual delights. Fourth, because His Majesty is not obliged to give them to us as He is to give us glory if we keep His commandments. (Without these favors we can be saved, and He knows better than we ourselves what is fitting for us and who of us truly loves Him. This is certain, I know. And I know persons who walk by the path of love as they ought to walk, that is, only so as to serve their Christ crucified; not only do these persons refuse to seek spiritual delights from Him or to desire them but they beseech Him not to give them these favors during their lifetime. This is true.) The fifth reason is that we would be laboring in vain; for since this water must not be drawn through aqueducts as was the previous water, we are little helped by tiring ourselves if the spring doesn't want to produce it. I mean that no matter how much we meditate or how much we try to squeeze something out and have tears, this water doesn't come in such a way. It is given only to whom God wills to give it and often when the soul is least thinking of it.

10. We belong to Him, daughters. Let Him do whatever He likes with us, bring us wherever He pleases. I really believe that whoever humbles himself and is detached (I mean in fact because the detachment and humility must not be just in our thoughts—for they often deceive us—but complete) will receive the favor of this water from the Lord and many other favors that we don't know how to desire. May He be forever praised and blessed, amen.

CHAPTER THREE

Deals with the prayer of recollection, which for the most part the Lord gives before the prayer just mentioned. Tells about its effects and about those that come from that spiritual delight, given by the Lord, that was discussed in the previous chapter.

1. The effects of this prayer are many. I shall mention some. But first, I want to mention another kind of prayer that almost always begins before this one. Since I have spoken of such a prayer elsewhere,[1] I shall say little. It is a recollection that also seems to me to be supernatural because it doesn't involve being in the dark or closing the eyes, nor does it consist in any exterior thing, since without first wanting to do so, one does close one's eyes and desire solitude. It seems that without any contrivance the edifice is being built, by means of this recollection, for the prayer that was mentioned. The senses and exterior things seem to be losing their hold because the soul is recovering what it had lost.

2. They say that the soul enters within itself and, at other times, that it rises above itself.[2] With such terminology I wouldn't know how to clarify anything. This is what's wrong with me: that I think you will understand by my way of explaining, while perhaps I'm the only one who will understand myself. Let us suppose that these senses and faculties (for I have already mentioned that these powers are the people of this castle,[3] which is the image I have taken for my explanation) have gone outside and have walked for days and years with strangers—enemies of the well-being of the castle. Having seen their perdition they've already begun to approach the castle even though they may not manage to remain inside because the habit of doing so is difficult to acquire. But still they are not traitors, and they walk in the environs of the castle. Once the great King, who is in the center dwelling place of this castle, sees their good will, He desires in His wonderful mercy to bring them back to Him. Like a good shepherd, with a whistle so gentle that even they themselves almost fail to hear it, He makes them recognize His voice and stops them from going so far astray and brings them back to their dwelling place. And this shepherd's whistle has such power that they abandon the exterior things in which they were estranged from Him and enter the castle.

3. I don't think I've ever explained it as clearly as I have now. When God grants the favor it is a great help to seek Him within where He is found more easily and in a way more beneficial to us than when sought in creatures, as Saint Augustine says after having looked for Him in many places.[4] Don't think this recollection is acquired by the intellect striving to think about God within itself, or by the imagination imagining Him within itself. Such efforts are good and an excellent kind of meditation because they are founded on a truth, which is that God is within us. But this isn't the prayer of recollection because it is something each one can do—with the help of God, as should be understood of everything. But what I'm speaking of comes in a different way. Sometimes before one begins to think of God, these people are already inside the castle. I don't know in what way or how they heard their shepherd's whistle. It wasn't through the ears, because nothing is heard. But one noticeably senses a gentle drawing inward, as anyone who goes

through this will observe, for I don't know how to make it clearer. It seems to me that I have read where it was compared to a hedgehog curling up or a turtle drawing into its shell.[5] (The one who wrote this example must have understood the experience well.) But these creatures draw inward whenever they want. In the case of this recollection, it doesn't come when we want it but when God wants to grant us the favor. I for myself hold that when His Majesty grants it, He does so to persons who are already beginning to despise the things of the world. I don't say that those in the married state do so in deed, for they cannot, but in desire; for He calls such persons especially so that they might be attentive to interior matters. So I believe that if we desire to make room for His Majesty, He will give not only this but more, and give it to those whom He begins to call to advance further.

4. May whoever experiences this within himself praise God greatly because it is indeed right to recognize the favor and give thanks, for doing so will dispose one for other greater favors. And this recollection is a preparation for being able to listen, as is counseled in some books,[6] so that the soul instead of striving to engage in discourse strives to remain attentive and aware of what the Lord is working in it. If His Majesty has not begun to absorb us, I cannot understand how the mind can be stopped. There's no way of doing so without bringing about more harm than good, although there has been a lengthy controversy on this matter among some spiritual persons. For my part I must confess my lack of humility, but those in favor of stopping the mind have never given me a reason for submitting to what they say. One of them tried to convince me with a certain book by the saintly Friar Peter of Alcántara[7]—for I believe he is a saint—to whom I would submit because I know that he knew. And we read it together, and he says the same thing I do, although not in my words. But it is clear in what he says that love must be already awakened. It could be that I'm mistaken, but I have the following reasons.

5. First, in this work of the spirit the one who thinks less and has less desire to act does more. What we must do is to beg like the needy poor before a rich and great emperor, and then lower our eyes and wait with humility. When through His secret paths it seems we understand that He hears us, then it is

good to be silent, since He has allowed us to remain near Him; and it will not be wrong to avoid working with the intellect—if we can work with it, I mean. But if we don't yet know whether this King has heard or seen us, we mustn't become fools. The soul does become quite a fool when it tries to induce this prayer, and it is left much drier; and the imagination perhaps becomes more restless through the effort made not to think of anything. But the Lord desires that we beseech Him and call to mind that we are in His presence; He knows what is suitable for us. I cannot persuade myself to use human diligence in a matter in which it seems that His Majesty has placed a limit, and I want to leave the diligence to Him. What He did not reserve to Himself are many other efforts we can make with His help, such as: penance, good deeds, and prayer—insofar as our wretchedness can do these things.

6. The second reason is that these interior works are all gentle and peaceful; doing something arduous would cause more harm than good. I call any force that we might want to use "something arduous"; for example, it would be arduous to hold one's breath. Leave the soul in God's hands, let Him do whatever He wants with it, with the greatest disinterest about your own benefit as is possible and the greatest resignation to the will of God.

The third reason is that the very care used not to think of anything will perhaps rouse the mind to think very much.

The fourth is that what is most essential and pleasing to God is that we be mindful of His honor and glory and forget ourselves and our own profit and comfort and delight. How is a person forgetful of self if he is so careful not to stir or even to allow his intellect or desires to be stirred to a longing for the greater glory of God, or if he rests in what he already has? When His Majesty desires the intellect to stop, He occupies it in another way and gives it a light so far above what we can attain that it remains absorbed. Then, without knowing how, the intellect is much better instructed than it was through all the soul's efforts not to make use of it. Since God gave us our faculties that we might work with them and in this work they find their reward, there is no reason to charm them; we should let them perform their task until God appoints them to another greater one.

7. What I understand to be most fitting for the soul the Lord has desired to put in this dwelling place is that which has been said.[8] And without any effort or noise the soul should strive to cut down the rambling of the intellect—but not suspend either it or the mind; it is good to be aware of who God is and that one is in God's presence. If what it feels within itself absorbs it, well and good. But let it not strive to understand the nature of this recollection, for this recollection is given to the will. Let the soul enjoy it without any endeavors other than some loving words, for even though we may not try in this prayer to go without thinking of anything, I know that often the intellect will be suspended, even though for only a very brief moment.

8. But as I said elsewhere,[9] the reason why in this kind of prayer, that is, the kind that is like the flowing spring in which the water does not come through aqueducts, the soul restrains itself or is restrained in its realization that it doesn't understand what it desires; and so the mind wanders from one extreme to the other, like a fool unable to rest in anything. (I am referring to the kind of prayer this dwelling place began with, for I have joined the prayer of recollection, which I should have mentioned first, with this one. The prayer of recollection is much less intense than the prayer of spiritual delight from God that I mentioned; but it is the beginning through which one goes to the other, for in the prayer of recollection meditation, or the work of the intellect, must not be set aside.) The will has such deep rest in its God that the clamor of the intellect is a terrible bother to it. There is no need to pay any attention to this clamor, for doing so would make the will lose much of what it enjoys. But one should let the intellect go and surrender oneself into the arms of love, for His Majesty will teach the soul what it must do at that point. Almost everything lies in finding oneself unworthy of so great a good and in being occupied with giving thanks.

9. In order to deal with the prayer of recollection I postponed mention of the effects or signs in souls to whom God, our Lord, gives this prayer of quiet. What an expansion or dilation of the soul is may be clearly understood from the example of a fount whose water doesn't overflow into a stream because the fount itself is constructed of such material that the

more water there is flowing into it the larger the trough becomes. So it seems is the case with this prayer and with many other marvels that God grants to the soul, for He enables and prepares it so that it can keep everything within itself. Hence this interior sweetness and expansion can be verified in the fact that the soul is not as tied down as it was before in things pertaining to the service of God, but has much more freedom. Thus, in not being constrained by the fear of hell (because although there is even greater fear of offending God, it loses servile fear here), this soul is left with great confidence that it will enjoy Him. The fear it used to have of doing penance and losing its health has disappeared, and it now thinks it will be able to do all things in God[10] and has greater desire for penance than previously. The fear it used to have of trials it now sees to be tempered. Its faith is more alive; it knows that if it suffers trials for God, His Majesty will give it the grace to suffer them with patience. Sometimes it even desires them because there also remains a strong will to do something for God. Since its knowledge of God's grandeur grows, it considers itself to be more miserable. Because it has already experienced spiritual delight from God, it sees that worldly delights are like filth. It finds itself withdrawing from them little by little, and it is more master of itself for so doing. In sum, there is an improvement in all the virtues. It will continue to grow if it doesn't turn back now to offending God; because if it does, then everything will be lost however high on the summit the soul may be. Nor should it be understood that if God grants this favor once or twice to a soul all these good effects will be caused. It must persevere in receiving them, for in this perseverance lies all our good.

10. One strong warning I give to whoever finds himself in this state is that he guard very carefully against placing himself in the occasion of offending God. In this prayer the soul is not yet grown but is like a suckling child. If it turns away from its mother's breasts, what can be expected for it but death? I am very much afraid that this will happen to anyone to whom God has granted this favor and who withdraws from prayer—unless he does so for a particularly special reason—or if he doesn't return quickly to prayer, for he will go from bad to worse. I know there is a great deal to fear in this matter. And I know

some persons for whom I have felt quite sorry—and I've seen what I'm speaking about—because they have turned away from one who with so much love wanted to be their friend and proved it by deeds. I advise them so strongly not to place themselves in the occasions of sin because the devil tries much harder for a soul of this kind than for very many to whom the Lord does not grant these favors. For such a soul can be of great benefit to God's Church and do a great deal of harm to the devil by getting others to follow it. And even though the devil may have no other reason than to see who it is to whom His Majesty shows particular love, that's sufficient for him to wear himself out trying to lead the soul to perdition. So these souls suffer much combat and if they go astray they do so much more than others.

You, Sisters, are free of dangers, from what we can know. From pride and vainglory may God deliver you. If the devil should counterfeit God's favors, this will be known by the fact that these good effects are not caused, but just the opposite.

11. There is one danger I want to warn you about (although I may have mentioned it elsewhere)[11] into which I have seen persons of prayer fall, especially women, for since we are weaker there is more occasion for what I'm about to say. It is that some have a weak constitution because of a great amount of penance, prayer, and keeping vigil, and even without these; in receiving some favor, their nature is overcome. Since they feel some consolation interiorly and a languishing and weakness exteriorly, they think they are experiencing a spiritual sleep (which is a prayer a little more intense than the prayer of quiet)[12] and they let themselves become absorbed. The more they allow this, the more absorbed they become because their nature is further weakened, and they fancy that they are being carried away in rapture. I call it being carried away in foolishness[13] because it amounts to nothing more than wasting time and wearing down one's health. These persons feel nothing through their senses nor do they feel anything concerning God. One person happened to remain eight hours in this state. By sleeping and eating and avoiding so much penance, this person got rid of the stupor, for there was someone who understood her. She had misled both her confessor and other persons, as well as herself—for she hadn't intended to deceive.

I truly believe that the devil was trying to gain ground, and in this instance indeed he was beginning to gain no small amount.

12. It must be understood that when something is truly from God there is no languishing in the soul, even though there may be interior and exterior languishing. The soul experiences deep feelings when it sees itself close to God. Nor does the experience last so long, but for a very short while—although one becomes absorbed again. In such prayer, if the cause of it is not weakness, as I said,[14] the body is not worn down nor is any external feeling produced. For this reason let them take the advice that when they feel this languishing in themselves they tell the prioress and distract themselves from it insofar as they can. The prioress should make them give up so many hours for prayer so that they have only a very few and try to get them to sleep and eat well until their natural strength begins to return, if it has been lost through a lack of food and sleep. If a Sister's nature is so weak that this is not enough, may she believe me that God does not want her to practice anything but the active life, which also must be practiced in monasteries. They should let her get busy with different duties, and always take care that she not have a great deal of solitude, for she would lose her health completely. It will be quite a mortification for her; in how she bears this absence is the way the Lord wants to test her love for Him. And He will be pleased to give her strength back after some time. If He doesn't, she will gain through vocal prayer and through obedience and will merit what she would have merited otherwise, and perhaps more.

13. There could also be some persons with such weak heads and imaginations—and I have known some—to whom it seems that everything they think about they see. This is very dangerous. Because I shall perhaps treat of it further on, I'll say no more here. I have greatly enlarged on this dwelling place because it is the one that more souls enter. Since it is, and since the natural and the supernatural are joined in it, the devil can do more harm. In those dwelling places still to be spoken of, the Lord doesn't give him so much leeway. May His Majesty be forever praised, amen.

THE FIFTH DWELLING PLACES

CONTAINS FOUR CHAPTERS

CHAPTER ONE

Begins to deal with how the soul is united to God in prayer. Tells how one discerns whether there is any illusion.

1. O Sisters, how can I explain the riches and treasures and delights found in the fifth dwelling places? I believe it would be better not to say anything about these remaining rooms, for there is no way of learning how to speak of them; neither is the intellect capable of understanding them nor can comparisons help in explaining them; earthly things are too coarse for such a purpose.

Send light from heaven, my Lord, that I might be able to enlighten these Your servants—for You have been pleased that some of them ordinarily enjoy these delights—so that they may not be deceived by the devil transforming himself into an angel of light.[1] For all their desires are directed toward pleasing You.

2. And although I have said "some," there are indeed only a few who fail to enter this dwelling place of which I shall now speak. There are various degrees, and for that reason I say that most enter these places. But I believe that only a few will experience some of the things that I will say are in this room. Yet even if souls do no more than reach the door, God is being very merciful to them; although many are called few are chosen.[2] So I say now that all of us who wear this holy habit of Carmel are called to prayer and contemplation. This call explains our origin; we are the descendants of men who felt this call, of those holy fathers on Mount Carmel who in such great

solitude and contempt for the world sought this treasure, this precious pearl of contemplation that we are speaking about. Yet few of us dispose ourselves that the Lord may communicate it to us. In exterior matters we are proceeding well so that we will reach what is necessary; but in the practice of the virtues that are necessary for arriving at this point we need very, very much and cannot be careless in either small things or great. So, my Sisters, since in some way we can enjoy heaven on earth, be brave in begging the Lord to give us His grace in such a way that nothing will be lacking through our own fault; that He show us the way and strengthen the soul that it may dig until it finds this hidden treasure.[3] The truth is that the treasure lies within our very selves. This is what I would like to know how to explain, if the Lord would enable me to do so.

3. I said "strengthen the soul" so that you will understand that bodily strength is not necessary for those to whom God does not give it. He doesn't make it impossible for anyone to buy His riches. He is content if each one gives what he has. Blessed be so great a God. But reflect, daughters, that He doesn't want you to hold on to anything, for if you avoid doing so you will be able to enjoy the favors we are speaking of. Whether you have little or much, He wants everything for Himself; and in conformity with what you know you have given you will receive greater or lesser favors. There is no better proof for recognizing whether our prayer has reached union or not. Don't think this union is some kind of dreamy state like the one I mentioned before.[4] I say "dreamy state" because it seems that the soul is as though asleep; yet neither does it really think it is asleep nor does it feel awake. There is no need here to use any technique to suspend the mind since all the faculties are asleep in this state—and truly asleep—to the things of the world and to ourselves. As a matter of fact, during the time that the union lasts the soul is left as though without its senses, for it has no power to think even if it wants to. In loving, if it does love, it doesn't understand how or what it is it loves or what it would want. In sum, it is like one who in every respect has died to the world so as to live more completely in God. Thus the death is a delightful one, an uprooting from the soul of all the operations the latter can have while being in the body. The death is a delightful one because in truth it seems

that in order to dwell more perfectly in God the soul is so separated from the body that I don't even know if it has life enough to breathe. (I was just now thinking about this, and it seems to me that it doesn't—at least if it does breathe, it is unaware that it is doing so.) Nonetheless, its whole intellect would want to be occupied in understanding something of what is felt. And since the soul does not have the energy to attain to this, it is so stunned that, even if it is not completely lost, neither a hand nor a foot stirs, as we say here below when a person is in such a swoon that we think he is dead.

O secrets of God! I would never tire of trying to explain them if I thought I could in some way manage to do so; thus I will say a thousand foolish things in order that I might at times succeed and that we might give great praise to the Lord.

4. I said that this union was not some kind of dreamy state,[5] because even if the experience in the dwelling place that was mentioned is abundant the soul remains doubtful that it was union. It doubts whether it imagined the experience; whether it was asleep; whether the experience was given by God; or whether the devil transformed himself into an angel of light.[6] It is left with a thousand suspicions. That it has them is good, for, as I have said,[7] even our own nature can sometimes deceive us in that dwelling place. Though there is not so much room for poisonous things to enter, some tiny lizards do enter; since these lizards have slender heads, they can poke their heads in anywhere. And even though they do no harm, especially if one pays no attention to them, as I said,[8] they are often a bother since they are little thoughts proceeding from the imagination and from what I mentioned. But however slender they may be, these little lizards cannot enter this fifth dwelling place; for there is neither imagination, nor memory, nor intellect that can impede this good. And I would dare say that if the prayer is truly union with God the devil cannot even enter or do any damage. His Majesty is so joined and united with the essence of the soul that the devil will not dare approach, nor will he even know about this secret. And this is obvious. Since, as they say, he doesn't know our mind, he will have less knowledge of something so secret; for God doesn't even entrust this to our own mind. Oh, what a great good, a state in which this accursed one does us no harm! Thus the soul is left with

such wonderful blessings because God works within it without anyone's disturbing Him, not even ourselves. What will He not give, who is so fond of giving and who can give all that He wants?

5. It seems that I have left you confused by saying "if it is union" and that there are other unions. And indeed how true it is that there are! Even though these unions regard vain things, the devil will use such things to transport us when they are greatly loved. But he doesn't do so in the way God does, or with the delight and satisfaction of soul, or with the peace and joy. This union is above all earthly joys, above all delights, above all consolations, and still more than that. It doesn't matter where those spiritual or earthly joys come from, for the feeling is very different, as you will have experienced. I once said[9] that the difference is like that between feeling something on the rough outer covering of the body or in the marrow of the bones. And that was right on the mark, for I don't know how to say it better.

6. It seems to me that you're still not satisfied, for you will think you can be mistaken and that these interior things are something difficult to examine. What was said will be sufficient for anyone who has experienced union. Yet, because the difference between union and the previous experience is great, I want to mention a clear sign by which you will be sure against error or doubts about whether the union is from God. His Majesty has brought it to my memory today, and in my opinion it is the sure sign. In difficult matters, even though it seems to me that I understand and that I speak the truth, I always use this expression "it seems to me." For if I am mistaken, I'm very much prepared to believe what those who have a great deal of learning say. Even though they have not experienced these things, very learned men have a certain I don't know what; for since God destines them to give light to His Church, He enlightens them that they might acknowledge a truth when presented with it. And if they do not live a dissipated life but are God's servants, they are never surprised by His grandeurs; they have come to understand well that He can do ever more and more. And, finally, even though some things are not so well explained, these learned men will find

others in their books through which they will see that these things could take place.

7. I have had a great deal of experience with learned men, and have also had experience with half-learned, fearful ones; these latter cost me dearly.[10] At least I think that anyone who refuses to believe that God can do much more or that He has considered and continues to consider it good sometimes to communicate favors to His creatures has indeed closed the door to receiving them. Therefore, Sisters, let this never happen to you, but believe that God can do far more and don't turn your attention to whether the ones to whom He grants His favors are good or bad; for His Majesty knows this, as I have told you.[11] There is no reason for us to meddle in the matter, but with humility and simplicity of heart we should serve and praise Him for His works and marvels.

8. Now then, to return to the sign that I say is the true one:[12] you now see that God has made this soul a fool with regard to all so as better to impress upon it true wisdom. For during the time of this union it neither sees, nor hears, nor understands, because the union is always short and seems to the soul even much shorter than it probably is. God so places Himself in the interior of that soul that when it returns to itself it can in no way doubt that it was in God and God was in it. This truth remains with it so firmly that even though years go by without God's granting that favor again, the soul can neither forget nor doubt that it was in God and God was in it. This is what matters now, for I shall speak of the effects of this prayer afterward.[13]

9. Now, you will ask me, how did the soul see this truth or understand if it didn't see or understand anything? I don't say that it then saw the truth but that afterward it sees the truth clearly, not because of a vision but because of a certitude remaining in the soul that only God can place there. I know a person who hadn't learned that God was in all things by presence, power, and essence, and through a favor of this kind that God granted her she came to believe it. After asking a half-learned man of the kind I mentioned[14]—he knew as little as she had known before God enlightened her—she was told that God was present only by grace. Such was her own conviction that

even after this she didn't believe him and asked others who told her the truth, with which she was greatly consoled.[15]

10. Don't be mistaken by thinking that this certitude has to do with a corporal form, as in the case of the bodily presence of our Lord Jesus Christ in the Most Blessed Sacrament even though we do not see Him. Here the matter isn't like that; it concerns only the divinity. How, then, is it that what we do not see leaves this certitude? I don't know; these are His works. But I do know I speak the truth. And I would say that whoever does not receive this certitude does not experience union of the whole soul with God, but union of some faculty, or that he experiences one of the many other kinds of favors God grants souls. In regard to all these favors we have to give up looking for reasons to see how they've come about. Since our intellect cannot understand this union, why do we have to make this effort? It's enough for us to see that He who is the cause of it is almighty. Since we have no part at all to play in bringing it about no matter how much effort we put forth, but it is God who does so, let us not desire the capacity to understand this union.

11. Now I recall, in saying that we have no part to play, what you have heard the Bride say in the Song of Songs: *He brought me into the wine cellar* (or, placed me there, I believe it says).[16] And it doesn't say that she went. And she says also that she went looking about in every part of the city for her Beloved.[17] I understand this union to be the wine cellar where the Lord wishes to place us when He desires and as He desires. But however great the effort we make to do so, we cannot enter. His Majesty must place us there and enter Himself into the center of our soul. And that He may show His marvels more clearly, He doesn't want our will to have any part to play, for it has been entirely surrendered to Him. Neither does He want the door of the faculties and of the senses to be opened, for they are all asleep. But He wants to enter the center of the soul without going through any door, as He entered the place where His disciples were when He said *pax vobis*;[18] or as He left the tomb without lifting away the stone. Further on you will see in the last dwelling place[19] how His Majesty desires that the soul enjoy Him in its own center even much more than here.

12. O daughters, how much we shall see if we don't want to have anything more to do with our own lowliness and misery and if we understand that we are unworthy of being servants of a Lord who is so great we cannot comprehend His wonders! May He be forever praised, amen.

CHAPTER TWO

Continues on the same topic. Explains the prayer of union through an exquisite comparison. Tells about the effects it leaves in the soul. The chapter is very important.

1. It will seem to you that everything has already been said about what there is to see in this dwelling place. Yet a lot is missing; for, as I said,[1] there are various degrees of intensity. With regard to the nature of union, I don't believe I'd know how to say anything more. But when souls to whom God grants these favors prepare themselves, there are many things to say about the Lord's work in them. I shall speak of some of these and tell about the state the soul is left in. To explain things better I want to use a helpful comparison; it is good for making us see how, even though we can do nothing in this work done by the Lord, we can do much by disposing ourselves so that His Majesty may grant us this favor.

2. You must have already heard about His marvels manifested in the way silk originates, for only He could have invented something like that. The silkworms come from seeds about the size of little grains of pepper. (I have never seen this but have heard of it, and so if something in the explanation gets distorted it won't be my fault.) When the warm weather comes and the leaves begin to appear on the mulberry tree, the seeds start to live, for they are dead until then. The worms nourish themselves on the mulberry leaves until, having grown to full size, they settle on some twigs. There with their little mouths they themselves go about spinning the silk and making some very thick little cocoons in which they enclose themselves. The silkworm, which is fat and ugly, then dies, and a little white butterfly, which is very pretty, comes forth from the cocoon. Now if this were not seen but recounted to us as having happened in other times, who would believe it? Or what reasonings could make us conclude that a thing as nonrational as a

worm or a bee could be so diligent in working for our benefit and with so much industriousness? And the poor little worm loses its life in the challenge. This is enough, Sisters, for a period of meditation even though I may say no more to you; in it you can consider the wonders and the wisdom of our God. Well now, what would happen if we knew the property of every created thing? It is very beneficial for us to busy ourselves thinking of these grandeurs and delighting in being brides of a King so wise and powerful.

3. Let's return to what I was saying. This silkworm, then, starts to live when by the heat of the Holy Spirit it begins to benefit through the general help given to us all by God and through the remedies left by Him to His Church, by going to confession, reading good books, and hearing sermons, which are the remedies that a soul, dead in its carelessness and sins and placed in the midst of occasions, can make use of. It then begins to live and to sustain itself by these things, and by good meditations, until it is grown. Its being grown is what is relevant to what I'm saying, for these other things have little importance here.

4. Well once this silkworm is grown—in the beginning I dealt with its growth[2]—it begins to spin the silk and build the house wherein it will die. I would like to point out here that this house is Christ. Somewhere, it seems to me, I have read or heard that our life is hidden in Christ or in God (both are the same), or that our life is Christ.[3] Whether the quotation is exact or not doesn't matter for what I intend.

5. Well see here, daughters, what we can do through the help of God: His Majesty Himself, as He does in this prayer of union, becomes the dwelling place we build for ourselves. It seems I'm saying that we can build up God and take Him away since I say that He is the dwelling place and we ourselves can build it so as to place ourselves in it. And, indeed, we can! Not that we can take God away or build Him up, but we can take away from ourselves and build up, as do these little silkworms. For we will not have finished doing all that we can in this work when, to the little we do, which is nothing, God will unite Himself, with His greatness, and give it such high value that the Lord Himself will become the reward of this work. Thus, since it was He who paid the highest price, His Majesty wants

to join our little labors with the great ones He suffered so that all the work may become one.

6. Therefore, courage, my daughters! Let's be quick to do this work and weave this little cocoon by taking away our self-love and self-will, our attachment to any earthly thing, and by performing deeds of penance, prayer, mortification, obedience, and of all the other things you know. Would to heaven that we would do what we know we must; and we are instructed about what we must do. Let it die; let this silkworm die, as it does in completing what it was created to do! And you will see how we see God, as well as ourselves placed inside His grandeur, as is this little silkworm within its cocoon. Keep in mind that I say "see God," in the sense of what I mentioned[4] concerning that which is felt in this kind of union.

7. Now, then, let's see what this silkworm does, for that's the reason I've said everything else. When the soul is, in this prayer, truly dead to the world, a little white butterfly comes forth. O greatness of God! How transformed the soul is when it comes out of this prayer after having been placed within the greatness of God and so closely joined with Him for a little while—in my opinion the union never lasts for as much as a half hour. Truly, I tell you that the soul doesn't recognize itself. Look at the difference there is between an ugly worm and a little white butterfly; that's what the difference is here. The soul doesn't know how it could have merited so much good—from where this good may have come I mean, for it well knows that it doesn't merit this blessing. It sees within itself a desire to praise the Lord; it would want to dissolve and die a thousand deaths for Him. It soon begins to experience a desire to suffer great trials without its being able to do otherwise. There are the strongest desires for penance, for solitude, and that all might know God; and great pain comes to it when it sees that He is offended. I shall treat of these things more particularly in the next dwelling place;[5] although what is in this dwelling place and the next are almost identical, the force of the effects is very different. As I have said,[6] if after God brings a soul here it makes the effort to advance, it will see great things.

8. Oh, now, to see the restlessness of this little butterfly, even though it has never been quieter and calmer in its life, is

something to praise God for! And the difficulty is that it doesn't know where to alight and rest. Since it has experienced such wonderful rest, all that it sees on earth displeases it, especially if God gives it this wine often. Almost each time it gains new treasures. It no longer has any esteem for the works it did while a worm, which was to weave the cocoon little by little; it now has wings. How can it be happy walking step by step when it can fly? On account of its desires, everything it can do for God becomes little in its own eyes. It doesn't wonder as much at what the saints suffered now that it understands through experience how the Lord helps and transforms a soul, for it doesn't recognize itself or its image. The weakness it previously seemed to have with regard to doing penance it now finds is its strength. Its attachment to relatives or friends or wealth (for neither its actions, nor its determination, nor its desire to withdraw were enough; rather, in its opinion, it was more attached to everything) is now so looked upon that it grieves when obliged to do what is necessary in this regard so as not to offend God. Everything wearies it, for it has learned through experience that creatures cannot give it true rest.

9. It seems I have been lengthy, but I could say much more; and whoever has received this favor from God will see that I've been brief. So, there is no reason to be surprised that this little butterfly seeks rest again since it feels estranged from earthly things. Well then, where will the poor little thing go? It can't return to where it came from; as was said,[7] we are powerless, however much we do, to bring about this favor until God is again pleased to grant it. O Lord, what new trials begin for this soul! Who would say such a thing after a favor so sublime? Briefly, in one way or another there must be a cross while we live, and with respect to anyone who says that after he arrived here he always enjoyed rest and delight I would say that he never arrived but that perhaps he had experienced some spiritual delight—if he had entered into the previous dwelling places and his experiences had been helped along by natural weakness or perhaps even by the devil who gives him peace so as afterward to wage much greater war against him.

10. I don't mean to say that those who arrive here do not have peace; they do have it, and it is very deep. For the trials themselves are so valuable and have such good roots that al-

though very severe they give rise to peace and happiness. From the very unhappiness caused by worldly things arises the ever so painful desire to leave this world. Any relief the soul has comes from the thought that God wants it to be living in this exile; yet even this is not enough, because in spite of all these benefits it is not entirely surrendered to God's will, as will be seen further on[8]—although it doesn't fail to conform itself. But it conforms with a great feeling that it can do no more because no more has been given it, and with many tears. Every time it is in prayer this regret is its pain. In some way perhaps the sorrow proceeds from the deep pain it feels at seeing that God is offended and little esteemed in this world and that many souls are lost, heretics as well as Moors; although those that grieve it most are Christians. Even though it sees that God's mercy is great—for, however wicked their lives, these Christians can make amends and be saved—it fears that many are being condemned.

11. O greatness of God! A few years ago—and even perhaps days—this soul wasn't mindful of anything but itself. Who has placed it in the midst of such painful concerns? Even were we to meditate for many years we wouldn't be able to feel them as painfully as does this soul now. Well, God help me, wouldn't it be enough if for many days and years I strove to think about the tremendous evil of an offense against God and that those souls who are condemned are His children and my brothers and about the dangers in which we live and how good it is for us to leave this miserable life? Not at all, daughters; the grief that is felt here is not like that of this world. We can, with God's favor, feel the grief that comes from thinking about these things a great deal, but such grief doesn't reach the intimate depths of our being as does the pain suffered in this state, for it seems that the pain breaks and grinds the soul into pieces, without the soul's striving for it or even at times wanting it. Well, what is this pain? Where does it come from? I shall tell you.

12. Haven't you heard it said of the bride—for I have already mentioned it elsewhere here but not in this sense[9]—that God brought her into the inner wine cellar and put charity in order within her?[10] Well, that is what I mean. Since that soul now surrenders itself into His hands and its great love makes it

so surrendered that it neither knows nor wants anything more than what He wants with her (for God will never, in my judgment, grant this favor save to a soul that He takes for His own), He desires that, without its understanding how, it may go forth from this union impressed with His seal. For indeed the soul does no more in this union than does the wax when another impresses a seal on it. The wax doesn't impress the seal upon itself; it is only disposed—I mean by being soft. And even in order to be disposed it doesn't soften itself but remains still and gives its consent. O goodness of God; everything must be at a cost to You! All You want is our will and that there be no impediment in the wax.

13. Well now, you see here, Sisters, what our God does in this union so that this soul may recognize itself as His own. He gives from what He has, which is what His Son had in this life. He cannot grant us a higher favor. Who could have had a greater desire to leave this life? And so His Majesty said at the Last Supper: *I have earnestly desired.*[11]

Well then, how is it, Lord, that You weren't thinking of the laborious death You were about to suffer, so painful and frightful? You answer: "No, my great love and the desire I have that souls be saved are incomparably more important than these sufferings; and the very greatest sorrows that I have suffered and do suffer, after being in the world, are not enough to be considered anything at all in comparison with this love and desire to save souls."

14. This is true, for I have often reflected on the matter. I know the torment a certain soul of my acquaintance[12] suffers and has suffered at seeing our Lord offended. The pain is so unbearable that she desires to die much more than to suffer it. If a soul with so little charity when compared with Christ's— for its charity could be then considered almost nonexistent— felt this torment to be so unbearable, what must have been the feeling of our Lord Jesus Christ? And what kind of life must He have suffered since all things were present to Him and He was always witnessing the serious offenses committed against His Father? I believe without a doubt that these sufferings were much greater than were those of His most sacred Passion. At the time of His Passion He already saw an end to these trials and with this awareness as well as the happiness of seeing a

remedy for us in His death and of showing us the love He had for His Father in suffering so much for Him, He tempered His sorrows. These sorrows are also tempered here below by those who with the strength that comes from love perform great penances, for they almost don't feel them; rather they would want to do more and more—and everything they do seems little to them. Well, what must it have been for His Majesty to find Himself with so excellent an occasion for showing His Father how completely obedient He was to Him, and with love for His neighbor? O great delight, to suffer in doing the will of God! But I consider it so difficult to see the many offenses committed so continually against His Majesty and the many souls going to hell that I believe only one day of that pain would have been sufficient to end many lives; how much more one life, if He had been no more than man.

CHAPTER THREE

Continues on the same subject. Tells about another kind of union the soul can reach with God's help and of how important love of neighbor is for this union. The chapter is very useful.

1. Well now let us get back to our little dove[1] and see something about what God gives it in this state. It must always be understood that one has to strive to go forward in the service of our Lord and in self-knowledge. For if a person does no more than receive this favor and if, as though already securely in possession of something, he grows careless in his life and turns aside from the heavenly path, which consists of keeping the commandments, that which happens to the silkworm will happen to him. For it gives forth the seed that produces other silkworms, and itself dies forever. I say that it "gives forth the seed" because I hold that it is God's desire that a favor so great not be given in vain; if a person doesn't himself benefit, the favor will benefit others. For since the soul is left with these desires and virtues that were mentioned, it always brings profit to other souls during the time that it continues to live virtuously; and they catch fire from its fire. And even when the soul has itself lost this fire, the inclination to benefit others will remain, and the soul delights in explaining the favors God grants to whoever loves and serves Him.

2. I know a person to whom this happened.[2] Although she had gone far astray, she enjoyed helping others through the favors God had granted her and showing the way of prayer to those who didn't understand it; and she did a great deal of good. Afterward the Lord again gave her light. It's true that she still hadn't experienced the effects that were mentioned; but how many there must be, like Judas, whom the Lord calls to the apostolate by communing with them, and, like Saul, whom He calls to be kings, who afterward through their own fault go astray! Thus we can conclude, Sisters, that, in order to merit more and more and to avoid getting lost like such persons, our security lies in obedience and refusal to deviate from God's law. I'm speaking to those to whom He has granted similar favors, and even to everyone.

3. It seems to me that despite all I've said about this dwelling place, the matter is still somewhat obscure. Since so much gain comes from entering this place, it will be good to avoid giving the impression that those to whom the Lord doesn't give things that are so supernatural are left without hope. True union can very well be reached, with God's help, if we make the effort to obtain it by keeping our wills fixed only on that which is God's will. Oh, how many of us there are who will say we do this, and it will seem to us that we don't want anything else and that we would die for this truth, as I believe I have said![3] Well I tell you, and I will often repeat it, that if what you say is true you will have obtained this favor from the Lord, and you needn't care at all about the other delightful union that was mentioned. That which is most valuable in the delightful union is what proceeds from this union of which I'm now speaking; and one cannot arrive at the delightful union if the union coming from being resigned to God's will is not very certain. Oh, how desirable is this union with God's will! Happy the soul that has reached it. Such a soul will live tranquilly in this life, and in the next as well. Nothing in earthly events afflicts it unless it finds itself in some danger of losing God or sees that He is offended: neither sickness, nor poverty, nor death—unless the death is of someone who will be missed by God's Church—for this soul sees well that the Lord knows what He is doing better than it knows what it is desiring.

4. You must note that there are different kinds of suffer-

ings. Some sufferings are produced suddenly by our human nature, and the same goes for consolations, and even by the charity of compassion for one's neighbor, as our Lord experienced when He raised Lazarus.[4] Being united with God's will doesn't take these experiences away, nor do they disturb the soul with a restless, disquieting passion that lasts a long while. These sufferings pass quickly. As I have said concerning consolations in prayer,[5] it seems they do not reach the soul's depth but only the senses and faculties. They are found in the previous dwelling places; but they do not enter the last ones still to be explained, since the suspension of the faculties is necessary in order to reach these, as has been said.[6] The Lord has the power to enrich souls through many paths and bring them to these dwelling places, without using the short cut that was mentioned.

5. Nonetheless, take careful note, daughters, that it is necessary for the silkworm to die, and, moreover, at a cost to yourselves. In the delightful union,[7] the experience of seeing oneself in so new a life greatly helps one to die; in the other union,[8] it's necessary that, while living in this life, we ourselves put the silkworm to death. I confess this latter death will require a great deal of effort, or more than that; but it has its value. Thus if you come out victorious the reward will be much greater. But there is no reason to doubt the possibility of this death any more than that of true union with the will of God. This union with God's will is the union I have desired all my life; it is the union I ask the Lord for always and the one that is clearest and safest.

6. But alas for us, how few there must be who reach it, although whoever guards himself against offending the Lord and has entered religious life thinks he has done everything! Oh, but there remain some worms, unrecognized until, like those in the story of Jonah that gnawed away the ivy,[9] they have gnawed away the virtues. This happens through self-love, self-esteem, judging one's neighbors, even though in little things, a lack of charity for them, and not loving them as ourselves. For even though, while crawling along, we fulfill our obligation and no sin is committed, we don't advance very far in what is required for complete union with the will of God.

7. What do you think His will is, daughters? That we be completely perfect. See what we lack to be one with Him and His Father as His Majesty asked.[10] I tell you I am writing this with much pain upon seeing myself so far away—and all through my own fault. The Lord doesn't have to grant us great delights for this union; sufficient is what He has given us in His Son, who would teach us the road. Don't think the matter lies in my being so conformed to the will of God that if my father or brother dies I don't feel it, or that if there are trials or sicknesses I suffer them happily. Such an attitude is good, and sometimes it's a matter of discretion because we can't do otherwise, and we make a virtue of necessity. How many things like these the philosophers did, or even, though not like these, other things, such as acquiring much learning. Here in our religious life the Lord asks of us only two things: love of His Majesty and love of our neighbor. These are what we must work for. By keeping them with perfection, we do His will and so will be united with Him. But how far, as I have said, we are from doing these two things for so great a God as we ought! May it please His Majesty to give us His grace so that we might merit, if we want, to reach this state that lies within our power.

8. The most certain sign, in my opinion, as to whether or not we are observing these two laws is whether we observe well the love of neighbor. We cannot know whether or not we love God, although there are strong indications for recognizing that we do love Him; but we can know whether we love our neighbor.[11] And be certain that the more advanced you see you are in love for your neighbor the more advanced you will be in the love of God, for the love His Majesty has for us is so great that to repay us for our love of neighbor He will in a thousand ways increase the love we have for Him. I cannot doubt this.

9. It's important for us to walk with careful attention to how we are proceeding in this matter, for if we practice love of neighbor with great perfection, we will have done everything. I believe that, since our nature is bad, we will not reach perfection in the love of neighbor if that love doesn't rise from love of God as its root. Since this is so important to us Sisters, let's try to understand ourselves even in little things, and pay no attention to any big plans that sometimes suddenly come to us during prayer in which it seems we will do wonders for our

neighbor and even for just one soul so that it may be saved. If afterward our deeds are not in conformity with those plans, there will be no reason to believe that we will accomplish the plans. I say the same about humility and all the virtues. Great are the wiles of the devil; to make us think we have one virtue—when we don't—he would circle hell a thousand times. And he is right because such a notion is very harmful, for these feigned virtues never come without some vainglory since they rise from that source, just as virtues from God are free of it as well as of pride.

10. I am amused sometimes to see certain souls who think when they are at prayer that they would like to be humiliated and publicly insulted for God, and afterward they would hide a tiny fault if they could; or, if they have not committed one and yet are charged with it—God deliver us! Well, let anyone who can't bear such a thing be careful not to pay attention to what he has by himself determined—in his opinion—to do. As a matter of fact, the determination was not in the will—for when there is a true determination of the will it's another matter—but a work of the imagination; it is in the imagination that the devil produces his wiles and deceits. And with women or unlearned people he can produce a great number, for we don't know how the faculties differ from one another and from the imagination, nor do we know about a thousand other things there are in regard to interior matters. O Sisters, how clearly one sees the degree to which love of neighbor is present in some of you, and how clearly one sees the deficiency in those who lack such perfection! If you were to understand how important this virtue is for us you wouldn't engage in any other study.

11. When I see souls very earnest in trying to understand the prayer they have and very sullen when they are in it—for it seems they don't dare let their minds move or stir lest a bit of their spiritual delight and devotion be lost—it makes me realize how little they understand of the way by which union is attained; they think the whole matter lies in these things. No, Sisters, absolutely not; works are what the Lord wants! He desires that if you see a Sister who is sick to whom you can bring some relief, you have compassion on her and not worry about losing this devotion; and that if she is suffering pain, you also feel it; and that, if necessary, you fast so that she might

eat—not so much for her sake as because you know it is your Lord's desire. This is true union with His will; and if you see a person praised, the Lord wants you to be much happier than if you yourself were being praised. This, indeed, is easy, for if you have humility you will feel sorry to see yourself praised. But this happiness that comes when the virtues of the Sisters are known is a very good thing; and when we see some fault in them, it is also a very good thing to be sorry and hide the fault as though it were our own.

12. I have said a lot on this subject elsewhere,[12] because I see, Sisters, that if we fail in love of neighbor we are lost. May it please the Lord that this will never be so; for if you do not fail, I tell you that you shall receive from His Majesty the union that was mentioned. When you see yourselves lacking in this love, even though you have devotion and gratifying experiences that make you think you have reached this stage, and you experience some little suspension in the prayer of quiet (for to some it then appears that everything has been accomplished), believe me, you have not reached union. And beg our Lord to give you this perfect love of neighbor. Let His Majesty have a free hand, for He will give you more than you know how to desire because you are striving and making every effort to do what you can about this love. And force your will to do the will of your Sisters in everything, even though you may lose your rights; forget your own good for their sakes no matter how much resistance your nature puts up; and, when the occasion arises, strive to accept work yourself so as to relieve your neighbor of it. Don't think that it won't cost you anything or that you will find everything done for you. Look at what our Spouse's love for us cost Him; in order to free us from death, He died that most painful death on the cross.

CHAPTER FOUR

Continues with the same subject, explaining further this kind of prayer.[1] *Tells how important it is to walk with care because the devil himself uses a great deal of care in trying to make one turn back from what was begun.*

1. It seems to me you have a desire to see what this little dove is doing and where it rests since as was explained it rests neither in spiritual delights nor in earthly consolations. Its

flight is higher, and I cannot satisfy your desire until the last dwelling place. May it please God that I then remember or have the time to write of this. About five months have passed since I began,[2] and because my head is in no condition to read over what I've written, everything will have to continue without order, and perhaps some things will be said twice. Since this work is for my Sisters, the disorder won't matter much.

2. Nonetheless, I want to explain more to you about what I think this prayer of union is. In accordance with my style, I shall draw a comparison. Later on we'll say more about this little butterfly. Although it is always bearing fruit by doing good for itself and for other souls, it never stops to rest, because it fails to find its true repose.

3. You've already often heard that God espouses souls spiritually. Blessed be His mercy that wants so much to be humbled! And even though the comparison may be a coarse one I cannot find another that would better explain what I mean than the sacrament of marriage. This spiritual espousal is different in kind from marriage, for in these matters that we are dealing with there is never anything that is not spiritual. Corporal things are far distant from them, and the spiritual joys the Lord gives when compared to the delights married people must experience are a thousand leagues distant. For it is all a matter of love united with love, and the actions of love are most pure and so extremely delicate and gentle that there is no way of explaining them, but the Lord knows how to make them very clearly felt.

4. It seems to me that the prayer of union does not yet reach the stage of spiritual betrothal. Here below when two people are to be engaged, there is discussion about whether they are alike, whether they love each other, and whether they might meet together so as to become more satisfied with each other. So, too, in the case of this union with God, the agreement has been made, and this soul is well informed about the goodness of her Spouse and determined to do His will in everything and in as many ways as she sees might make Him happy. And His Majesty, as one who understands clearly whether these things about His betrothed are so, is happy with her. As a result He grants this mercy, for He desired her to know Him more and that they might meet together, as they

say, and be united.[3] We can say that union is like this, for it passes in a very short time. In it there no longer takes place the exchanging of gifts, but the soul sees secretly who this Spouse is that she is going to accept. Through the work of the senses and the faculties she couldn't in any way or in a thousand years understand what she understands here in the shortest time. But being who He is, the Spouse from that meeting alone leaves her more worthy for the joining of hands, as they say. The soul is left so much in love that it does for its part all it can to avoid disturbing this divine betrothal. But if it is careless about placing its affection in something other than Him, it loses everything. And the loss is as great as the favors He was granting her, and cannot be exaggerated.

5. For this reason, I ask Christian souls whom the Lord has brought to these boundaries that for His sake they not grow careless but withdraw from occasions. Even in this state the soul is not so strong that it can place itself in the occasions as it will be after the betrothal is made. The betrothal belongs to the dwelling place we shall speak of after this one. This present communication amounts to no more than a meeting, as they say. And the devil will go about very carefully in order to fight against and prevent this betrothal. Afterward, since he sees the soul entirely surrendered to the Spouse, he doesn't dare do so much, because he fears it. He has experienced that if sometimes he tries he is left with a great loss, and the soul with further gain.

6. I tell you, daughters, that I have known persons who had ascended high and had reached this union, who were turned back and won over by the devil with his deep cunning and deceit. All hell must join for such a purpose because, as I have often said,[4] in losing one soul of this kind, not only one is lost but a multitude. The devil already has experience in this matter. Look at the multitude of souls God draws to Himself by means of one. He is to be greatly praised for the thousands converted by the martyrs: for a young girl like Saint Ursula; for those the devil must have lost through Saint Dominic, Saint Francis, and other founders of religious orders, and those he now loses through Father Ignatius, the one who founded the Society. Clearly, all of these received, as we read, similar favors from God. How would this have come about if they hadn't

made the effort not to lose through their own fault so divine an espousal? O my daughters, how prepared this Lord is to grant us favors now just as He has granted them to others in the past. And, in part, He is even more in need that we desire to receive them, for there are fewer now who care about His honor than there were then. We love ourselves very much; there's an extraordinary amount of prudence we use so as not to lose our rights. O what great deception! May the Lord through His mercy enlighten us so that we do not fall into similar darknesses.

7. You will ask me or be in doubt concerning two things: First, if the soul is as ready to do the will of God as was mentioned,[5] how can it be deceived since it doesn't want to do anything but His will in all? Second, what are the ways in which the devil can enter so dangerously that your soul goes astray? For you are so withdrawn from the world, so close to the sacraments, and in the company, we could say, of angels, and through the Lord's goodness you have no other desire than to serve God and please Him in everything. With those who are already in the midst of worldly occasions such a turn backward would not be surprising. I say that you are right about this, for God has granted us a great deal of mercy. But when I see, as I have said,[6] that Judas was in the company of the apostles and conversing always with God Himself and listening to His words, I understand that there is no security in these things.

8. In answer to the first, I say that if this soul were always attached to God's will it is clear that it would not go astray. But the devil comes along with some skillful deception and, under the color of good, confuses it with regard to little things and induces it to get taken up with some of them that he makes it think are good. Then little by little he darkens the intellect, cools the will's ardor, and makes self-love grow until in one way or another he withdraws the soul from the will of God and brings it to his own.

Thus, we have an answer to the second doubt. There is no enclosure so fenced in that he cannot enter, or desert so withdrawn that he fails to go there. And I still have something more to say: Perhaps the Lord permits this so as to observe the behavior of that soul He wishes to set up as a light for others. If there is going to be a downfall, it's better that it happen in the beginning rather than later, when it would be harmful to many.

9. The diligence on our part that comes to my mind as being the most effective is the following. First, we must always ask God in prayer to sustain us, and very often think that if He abandons us we will soon end in the abyss, as is true; and we must never trust in ourselves since it would be foolish to do so. Then, we should walk with special care and attention, observing how we are proceeding in the practice of virtue: whether we are getting better or worse in some area, especially in love for one another, in the desire to be considered the least among the Sisters, and in the performance of ordinary tasks. For if we look out for these things and ask the Lord to enlighten us, we will soon see the gain or the loss. Don't think that a soul that comes so close to God is allowed to lose Him so quickly, that the devil has an easy task. His Majesty would regret the loss of this soul so much that He gives it in many ways a thousand interior warnings, so that the harm will not be hidden from it.

10. Let this, in sum, be the conclusion: that we strive always to advance. And if we don't advance, let us walk with great fear. Without doubt the devil wants to cause some lapse, for it is not possible that after having come so far, one will fail to grow. Love is never idle, and such a failure would be a very bad sign. A soul that has tried to be the betrothed of God Himself, that is now intimate with His Majesty, and has reached the boundaries that were mentioned must not go to sleep.

That you, daughters, may see what He does with those He now considers to be His betrothed ones, we shall begin to speak of the sixth dwelling places. And you will see how little it all is that we can do to serve and suffer and accomplish so as to dispose ourselves for such great favors. It could be that our Lord ordained that they command me to write so that we might forget our little earthly joys and with our eyes set on the reward, seeing how unmeasurable is His mercy—since He desires to commune with and reveal Himself to some worms—and having them fixed also on His grandeur, we may run along enkindled in His love.

11. May He be pleased that I manage to explain something

about these very difficult things. I know well that this will be impossible if His Majesty and the Holy Spirit do not move my pen. And if what I say will not be for your benefit, I beg Him that I may not succeed in saying anything. His Majesty knows that I have no other desire, insofar as I can understand myself, but that His name be praised and that we strive to serve a Lord who even here on earth pays like this. Through His favors we can understand something of what He will give us in heaven without the intervals, trials, and dangers that there are in this tempestuous sea. If there were no danger of losing or offending Him, it would be easy to endure life until the end of the world so as to labor for so great a God and Lord and Spouse.

May it please His Majesty that we may merit to render Him some service, without as many faults as we always have, even in good works, amen.

THE SIXTH DWELLING PLACES

CONTAINS ELEVEN CHAPTERS

CHAPTER ONE

Discusses how greater trials come when the Lord begins to grant greater favors. Mentions some and how those who are now in this dwelling place conduct themselves. This chapter is good for souls undergoing interior trials.

1. Well then, let us, with the help of the Holy Spirit, speak of the sixth dwelling places, where the soul is now wounded with love for its Spouse and strives for more opportunities to be alone and, in conformity with its state, to rid itself of everything that can be an obstacle to this solitude.

That meeting[1] left such an impression that the soul's whole desire is to enjoy it again. I have already said that in this prayer nothing is seen in a way that can be called seeing, nor is anything seen with the imagination. I use the term "meeting" because of the comparison I made.[2] Now the soul is fully determined to take no other spouse. But the Spouse does not look at the soul's great desires that the betrothal take place, for He still wants it to desire this more, and He wants the betrothal to take place at a cost; it is the greatest of blessings. And although everything is small when it comes to paying for this exceptional benefit, I tell you, daughters, that for the soul to endure such delay it needs to have that token or pledge of betrothal that it now has. O God help me, what interior and exterior trials the soul suffers before entering the seventh dwelling place!

2. Indeed, sometimes I reflect and fear that if a soul knew beforehand, its natural weakness would find it most difficult to have the determination to suffer and pass through these trials, no matter what blessings were represented to it—unless it had arrived at the seventh dwelling place. For once it has arrived there, the soul fears nothing and is absolutely determined to overcome every obstacle for God.[3] And the reason is that it is always so closely joined to His Majesty that from this union comes its fortitude. I believe it will be well to recount some of those trials that I know one will certainly undergo. Perhaps not all souls will be led along this path, although I doubt very much that those persons who sometimes enjoy so truly the things of heaven will live free of earthly trials that come in one way or another.

3. Although I hadn't intended to treat of these, I thought doing so would bring great consolation to some soul going through them, for it would learn that these trials take place in souls to whom God grants similar favors; for truly when one is suffering the trials, it then seems that everything is lost. I will not deal with them according to the order in which they happen, but as they come to mind. And I want to begin with the smallest trials. There is an outcry by persons a Sister is dealing with and even by those she does not deal with and who, it seems to her, would never even think of her; gossip like the following: "She's trying to make out she's a saint; she goes to extremes to deceive the world and bring others to ruin; there are other better Christians who don't put on all this outward show." (And it's worth noting that she is not putting on any outward show but just striving to fulfill well her state in life.) Those she considered her friends turn away from her, and they are the ones who take the largest and most painful bite at her, "That soul has gone astray and is clearly mistaken; these are things of the devil; she will turn out like this person or that other that went astray, and will bring about a decline in virtue; she has deceived her confessors" (and they go to these confessors, telling them so, giving them examples of what happened to some that were lost in this way); a thousand kinds of ridicule and sayings like the above.

4. I know a person who had great fear that there would be

no one who would hear her confession because of such gossip[4]—so much gossip that there's no reason to go into it all here. And what is worse these things do not pass quickly, but go on throughout the person's whole life including the advice to others to avoid any dealings with such persons.

You will tell me that there are also those who will speak well of that soul. O daughters, how few there are who believe in such favors in comparison with the many who denigrate them! Moreover, praise is just another trial greater than those mentioned! Since the soul sees clearly that if it has anything good this is given by God and is by no means its own—for just previously it saw itself to be very poor and surrounded by great sins—praise is an intolerable burden to it, at least in the beginning. Later on, for certain reasons, praise is not so intolerable. First, because experience makes the soul see clearly that people are as quick to say good things as bad, and so it pays no more attention to the good things than to the bad. Second, because it has been more enlightened by the Lord that no good thing comes from itself but is given by His Majesty; and it turns to praise God, forgetful that it has had any part to play, just as if it had seen the gift in another person. Third, if it sees that some souls have benefitted from seeing the favors God grants it, it thinks that His Majesty used this means, of its being falsely esteemed as good, so that some blessings might come to those souls. Fourth, since it looks after the honor and glory of God more than its own, the temptation, which came in the beginning, that these praises will destroy it is removed; little does dishonor matter to it if in exchange God might perhaps thereby just once be praised—afterward, let whatever comes come.

5. These reasons and others mitigate the great pain these praises cause, although some pain is almost always felt, except when one is paying hardly any attention. But it is an incomparably greater trial to see oneself publicly considered as good without reason than the trials mentioned. And when the soul reaches the stage at which it pays little attention to praise, it pays much less to disapproval; on the contrary, it rejoices in this and finds it a very sweet music. This is an amazing truth. Blame does not intimidate the soul but strengthens it. Experience has already taught it the wonderful gain that comes through this path. It feels that those who persecute it do not

offend God; rather that His Majesty permits persecution for the benefit of the soul. And since it clearly experiences the benefits of persecution, it acquires a special and very tender love for its persecutors. It seems to it that they are greater friends and more advantageous than those who speak well of it.

6. The Lord is wont also to send it the severest illnesses. This is a much greater trial, especially when the pains are acute. For, in some way, if these pains are severe, the trial is, it seems to me, the greatest on earth—I mean the greatest exterior trial, however many the other pains. I say "if the pains are severe, " because they then afflict the soul interiorly and exteriorly in such a way that it doesn't know what to do with itself. It would willingly accept at once any martyrdom rather than these sharp pains, although they do not last long in this extreme form. After all, God gives no more than what can be endured; and His Majesty gives patience first. But other great sufferings and illnesses of many kinds are the usual thing.

7. I know a person who cannot truthfully say that from the time the Lord began forty years ago to grant the favor that was mentioned she spent even one day without pains and other kinds of suffering (from lack of bodily health, I mean) and other great trials.[5] It's true that she had been very wretched and that everything seemed small to her in comparison with the hell she deserved. Others, who have not offended our Lord so much, will be led by another path. But I would always choose the path of suffering, if only to imitate our Lord Jesus Christ if there were no other gains, especially since there are always so many other things to gain.

Oh, were we to treat of interior sufferings these others would seem small if the interior ones could be clearly explained; but it is impossible to explain the way in which they come to pass.

8. Let us begin with the torment one meets with from a confessor who is so discreet and has so little experience that there is nothing he is sure of: He fears everything and finds in everything something to doubt because he sees these unusual experiences. He becomes especially doubtful if he notices some imperfection in a soul that has them, for it seems to such confessors that the ones to whom God grants these favors must be angels—but that is impossible as long as they are in this

body. Everything is immediately condemned as from the devil or melancholy. And the world is so full of this melancholy that I am not surprised. There is so much of it now in the world, and the devil causes so many evils through this means that confessors are very right in fearing it and considering it carefully. But the poor soul that walks with the same fear and goes to its confessor as to its judge, and is condemned by him, cannot help but be deeply tormented and disturbed. Only the one who has passed through this will understand what a great torment it is. For this is another one of the terrible trials these souls suffer, especially if they have lived wretched lives, thinking that because of their sins God will allow them to be deceived. Even though they feel secure and cannot believe that the favor, when granted by His Majesty, is from any other spirit than from God, the torment returns immediately since the favor is something that passes quickly, and the remembrance of sins is always present, and the soul sees faults in itself, which are never lacking. When the confessor assures it, the soul grows calm, although the disturbance will return. But when the confessor contributes to the torment with more fear, this trial becomes something almost unbearable—especially when some dryness comes between the times of these favors. It then seems to the soul that it has never been mindful of God and never will be; and when it hears His Majesty spoken of, it seems to it as though it were hearing about a person far away.

9. All this would amount to nothing if it were not for the fact that in addition comes the feeling that it is incapable of explaining things to its confessors, that it has deceived them. And even though it thinks and sees that it tells its confessors about every stirring, even the first ones, this doesn't help. The soul's understanding is so darkened that it becomes incapable of seeing the truth and believes whatever the imagination represents to it (for the imagination is then its master) or whatever foolish things the devil wants to represent. The Lord, it seems, gives the devil license so that the soul might be tried and even be made to think it is rejected by God. Many are the things that war against it with an interior oppression so keen and unbearable that I don't know what to compare this experience to if not to the oppression of those that suffer in hell, for no consolation is allowed in the midst of this tempest. If they

desire to be consoled by their confessor, it seems the devils assist him to torment it more. Thus, when a confessor was dealing with a person after she had suffered this torment (for it seems a dangerous affliction since there are so many things involved in it), he told her to let him know when she was in this state; but the torment was always so bad that he came to realize there was nothing he could do about it.[6] Well then, if a person in this state who knows how to read well takes up a book in the vernacular, he will find that he understands no more of it than if he didn't know how to read even one of the letters, for the intellect is incapable of understanding.[7]

10. In sum, there is no remedy in this tempest but to wait for the mercy of God. For at an unexpected time, with one word alone or a chance happening, He so quickly calms the storm that it seems there had not been even as much as a cloud in that soul, and it remains filled with sunlight and much more consolation. And like one who has escaped from a dangerous battle and been victorious, it comes out praising our Lord; for it was He who fought for the victory. It knows very clearly that it did not fight, for all the weapons with which it could have defended itself are seen to be, it seems, in the hands of its enemies. Thus, it knows clearly its wretchedness and the very little we of ourselves can do if the Lord abandons us.

11. It seems the soul has no longer any need of reflection to understand this, for the experience of having suffered through it, having seen itself totally incapacitated, made it understand our nothingness and what miserable things we are. For in this state grace is so hidden (even though the soul must not be without grace since with all this torment it doesn't offend God nor would it offend Him for anything on earth) that not even a very tiny spark is visible. The soul doesn't think that it has any love of God or that it ever had any, for if it has done some good, or His Majesty has granted it some favor, all of this seems to have been dreamed up or fancied. As for sins, it sees certainly that it has committed them.

12. O Jesus, and what a thing it is to see this kind of forsaken soul; and, as I have said,[8] what little help any earthly consolation is for it! Hence, do not think, Sisters, if at some time you find yourselves in this state, that the rich and those who are free will have a better remedy for these times of

suffering. Absolutely not, for being rich in this case seems to me like the situation of a person condemned to die who has all the world's delights placed before him. These delights would not be sufficient to alleviate his suffering; rather, they would increase the torment. So it is with this torment; it comes from above, and earthly things are of no avail in the matter. Our great God wants us to know our own misery and that He is king; and this is very important for what lies ahead.

13. Well then, what will this poor soul do when the torment goes on for many days? If it prays, it feels as though it hasn't prayed—as far as consolation goes, I mean. For consolation is not admitted into the soul's interior, nor is what one recites to oneself, even though vocal, understood. As for mental prayer, this definitely is not the time for that, because the faculties are incapable of the practice; rather, solitude causes greater harm—and also another torment for this soul is that it be with anyone or that others speak to it. And thus however much it forces itself not to do so, it goes about with a discontented and ill-tempered mien that is externally very noticeable.

Is it true that it will know how to explain its experiences? They are indescribable, for they are spiritual afflictions and sufferings that one doesn't know what to call. The best remedy (I don't mean for getting rid of them, because I don't find any, but so that they may be endured) is to engage in external works of charity and to hope in the mercy of God, who never fails those who hope in Him. May He be forever blessed, amen.

14. Other exterior trials the devils cause must be quite unusual; and so there's no reason to speak of them. Nor are they, for the most part, so painful; for, however much the devils do, they do not, in my opinion, manage to disable the faculties or disturb the soul in this way. In sum, there's reason for thinking that they can do no more than what the Lord allows them to do; and provided one doesn't lose one's mind, everything is small in comparison with what was mentioned.

15. We shall be speaking in these dwelling places of other interior sufferings, and dealing with different kinds of prayer and favors from the Lord. For even though some favors cause still more severe suffering than those mentioned, as will be seen from the condition in which the body is left, they do not deserve to be called trials. Nor is there any reason for us to

write of them since they are such great favors from the Lord. In the midst of receiving them the soul understands that they are great favors and far beyond its merits. This severe suffering comes so that one may enter the seventh dwelling place. It comes along with many other sufferings, only some of which I shall speak of[9] because it would be impossible to speak of them all, or even to explain what they are; for they are of a different, much higher level than those mentioned in this chapter. And if I haven't been able to explain any more than I did about those of a lower kind, less will I be able to say of the others. May the Lord give His help for everything through the merits of His Son, amen.

CHAPTER TWO

Deals with some of the ways in which our Lord awakens the soul. It seems that there is nothing in these awakenings to fear even though the experience is sublime and the favors are great.

1. Seemingly we have left the little dove far behind; but we have not, for these are the trials that make it fly still higher. Well let us begin, then, to discuss the manner in which the Spouse deals with it and how before He belongs to it completely He makes it desire Him vehemently by certain delicate means the soul itself does not understand. (Nor do I believe I'll be successful in explaining them save to those who have experienced them.) These are impulses so delicate and refined, for they proceed from very deep within the interior part of the soul, that I don't know any comparison that will fit.

2. They are far different from all that we can acquire of ourselves here below and even from the spiritual delights that were mentioned.[1] For often when a person is distracted and forgetful of God, His Majesty will awaken it. His action is as quick as a falling comet. And as with a thunderclap, even though no sound is heard, the soul understands very clearly that it was called by God. So well does it understand that sometimes, especially in the beginning, it is made to tremble and even complain without there being anything that causes it pain. It feels that it is wounded in the most delightful way, but it doesn't learn how or by whom it was wounded. It knows clearly that the wound is something precious, and it would

115

never want to be cured. It complains to its Spouse with words of love, even outwardly, without being able to do otherwise. It knows that He is present, but He doesn't want to reveal the manner in which He allows Himself to be enjoyed. And the pain is great, although delightful and sweet. And even if the soul does not want this wound, the wound cannot be avoided. But the soul, in fact, would never want to be deprived of this pain. The wound satisfies it much more than the delightful and painless absorption of the prayer of quiet.[2]

3. I am struggling, Sisters, to explain for you this action of love, and I don't know how. For it seems a contradiction that the Beloved would give the soul clear understanding that He is with it and yet make it think that He is calling it by a sign so certain that no room is left for doubt and a whisper so penetrating that the soul cannot help but hear it. For it seems that when the Spouse, who is in the seventh dwelling place, communicates in this manner (for the words are not spoken), all the people in the other dwelling places keep still; neither the senses, nor the imagination, nor the faculties stir.

O my powerful God, how sublime are your secrets, and how different spiritual things are from all that is visible and understandable here below. There is nothing that serves to explain this favor, even though the favor is a very small one when compared with the very great ones You work in souls.

4. This action of love is so powerful that the soul dissolves with desire, and yet it doesn't know what to ask for since clearly it thinks that its God is with it.

You will ask me: Well, if it knows this, what does it desire or what pains it? What greater good does it want? I don't know. I do know that it seems this pain reaches to the soul's very depths and that when He who wounds it draws out the arrow, it indeed seems in accord with the deep love the soul feels that God is drawing these very depths after Him.[3] I was thinking now that it's as though from this fire enkindled in the brazier that is my God a spark leapt forth and so struck the soul that the flaming fire was felt by it. And since the spark was not enough to set the soul on fire, and the fire is so delightful, the soul is left with that pain; but the spark merely by touching the soul produces that effect. It seems to me this is the best comparison I have come up with. This delightful pain—and it is not pain—is not continuous, although sometimes it lasts a long while; at other times it goes away quickly. This depends on the way the Lord wishes to communicate it, for it is not something that can be procured in any human way. But even though it sometimes lasts for a long while, it comes and goes. To sum up, it is never permanent. For this reason it doesn't set the soul on fire; but just as the fire is about to start, the spark goes out and the soul is left with the desire to suffer again that loving pain the spark causes.

5. Here there is no reason to wonder whether the experience is brought on naturally or caused by melancholy, or whether it is some trick of the devil or some illusion. It is something that leaves clear understanding of how this activity comes from the place where the Lord, who is unchanging, dwells. The activity is not like that found in other feelings of devotion, where the great absorption in delight can make us doubtful. Here all the senses and faculties remain free of any absorption, wondering what this could be, without hindering anything or being able, in my opinion, to increase or take away that delightful pain.

Anyone to whom our Lord may have granted this favor—for if He has, that fact will be recognized on reading this—should thank Him very much. Such a person doesn't have to fear deception. Let his great fear be that he might prove ungrateful for so generous a favor, and let him strive to better his entire life, and to serve, and he will see the results and how he receives more and more. In fact, I know a person[4] who received this favor for some years and was so pleased with it that had she served the Lord through severe trials for a great number of years she would have felt well repaid by it. May He be blessed forever, amen.

6. You may wonder why greater security is present in this favor than in other things. In my opinion, these are the reasons: First, the devil never gives delightful pain like this. He can give the savor and delight that seem to be spiritual, but he doesn't have the power to join pain—and so much of it—to the spiritual quiet and delight of the soul. For all of his powers are on the outside, and the pains he causes are never, in my

opinion, delightful or peaceful, but disturbing and contentious. Second, this delightful tempest comes from a region other than those regions of which he can be lord. Third, the favor brings wonderful benefits to the soul, the more customary of which are the determination to suffer for God, the desire to have many trials, and the determination to withdraw from earthly satisfactions and conversations and other similar things.

7. That this favor is no fancy is very clear. Although at other times the soul may strive to experience this favor, it will not be able to counterfeit one. And the impulse is something so manifest that it can in no way be fancied. I mean, one cannot think it is imagined, when it is not, or have doubts about it. If some doubt should remain, one must realize that the things experienced are not true impulses—I mean if there should be doubt about whether the favor was experienced or not. The favor is felt as clearly as a loud voice is heard. There's no basis for thinking it is caused by melancholy, because melancholy does not produce or fabricate its fancies save in the imagination. This favor proceeds from the interior part of the soul.

Now it could be that I'm mistaken, but until I hear other reasons from someone who understands the experience I will always have this opinion. And so I know a person who was quite fearful about being deceived but who never had any fear of this prayer.[5]

8. The Lord also has other ways of awakening the soul: unexpectedly when it is praying vocally and without thinking of anything interior, it seems a delightful enkindling will come upon it as though a fragrance were suddenly to become so powerful as to spread through all the senses. (I don't say that it is a fragrance but am merely making this comparison.) Or the experience is something like this, and it is communicated only for the sake of making one feel the Spouse's presence there. It moves the soul to a delightful desire of enjoying Him, and thereby the soul is prepared to make intense acts of love and praise of our Lord. This favor rises out of that place I mentioned;[6] but there is nothing in it that causes pain, nor are the desires themselves to enjoy God painful. Such is the way the soul usually experiences it. Neither does it seem to me, for some of the reasons mentioned,[7] there is anything to fear; but one should try to receive this favor with gratitude.

THE INTERIOR CASTLE

CHAPTER THREE

Deals with the same subject and tells of the manner in which God, when pleased, speaks to the soul. Gives counsel about how one should behave in such a matter and not follow one's own opinion. Sets down some signs for discerning when there is deception and when not. This chapter is very beneficial.[1]

1. God has another way of awakening the soul. Although it somehow seems to be a greater favor than those mentioned,[2] it can be more dangerous, and therefore I shall spend some time considering it. There are many kinds of locutions given to the soul. Some seem to come from outside oneself; others, from deep within the interior part of the soul; others, from the superior part; and some are so exterior that they come through the sense of hearing, for it seems there is a spoken word. Sometimes, and often, the locution can be an illusion, especially in persons with a weak imagination or in those who are melancholic, I mean who suffer noticeably from melancholy.

2. In my opinion no attention should be paid to these latter two kinds of persons even if they say they see and hear and understand. But neither should one disturb these persons by telling them their locutions come from the devil; one must listen to them as to sick persons. The prioress or confessor to whom they relate their locutions should tell them to pay no attention to such experiences, that these locutions are not essential to the service of God, and that the devil has deceived many by such means, even though this particular person, perhaps, may not be suffering such deception. This counsel should be given so as not to aggravate the melancholy, for if they tell her the locution is due to melancholy, there will be no end to the matter; she will swear that she sees and hears, for it seems to her that she does.

3. It is true that it's necessary to be firm in taking prayer away from her and to insist strongly that she pay no attention to locutions; for the devil is wont to profit from these souls that are sick in this way, even though what he does may not be to their harm but to the harm of others. But for both the sick and the healthy there is always reason to fear these things until the spirit of such persons is well understood. And I say that in the beginning it is always better to free these persons from such

119

experiences, for if the locutions are from God, doing so is a greater help toward progress, and a person even grows when tested. This is true; nonetheless, one should not proceed in a way that is distressing or disturbing to a soul, because truly the soul can't help it if these locutions come.

4. Now then, to return to what I was saying about locutions, all the kinds I mentioned[3] can be from God or from the devil or from one's own imagination. If I can manage to do so, I shall give, with the help of the Lord, the signs as to when they come from these different sources and when they are dangerous; for there are many souls among prayerful people who hear them. My desire, Sisters, is that you realize you are doing the right thing if you refuse to give credence to them, even when they are destined just for you (such as some consolation, or advice about your faults), no matter who tells you about them, or if they are an illusion, for it doesn't matter where they come from. One thing I advise you: do not think, even if the locutions are from God, that you are better because of them, for He spoke frequently with the Pharisees. All the good comes from how one benefits by these words; and pay no more attention to those that are not in close conformity with Scripture than you would to those heard from the devil himself. Even if they come from your weak imagination, it's necessary to treat them as if they were temptations in matters of faith, and thus resist them always. They will then go away because they will have little effect on you.

5. Returning, then, to the first of the different kinds of locutions; whether or not the words come from the interior part of the soul, from the superior part, or from the exterior part doesn't matter in discerning whether or not they are from God. The surest signs they are from God that can be had, in my opinion, are these: the first and truest is the power and authority they bear, for locutions from God effect what they say. Let me explain myself better. A soul finds itself in the midst of all the tribulation and disturbance that was mentioned,[4] in darkness of the intellect and in dryness; with one word alone of these that the Lord says ("don't be distressed"), it is left calm and free from all distress, with great light, and without all that suffering in which it seemed to it that all the learned men and all who might come together to give it reasons

for not being distressed would be unable to remove its affliction no matter how hard they tried. Or, it is afflicted because its confessor and others have told it that its spirit is from the devil, and it is all full of fear; with one word alone ("It is I, fear not"), the fear is taken away completely, and the soul is most comforted, thinking that nothing would be sufficient to make it believe anything else. Or, it is greatly distressed over how certain serious business matters will turn out; it hears that it should be calm, that everything will turn out all right. It is left certain and free of anxiety. And this is the way in many other instances.[5]

6. The second sign is the great quiet left in the soul, the devout and peaceful recollection, the readiness to engage in the praises of God. O Lord, if a word sent to be spoken through one of Your attendants (for the Lord Himself does not speak the words—at least not in this dwelling place—but an angel) has such power, what will be the power You leave in the soul that is attached to You, and You to it, through love?

7. The third sign is that these words remain in the memory for a very long time, and some are never forgotten, as are those we listen to here on earth—I mean those we hear from men. For even if the words are spoken by men who are very important and learned, or concern the future, we do not have them engraved on our memory, or believe them, as we do these. The certitude is so strong that even in things that in one's own opinion sometimes seem impossible and there is doubt as to whether they will or will not happen, and the intellect wavers, there is an assurance in the soul itself that cannot be overcome. Even though it seems that everything is going contrary to what the soul understood, and years go by, the thought remains that God will find other means than those men know of and that in the end the words will be accomplished; and so they are. Although, as I say, the soul still suffers when it sees the many delays, for since time has passed since it heard the words, and the effects and the certitude that were present about their being from God have passed, these doubts take place. The soul wonders whether the locutions might have come from the devil or from the imagination. Yet, none of these doubts remain in the soul, but it would at present die a thousand deaths for that truth. But, as I say, what won't the devil do with all these

imaginings so as to afflict and intimidate the soul, especially if the words regard a business matter that when carried out will bring many blessings to souls, and works that will bring great honor and service to God, and if there is great difficulty involved? At least he weakens faith, for it does great harm not to believe that God has the power to do things that our intellects do not understand.

8. Despite all these struggles and even the persons who tell one that the locutions are foolishness (I mean the confessors with whom one speaks about these things), and despite the many unfortunate occurrences that make it seem the words will not be fulfilled, there remains a spark of assurance so alive—I don't know from where—that the words will be fulfilled, though all other hopes are dead, that even should the soul desire otherwise, that spark will stay alive. And in the end, as I have said,[6] the words of the Lord are fulfilled, and the soul is so consoled and happy that it wouldn't want to do anything but always praise His Majesty and praise Him more for the fact that what He had told it was fulfilled than for the work itself, no matter how important the work is to the soul.

9. I don't know why it is so important to the soul that these words turn out to be true, for if that soul were itself caught in some lies, I don't think it would regret the fact as much. And yet, there is nothing else it can do, for it merely says what it hears. Countless times, in this regard, a certain person thought of how the prophet Jonah feared that Nineveh would not be destroyed.[7] In sum, since the spirit is from God, it is right that the soul be faithful in its desire that the words be considered true, for God is the supreme truth. And so its happiness is great when through a thousand roundabout ways and in most difficult circumstances it sees them fulfilled. Even though great trials should come to the person herself from them, she would rather suffer such trials than the trial of seeing that what the Lord told her fails in fact to happen. Perhaps not all persons will have this weakness—if it is a weakness, for I cannot condemn it as bad.

10. If the locutions come from the imagination, there are none of these signs; neither certitude, nor peace, nor interior delight. But it could happen—and I even know some persons to whom it has happened—that while these imaginings come a

person may be very absorbed in the prayer of quiet and spiritual sleep. Some have such a weak constitution and imagination, or I don't know the cause, that indeed in this deep recollection they are so outside themselves (for they don't feel anything exteriorly and all the senses are put to sleep) that they think as when they are asleep and dreaming (and perhaps it is true that they are asleep) that these locutions are spoken to them and even that they see things. And they think these things are from God, but in the end the effects are like those of sleep. It can also happen that while with affection they are begging our Lord for something, they think the locution is telling them what they want to hear; this sometimes happens. But anyone who has had much experience of God's locutions will not be deceived by these that come, in my opinion, from the imagination.

11. With those locutions coming from the devil there is more to fear. But if the signs mentioned[8] are present, there can be a great deal of certainty that the locutions are from God. But the certainty shouldn't be so strong that if the locution concerns something serious about oneself and has to be carried out in deed, or business affairs involving third parties, anything should ever be done or pass through one's mind without the opinion of a learned and prudent confessor and servant of God. This is so even if the soul increasingly understands and thinks the locution is clearly from God. His Majesty wants the soul to consult in this way; and that it does so does not mean it is failing to carry out the Lord's commands, for He has told us, where the words are undoubtedly His, to hold the confessor in His place.[9] And these words of His help to give courage if the task is a difficult one, and our Lord when He so desires will make the confessor believe that the locution comes from His spirit. If He doesn't, the confessor and the soul are no longer under obligation. To do otherwise and follow nothing but your own opinion in this, I hold to be very dangerous. And so, Sisters, I warn you, on the part of our Lord, that this never happen to you.

12. There is another way in which the Lord speaks to the soul—for I hold that it is very definitely from Him—with a certain intellectual vision, the nature of which I will explain further on.[10] The locution takes place in such intimate depths and a person with the ears of the soul seems to hear those

words from the Lord Himself so clearly and so in secret that this very way in which they are heard, together with the acts that the vision itself produces, assures that person and gives him certitude that the devil can have no part to play in the locution. Wonderful effects are left so that the soul may believe; at least there is assurance that the locution doesn't come from the imagination. Furthermore, if the soul is attentive, it can always have assurance for the following reasons: First, there is a difference because of the clarity of the locution. It is so clear that the soul remembers every syllable and whether it is said in one style or another, even if it is a whole sentence. But in a locution fancied by the imagination the words will not be so clear or distinct but like something half-dreamed.

13. Second, in these locutions one often is not thinking about what is heard (I mean that it comes unexpectedly and even sometimes while one is in conversation), although many times it is a response to what passes quickly through the mind or to what did so previously. But it often refers to things about the future that never entered the mind, and so the imagination couldn't have fabricated it in such a way that the soul could be deceived in fancying what was not desired or wanted or thought of.

14. Third, the one locution comes as in the case of a person who hears, and that of imagination comes as in the case of a person who gradually composes what he himself wants to be told.

15. Fourth, the words are very different, and with one of them much is comprehended. Our intellect could not compose them so quickly.

16. Fifth, together with the words, in a way I wouldn't know how to explain, there is often given much more to understand than is ever dreamed of without words.

I shall speak more about this mode of understanding elsewhere,[11] for it is something very delicate and to the praise of our Lord. For in regard to these different kinds of locutions, there have been persons who were very doubtful and unable to understand themselves. A certain person, especially, experienced this doubt,[12] and so there will be others. And thus I know that she observed the differences with close attention because the Lord has often granted her this favor, and the greatest doubt she had in the beginning was whether she had imagined the locution. That the words come from the devil can be more quickly understood, even though his wiles are so many, for he knows well how to counterfeit the Spirit of light. In my opinion the devil will say the words very clearly so that there will be certitude about their meaning, as is so with those coming from the Spirit of truth. But he will not be able to counterfeit the effects that were mentioned[13] or leave this peace or light in the soul; on the contrary he leaves restlessness and disturbance. But he can do little or no harm if the soul is humble and does what I have mentioned,[14] that is, doesn't make a move to do a thing of what it hears.

17. If the locutions contain words of favor and consolation from the Lord, let the soul look attentively to see if it thinks that because of them it is better than others. The more it hears words of favor the more humble it should be left; if it isn't, let it believe that the spirit is not from God. One thing very certain is that when the spirit is from God the soul esteems itself less, the greater the favor He granted, and it has more awareness of its sins and is more forgetful of its own gain, and its will and memory are employed more in seeking only the honor of God, nor does it think about its own profit, and it walks with greater fear lest its will deviate in anything, and with greater certitude that it never deserved any of those favors but deserved hell. Since all the favors and things it experienced in prayer produce these effects, the soul does not walk fearfully but with confidence in the mercy of the Lord, who is faithful[15] and will not let the devil deceive it; although walking with fear is always good.

18. It could be that those whom the Lord does not lead along this path think that such souls could refuse to listen to these words spoken to them—and if the words are interior distract themselves in such a way that they not be admitted— and as a result go about free of these dangers.

To this I reply that it is impossible. I'm not speaking of imaginary locutions, for by not being so desirous of a thing or wanting to pay attention to their imaginings souls have a remedy. In locutions from the Lord, they have none. For the very spirit that speaks puts a stop to all other thoughts and makes the soul attend to what is said. It does this in such a way that I think, and I believe truly, that somehow it would be more possible for a person with very good hearing not to hear someone else speaking in a loud voice. In this latter instance the person would be able to turn his attention away and center his mind and intellect on something else. But in the locution we are speaking about this cannot be done; there are no ears to stop, nor is there the power to think of anything but what is said to the soul. For He who was able to stop the sun (through Joshua's prayer, I believe)[16] can make the faculties and the whole interior stop in such a way that the soul sees clearly that another greater Lord than itself governs that castle. And this brings it deep devotion and humility. So there's no remedy for this kind of locution. May the divine Majesty provide a remedy that will enable us to place our eyes only on pleasing Him and to be forgetful of ourselves, as I said, amen.

Please God that I may have succeeded in explaining what I set out to; may it be helpful for whoever has had such experience.

CHAPTER FOUR

Treats of when God suspends the soul in prayer with rapture or ecstasy or transport, which are all the same in my opinion,[1] and how great courage is necessary to receive sublime favors from His Majesty.

1. With these trials and the other things that were mentioned, what kind of calm can the poor little butterfly have? All these sufferings are meant to increase one's desire to enjoy the Spouse. And His Majesty, as one who knows our weakness, is enabling the soul through these afflictions and many others to have the courage to be joined with so great a Lord and to take Him as its Spouse.[2]

2. You will laugh at my saying this and will think it's foolishness; it will seem to any one of you that such courage is unnecessary and that there's no woman so miserable who wouldn't have the courage to be married to the king. I believe this is true with respect to kings here on earth; but with respect to the King of heaven, I tell you there is need for more courage than you think. Our nature is very timid and lowly when it comes to something so great, and I am certain that if God were not to give the courage, no matter how much you might see

that the favor is good for us, it would be impossible for you to receive that favor. And thus you will see what His Majesty does to conclude this betrothal, which I understand must be established when He gives the soul raptures that draw it out of its senses. For if it were to see itself so near this great majesty while in its senses, it would perhaps die. Let it be understood that I mean true raptures and not the weaknesses women experience here below, for everything seems to us to be a rapture or an ecstasy. And, as I believe I have said,[3] some have constitutions so weak that the prayer of quiet is enough to make them die.

I want to put down here some kinds of rapture that I've come to understand because I've discussed them with so many spiritual persons. But I don't know whether I shall succeed as I did when I wrote elsewhere about them[4] and other things that occur in this dwelling place. On account of certain reasons it seems worthwhile to speak of these kinds of rapture again—if for no other reason, so that everything related to these dwelling places will be put down here together.

3. One kind of rapture is that in which the soul even though not in prayer is touched by some word it remembers or hears about God. It seems that His Majesty from the interior of the soul makes the spark we mentioned[5] increase, for He is moved with compassion in seeing the soul suffer so long a time from its desire. All burnt up, the soul is renewed like the phoenix, and one can devoutly believe that its faults are pardoned. Now that it is so pure, the Lord joins it with Himself, without anyone understanding what is happening except these two; nor does the soul itself understand in a way that can afterward be explained. Yet, it does have interior understanding, for this experience is not like that of fainting or convulsion; in these latter nothing is understood inwardly or outwardly.

4. What I know in this case is that the soul was never so awake to the things of God nor did it have such deep enlightenment and knowledge of His Majesty. This will seem impossible, for if the faculties are so absorbed that we can say they are dead, and likewise the senses, how can a soul know that it understands this secret? I don't know, nor perhaps does any creature but only the Creator. And this goes for many other

things that take place in this state—I mean in these two dwelling places, for there is no closed door between the one and the other. Because there are things in the last that are not revealed to those who have not yet reached it, I thought I should divide them.

5. When the soul is in this suspension, the Lord likes to show it some secrets, things about heaven, and imaginative visions. It is able to tell of them afterward, for these remain so impressed on the memory that they are never forgotten. But when the visions are intellectual, the soul doesn't know how to speak of them. For there must be some visions during these moments that are so sublime that it's not fitting for those who live on this earth to have the further understanding necessary to explain them. However, since the soul is in possession of its senses, it can say many things about these intellectual visions.

It could be that some of you do not know what a vision is, especially an intellectual one. I shall explain at the proper time,[6] for one who has the authority ordered me to do so.[7] And although the explanation may not seem pertinent, it will perhaps benefit some souls.

6. Well now you will ask me: If afterward there is to be no remembrance of these sublime favors granted by the Lord to the soul in this state, what benefit do they have? O daughters, they are so great one cannot exaggerate! For even though they are unexplainable, they are well inscribed in the very interior part of the soul and are never forgotten.

But, you will insist, if there is no image and the faculties do not understand, how can the visions be remembered? I don't understand this either; but I do understand that some truths about the grandeur of God remain so fixed in this soul that even if faith were not to tell it who God is and of its obligation to believe that He is God, from that very moment it would adore Him as God, as did Jacob when he saw the ladder. By means of the ladder Jacob must have understood other secrets that he didn't know how to explain, for by seeing just a ladder on which angels descended and ascended he would not have understood such great mysteries if there had not been deeper interior enlightenment.[8] I don't know if I'm guessing right in what I say, for although I have heard this story about Jacob, I don't know if I'm remembering it correctly.

7. Nor did Moses know how to describe all that he saw in the bush, but only what God wished Him to describe.[9] But if God had not shown secrets to his soul along with a certitude that made him recognize and believe that they were from God, Moses could not have entered into so many severe trials. But he must have understood such deep things among the thorns of that bush that the vision gave him the courage to do what he did for the people of Israel. So, Sisters, we don't have to look for reasons to understand the hidden things of God. Since we believe He is powerful, clearly we must believe that a worm with as limited a power as ours will not understand His grandeurs. Let us praise Him, for He is pleased that we come to know some of them.

8. I have been wanting to find some comparison by which to explain what I'm speaking about, and I don't think there is any that fits. But let's use this one: You enter into the room of a king or great lord, or I believe they call it the treasure chamber, where there are countless kinds of glass and earthen vessels and other things so arranged that almost all of these objects are seen upon entering. Once I was brought to a room like this in the house of the Duchess of Alba where, while I was on a journey, obedience ordered me to stay because of this lady's insistence with my superiors.[10] I was amazed on entering and wondered what gain could be gotten from that conglomeration of things, and I saw that one could praise the Lord at seeing so many different kinds of objects, and now I laugh to myself on realizing how the experience has helped me here in my explanation. Although I was in that room for a while, there was so much there to see that I soon forgot it all; none of those pieces has remained in my memory any more than if I had never seen them, nor would I know how to explain the workmanship of any of them. I can only say in general that I remember seeing everything. Likewise with this favor, the soul, while it is made one with God, is placed in this empyreal room that we must have interiorly. For, clearly, the soul has some of these dwelling places since God abides within it. And although the Lord must not want the soul to see these secrets every time it is in this ecstasy, for it can be so absorbed in enjoying Him that a sublime good like that is sufficient for it, sometimes He is pleased that the absorption decrease and the soul see at once

what is in that room. After it returns to itself, the soul is left with that representation of the grandeurs it saw; but it cannot describe any of them, nor do its natural powers grasp any more than what God wished that it see supernaturally.

9. You, therefore, might object that I admit that the soul sees and that the vision is an imaginative one. But I'm not saying that, for I'm not dealing with an imaginative vision but with an intellectual one. Since I have no learning, I don't know how in my dullness to explain anything. If what I have said up to now about this prayer is worthwhile, I know clearly that I'm not the one who has said it.

I hold that if at times in its raptures the soul doesn't understand these secrets, its raptures are not given by God but are caused by some natural weakness. It can happen to persons with a weak constitution, as is so with women, that any spiritual force will overcome the natural powers, and the soul will be absorbed as I believe I mentioned in reference to the prayer of quiet.[11] These experiences have nothing to do with rapture. In a rapture, believe me, God carries off for Himself the entire soul, and, as to someone who is His own and His spouse, He begins showing it some little part of the kingdom that it has gained by being espoused to Him. However small that part of His kingdom may be, everything that there is in this great God is magnificent. And He doesn't want any hindrance from anyone, neither from the faculties nor from the senses, but He immediately commands the doors of all these dwelling places to be closed; and only that door to His room remains open so that we can enter. Blessed be so much mercy; they will be rightly cursed who have not wanted to benefit by it and who have lost this Lord.

10. O my Sisters, what nothingness it is, that which we leave! Nor is what we do anything, nor all that we could do for a God who thus wishes to communicate Himself to a worm! And if we hope to enjoy this blessing even in this present life, what are we doing? What is causing us to delay? What is enough to make us, even momentarily, stop looking for this Lord as did the bride in the streets and in the squares?[12] Oh, what a mockery everything in the world is if it doesn't lead us and help us toward this blessing even if its delights and riches and joys, as much of them as imaginable, were to last forever! It

is all loathsome dung compared to these treasures that will be enjoyed without end. Nor are these anything in comparison with having as our own the Lord of all the treasures of heaven and earth.

11. O human blindness! How long, how long before this dust will be removed from our eyes! Even though among ourselves the dust doesn't seem to be capable of blinding us completely, I see some specks, some tiny pebbles that if we allow them to increase will be enough to do us great harm. On the contrary, for the love of God, Sisters, let us benefit by these faults so as to know our misery, and they will give us clearer vision as did the mud to the blind man cured by our Spouse.[13] Thus, seeing ourselves so imperfect, let us increase our supplications that His Majesty may draw good out of our miseries so that we might be pleasing to Him.

12. I have digressed a great deal without realizing it. Pardon me, Sisters, and believe me that having reached these grandeurs of God (I mean, reached the place where I must speak of them), I cannot help but feel very sorry to see what we lose through our own fault. Even though it is true that these are blessings the Lord gives to whomever He wills, His Majesty would give them all to us if we loved Him as He loves us. He doesn't desire anything else than to have those to whom to give. His riches do not lessen because He gives them away.

13. Well now, to get back to what I was saying,[14] the Spouse commands that the doors of the dwelling places be closed and even those of the castle and the outer wall. For in desiring to carry off this soul, He takes away the breath so that, even though the other senses sometimes last a little longer, a person cannot speak at all; although at other times everything is taken away at once, and the hands and the body grow cold so that the person doesn't seem to have any life; nor sometimes is it known whether he is breathing. This situation lasts but a short while, I mean in its intensity; for when this extreme suspension lets up a little, it seems that the body returns to itself somewhat and is nourished so as to die again and give more life to the soul. Nevertheless, so extreme an ecstasy doesn't last long.

14. But it will happen that even though the extreme ecstasy ends, the will remains so absorbed and the intellect so

withdrawn, for a day and even days, that the latter seems incapable of understanding anything that doesn't lead to awakening the will to love; and the will is wide awake to this love and asleep to becoming attached to any creature.

15. Oh, when the soul returns completely to itself, what bewilderment and how intense its desires to be occupied in God in every kind of way He might want! If the effects that were mentioned were produced by the former kinds of prayer, what will be the effects of a favor as sublime as this? The soul would desire to have a thousand lives so as to employ them all for God and that everything here on earth would be a tongue to help it praise Him. The desires to do penance are most strong, but not much help comes from performing it, because the strength of love makes the soul feel that all that is done amounts to little and see clearly that the martyrs did not accomplish much in suffering the torments they did because with this help from our Lord such suffering is easy. Hence these souls complain to His Majesty when no opportunity for suffering presents itself.

16. When this favor is granted them in secret their esteem for it is great; when it is given in the presence of other persons their embarrassment and shame are so strong that the pain and worry over what those who saw it will think somehow take the soul away from what was being enjoyed.[15] For these persons know the malice of the world, and they understand that the world will not perhaps regard the experience for what it is, but that what the Lord should be praised for will perhaps be the occasion for rash judgments. In some ways it seems to me that this pain and embarrassment amount to a lack of humility, for if this person desires to be reviled, what difference does it make what others think? But the soul cannot control such feelings. One who was in this affliction heard from the Lord: "Don't be afflicted, either they will praise Me or criticize you; and in either case you gain."[16] I learned afterward that this person was very much consoled and encouraged by these words, and I put them down here in case one of you might find herself in this affliction. It seems that our Lord wishes all to understand that that soul is now His, that no one should touch it. Well and good if its body, or honor, or possessions are touched for this soul draws honor for His Majesty out of everything. But that

one touch the soul—absolutely not; for if the soul does not withdraw from its Spouse through a very culpable boldness, He will protect it from the whole world and even from all hell.

17. I don't know if anything has been explained about the nature of rapture, for to explain it is completely impossible, as I have said.[17] But I don't believe anything has been lost by trying. For there are effects that are very different in feigned raptures. I do not say "feigned" because the one who has the experience wants to deceive but because that person is deceived. And since the signs and effects of the feigned raptures are not in conformity with such a great blessing, the true rapture is looked on unfavorably; and afterward the one to whom the Lord grants it justifiably is not believed. May He be blessed and praised forever, amen, amen.

CHAPTER FIVE

Continues on the same subject and deals with a kind of rapture in which God raises up the soul through a flight of the spirit, an experience different from that just explained. Tells why courage is necessary. Explains something about this delightful favor the Lord grants. The chapter is a very beneficial one.

1. There is another kind of rapture—I call it flight of the spirit—that, though substantially the same as other raptures, is interiorly experienced very differently.[1] For sometimes suddenly a movement of the soul is felt that is so swift it seems the spirit is carried off, and at a fearful speed especially in the beginning. This is why I have told you[2] that strong courage is necessary for the one to whom God grants these favors, and even faith and confidence and a full surrender to our Lord so that He may do what He wants with the soul. Do you think it is a small disturbance for a person to be very much in his senses and see his soul carried off (and in the case of some, we have read, even the body with the soul) without knowing where that soul is going, what or who does this, or how? At the beginning of this swift movement there is not so much certitude that the rapture is from God.[3]

2. Well, now, is there some means by which one can resist it? None at all; rather, to resist makes matters worse, for I know this was so with a certain person.[4] It seems God wishes

that the soul that has so often, so earnestly, and with such complete willingness offered everything to Him should understand that in itself it no longer has any part to play; and it is carried off with a noticeably more impetuous movement. It is determined now to do no more than what the straw does when drawn by the amber—if you have noticed—and abandon itself into the hands of the One who is all powerful, for it sees that the safest thing to do is to make a virtue of necessity. And that I mentioned a straw is certainly appropriate, for as easily as a huge giant snatches up a straw, this great and powerful Giant of ours carries away the spirit.[5]

3. It seems that the trough of water we mentioned (I believe it was in the fourth dwelling place, for I don't recall exactly)[6] filled so easily and gently, I mean without any movement. Here this great God, who holds back the springs of water and doesn't allow the sea to go beyond its boundaries,[7] lets loose the springs from which the water in this trough flows. With a powerful impulse, a huge wave rises up so forcefully that it lifts high this little bark that is our soul. A bark cannot prevent the furious waves from leaving it where they will; nor does the pilot have the power, nor do those who take part in controlling the little ship. So much less can the interior part of the soul stay where it will, or make its senses or faculties do other than what they are commanded; here the soul doesn't care what happens outwardly.

4. It is certain, Sisters, that just from writing about it I am amazed at how the immense power of this great King and Emperor is shown here. What will be the amazement of the one who experiences it! I hold that if His Majesty were to reveal this power to those who go astray in the world as He does to these souls, the former would not dare offend Him; this out of fear if not out of love. Oh, how obliged, then, will those persons be who have been informed through so sublime a path to strive with all their might not to displease this Lord! For love of Him, Sisters, I beg you, those of you to whom His Majesty has granted these favors, or others like them, that you don't grow careless, doing nothing but receive. Reflect that the one who owes a lot must pay a lot.[8]

5. In this respect, too, great courage is necessary, for this favor is something frightening. If our Lord were not to give

such courage, the soul would always go about deeply distressed. For it reflects on what His Majesty does for it and turns back to look at itself, at how little it serves in comparison with its obligation, and at how the tiny bit it does is full of faults, failures, and weaknesses. So as not to recall how imperfectly it performs some work—if it does—it prefers striving to forget its works, keeping in mind its sins, and placing itself before the mercy of God. Since it doesn't have anything with which to pay, it begs for the pity and mercy God has always had toward sinners.

6. Perhaps He will respond as He did to a person who before a crucifix was reflecting with deep affliction that she had never had anything to give to God, or anything to give up for Him. The Crucified Himself in consoling her told her He had given her all the sufferings and trials He had undergone in His Passion so that she could have them as her own to offer His Father.[9] The comfort and enrichment was such that, according to what I have heard from her, she cannot forget the experience. Rather, every time she sees how miserable she is, she gets encouragement and consolation from remembering those words.

I could mention here some other experiences like this, for since I have dealt with so many holy and prayerful persons, I know about many such experiences; but I want to limit myself lest you think I am speaking of myself. What I said seems to me very beneficial to help you understand how pleased our Lord is that we know ourselves and strive to reflect again and again on our poverty and misery and on how we possess nothing that we have not received. So, my Sisters, courage is necessary for this knowledge and for the many other graces given to the soul the Lord has brought to this stage. And when there is humility, courage, in my opinion, is even more necessary for this knowledge of one's own misery. May the Lord give us this humility because of who He is.

7. Well, now, to return to this quick rapture of the spirit.[10] It is such that the spirit truly seems to go forth from the body. On the other hand, it is clear that this person is not dead; at least, he cannot say whether for some moments he was in the body or not. It seems to him that he was entirely in another region different from this in which we live, where there is

shown another light so different from earth's light that if he were to spend his whole life trying to imagine that light, along with the other things, he would be unable to do so. It happens that within an instant so many things together are taught him that if he were to work for many years with his imagination and mind in order to systematize them he wouldn't be able to do so, not with even one thousandth part of one of them. This is not an intellectual but an imaginative vision, for the eyes of the soul see much better than do bodily eyes here on earth, and without words understanding of some things is given; I mean that if a person sees some saints, he knows them as well as if he had often spoken with them.

8. At other times, along with the things seen through the eyes of the soul by an intellectual vision, other things are represented, especially a multitude of angels with their Lord. And without seeing anything with the eyes of the body or the soul, through an admirable knowledge I will not be able to explain, there is represented what I'm saying and many other things not meant to be spoken of. Anyone who experiences them, and has more ability than I, will perhaps know how to explain them, although doing so seems to me very difficult indeed. Whether all this takes place in the body or not, I wouldn't know; at least I wouldn't swear that the soul is in the body or that the body is without the soul.[11]

9. I have often thought that just as the sun while in the sky has such strong rays that, even though it doesn't move from there, the rays promptly reach the earth, so the soul and the spirit, which are one,[12] could be like the sun and its rays. Thus, while the soul remains in its place, the superior part rises above it. In a word, I don't know what I'm saying. What is true is that with the speed of a ball shot from an arquebus, when fire is applied, an interior flight is experienced—I don't know what else to call it—which, though noiseless, is so clearly a movement that it cannot be the work of the imagination. And while the spirit is far outside itself, from all it can understand, great things are shown to it. When it again senses that it is within itself, the benefits it feels are remarkable, and it has so little esteem for all earthly things in comparison to the things it has seen that the former seem like dung. From then on its life on earth is very painful, and it doesn't see anything good in those things that used to seem good to it. The experience causes it to

care little about them. It seems that the Lord, like those Israelites who brought back signs from the promised land,[13] has desired to show it something about its future land so that it may suffer the trials of this laborious path, knowing where it must go to get its final rest. Even though something that passes so quickly will not seem to you very beneficial, the blessings left in the soul are so great that only the person who has this experience will be able to understand its value.

10. Wherefore, the experience, obviously, is not from the devil; it would be impossible for the imagination or the devil to represent things that leave so much virtue, peace, calm, and improvement in the soul. Three things, especially, are left in it to a very sublime degree: knowledge of the grandeur of God, because the more we see of this grandeur the greater is our understanding; self-knowledge and humility on seeing that something so low in comparison with the Creator of so many grandeurs dared to offend Him (and neither does the soul dare look up at Him); the third, little esteem of earthly things save for those that can be used for the service of so great a God.

11. These are the jewels the Spouse begins to give the betrothed, and their value is such that the soul will not want to lose them. For these meetings[14] remain so engraved in the memory that I believe it's impossible to forget them until one enjoys them forever, unless they are forgotten through one's own most serious fault. But the Spouse who gives them has the power to give the grace not to lose them.

12. Well to get back to the courage that is necessary,[15] does it seem to you that this is so trivial a thing? For it truly seems that because the soul loses its senses, and doesn't understand why, it is separated from the body. It's necessary that He who gives everything else give the courage also. You will say that this fear is well paid. So do I. May it please His Majesty to give us the courage so that we may merit to serve Him, amen.

CHAPTER SIX

Tells about an effect of the prayer discussed in the previous chapter. How to understand whether this effect is true rather than deceptive. Discusses another favor the Lord grants so that the soul might be occupied in praising Him.

1. As a result of these wonderful favors the soul is left so

full of longings to enjoy completely the One who grants them that it lives in a great though delightful torment. With the strongest yearnings to die, and thus usually with tears, it begs God to take it from this exile. Everything it sees wearies it. When it is alone it finds some relief, but soon this torment returns; yet when the soul does not experience this pain, something is felt to be missing. In sum, this little butterfly is unable to find a lasting place of rest; rather, since the soul goes about with such tender love, any occasion that enkindles this fire more makes the soul fly aloft. As a result, in this dwelling place the raptures are very common and there is no means to avoid them even though they may take place in public. Hence, persecutions and criticism. Even though the soul may want to be free from fears, others do not allow this freedom. For there are many persons who cause these fears, especially confessors.

2. And even though on the one hand the soul seems to feel very secure in its interior part, especially when it is alone with God, on the other hand it goes about in deep distress because it fears the devil may in some way beguile it into offending the One whom it loves so much. Little does it suffer over criticism, unless the confessor himself distresses it, as if it could do more. It does nothing but ask prayers from all and beg His Majesty to lead it by another path, for they all tell it to take another; they say that the path it is on is very dangerous. But since the soul has found this path to be so greatly beneficial, it sees that such a path is leading it along the way to heaven, according to what it reads, hears, and knows about God's commandments. Even if it wanted to, it could not really desire anything else but to abandon itself into God's hands. And even this powerlessness distresses it, for it thinks it is not obeying its confessor. Obeying and not offending our Lord, it thinks, is the complete remedy against deception. Thus, in its opinion, it would not commit knowingly a venial sin even were others to crush it to pieces. It is intensely afflicted upon seeing that it cannot free itself from unknowingly committing many venial sins.

3. God gives these souls the strongest desire not to displease Him in anything, however small, and the desire to avoid if possible every imperfection. For this reason alone, if for no other, the soul wants to flee people, and it has great envy of those who have lived in deserts. On the other hand, it would

want to enter into the midst of the world to try to play a part in getting even one soul to praise God more. A woman in this stage of prayer is distressed by the natural hindrance there is to her entering the world, and she has great envy of those who have the freedom to cry out and spread the news abroad about who this great God of hosts is.

4. O poor little butterfly, bound with so many chains that do not let you fly where you would like! Have pity on it, my God! Ordain that it might somehow fulfill its desires for your honor and glory. Do not be mindful of the little it deserves and of its lowly nature. You have the power, Lord, to make the great sea and the large river Jordan roll back and allow the children of Israel to pass.[1] Yet, do not take pity on this little butterfly! Helped by your strength, it can suffer many trials; it is determined to do so and desires to suffer them. Extend Your powerful arm,[2] Lord, that this soul might not spend its life in things so base. Let Your grandeur appear in a creature so feminine and lowly, whatever the cost to her, so that the world may know that this grandeur is not hers at all and may praise You. This praise is what she desires, and she would give a thousand lives—if she had that many—if one soul were to praise You a little more through her; and she would consider such lives very well spent. She understands in all truth that she doesn't deserve to suffer for You a tiny trial, much less die.

5. I don't know what my goal was in saying this, Sisters, nor why I said it, for these words were not planned. Let us realize that such effects are undoubtedly left by these suspensions and ecstasies. The desires are not passing but remain, and when an occasion arises to manifest their presence, one sees that they are not feigned. Why do I say they remain? Sometimes the soul feels, and in the smallest things, that it is a coward and so timid and frightened it doesn't think that it has the courage to do anything. I understand that the Lord leaves it then to its own human nature for its own greater good. It then sees that if it had been able to do something, the power was given by His Majesty. This truth is seen with a clarity that leaves the soul annihilated within itself and with deeper knowledge of God's mercy and grandeur—attributes the Lord desired to show to something so low. But usually its state is like that we've just mentioned.

6. Note one thing, Sisters, about these great desires to see our Lord: They sometimes afflict so much that you must necessarily avoid fostering them and must distract yourselves; if you can, I mean, for in other instances that I shall mention further on[3] this cannot be done, as you will see. As for these initial desires, it's sometimes possible to distract oneself from them because there is every reason to be conformed to the will of God and say what Saint Martin said.[4] A person can reflect on Saint Martin's words if the desires afflict a great deal. Since it seems that these desires are characteristic of very advanced persons, the devil could instigate them so that we might think we are advanced. It is always good to walk with fear. But my opinion is that he would not be able to give the quiet and peace this suffering gives the soul; he would be stirring some passion, as happens when we suffer over worldly things. But a person who has no experience of the authentic and the inauthentic desires will think his desires are something great and will help them along as much as he can and will do serious harm to his health. For this suffering is continual, or at least very habitual.

7. Also note that a weak constitution is wont to cause these kinds of suffering, especially in the case of tender persons who will weep over every little thing. A thousand times they will be led to think they weep for God, but they will not be doing so. And it can even happen, when tears flow in abundance (I mean, that for a time every little word the soul hears or thinks concerning God becomes irresistible to tears), that some humor has reached the heart, thereby contributing more to the tears than does love for God; for seemingly these persons will never finish weeping. Since they have already heard that tears are good, they will not restrain themselves nor would they desire to do anything else; and they help the tears along as much as they can. The devil's aim here is that these persons become so weak they will afterward be unable either to pray or to keep their rule.

8. It seems to me I can see you asking what you should do since I mark danger everywhere and in something as good as tears I think there can be deception; you are wondering if I may be the one who is deceived. And it could be that I am. But believe me, I do not speak without having seen that these false tears can be experienced by some persons; although not by me,

for I am not at all tender. Rather, I have a heart so hard that sometimes I am distressed; although when the inner fire is intense, the heart, no matter how hard, distills like an alembic. You will indeed know when this fire is the source of the tears, for they are then more comforting and bring peace, not turbulence, and seldom cause harm. The good that lies in the false tears—when there is any good—is that the damage is done to the body (I mean when there is humility) and not to the soul. But even if there is no harm done to the body, it won't be wrong to be suspicious about tears.

9. Let's not think that everything is accomplished through much weeping but set our hands to the task of hard work and virtue. These are what we must pay attention to; let the tears come when God sends them and without any effort on our part to induce them. These tears from God will irrigate this dry earth, and they are a great help in producing fruit. The less attention we pay to them the more there are, for they are the water that falls from heaven. The tears we draw out by tiring ourselves in digging cannot compare with the tears that come from God, for often in digging we shall get worn out and not find even a puddle of water, much less a flowing well. Therefore, Sisters, I consider it better for us to place ourselves in the presence of the Lord and look at His mercy and grandeur and at our own lowliness, and let Him give us what He wants, whether water or dryness. He knows best what is suitable for us. With such an attitude we shall go about refreshed, and the devil will not have so much chance to play tricks on us.

10. In the midst of these experiences that are both painful and delightful together, our Lord sometimes gives the soul feelings of jubilation and a strange prayer it doesn't understand. I am writing about this favor here so that if He grants it to you, you may give Him much praise and know what is taking place. It is, in my opinion, a deep union of the faculties; but our Lord nonetheless leaves them free that they might enjoy this joy—and the same goes for the senses—without understanding what it is they are enjoying or how they are enjoying. What I'm saying seems like gibberish, but certainly the experience takes place in this way, for the joy is so excessive the soul wouldn't want to enjoy it alone but wants to tell everyone about it so that they might help this soul praise our Lord. All

its activity is directed to this praise. Oh, how many festivals and demonstrations the soul would organize, if it could, that all might know its joy! It seems it has found itself and that, like the father of the prodigal son, it would want to prepare a festival and invite all[5] because it sees itself in an undoubtedly safe place, at least for the time being. And I hold that there is reason for its desires. The devil cannot give this experience, because there is so much interior joy in the very intimate part of the soul and so much peace; and all the happiness stirs the soul to the praises of God.

11. To be silent and conceal this great impulse of happiness, when experiencing it, is no small pain. Saint Francis must have felt this impulse when the robbers struck him, for he ran through the fields crying out and telling them that he was the herald of the great King; and also other saints must feel it who go to deserts to be able to proclaim as Saint Francis these praises of their God. I knew a saint named Friar Peter of Alcántara—for I believe from the way he lived that he was one—who did this very thing,[6] and those who at one time listened to him thought he was crazy. Oh, what blessed madness, Sisters! If only God would give it to us all! And what a favor He has granted you by bringing you to this house where, when the Lord gives you this favor and you tell others about it, you will receive help rather than the criticism you would receive in the world. This proclamation is so unusual there that one is not at all surprised at the criticism.

12. Oh, how unfortunate the times and miserable the life in which we now live; happy are they whose good fortune it is to remain apart from the world. Sometimes it is a particular joy for me to see these Sisters gathered together and feeling such great joy at being in the monastery that they praise our Lord as much as possible. It is seen very clearly that their praises rise from the interior of the soul. I would want you to praise Him often, Sisters; for the one who begins awakens the others. In what better way can you, when together, use your tongues than in the praises of God, since we have so many reasons for praising Him?

13. May it please His Majesty to give us this prayer often since it is so safe and beneficial; to acquire it is impossible because it is something very supernatural. And it may last a

whole day. The soul goes about like a person who has drunk a great deal but not so much as to be drawn out of his senses; or like a person suffering melancholy who has not lost his reason completely but cannot free himself from what is in his imagination—nor can anyone else.

These are inelegant comparisons for something so precious, but I can't think up any others. The joy makes a person so forgetful of self and of all things that he doesn't advert to, nor can he speak of anything other than, the praises of God that proceed from his joy.

Let us all help this soul, my daughters. Why do we want to have more discretion? What can give us greater happiness? And may all creatures help us forever and ever, amen, amen, amen!

CHAPTER SEVEN

Discusses the kind of suffering those souls to whom God grants the favors mentioned feel concerning their sins. Tells what a great mistake it is, however spiritual one may be, not to practice keeping the humanity of our Lord and Savior Jesus Christ present in one's mind; also His most sacred Passion and life, His glorious Mother, and the saints. The chapter is very helpful.

1. You will think, Sisters, that these souls to whom the Lord communicates Himself in this unusual way will already be so sure of enjoying Him forever that they will have nothing to fear nor sins to weep over. Those especially who have not attained these favors from God will think this, for if they had enjoyed them, they would know what I'm going to say. But to think the above would be a great mistake because suffering over one's sins increases the more one receives from our God. And, for my part, I hold that until we are there where nothing can cause pain this suffering will not be taken away.

2. True, sometimes there is greater affliction than at other times; and the affliction is also of a different kind, for the soul doesn't think about the suffering it will undergo on account of its sins but of how ungrateful it has been to One to whom it owes so much and who deserves so much to be served. For in these grandeurs God communicates to it, it understands much more about Him. It is astonished at how bold it was; it weeps over its lack of respect; it thinks its foolishness was so excessive

that it never finishes grieving over that foolishness when it recalls that for such base things it abandoned so great a Majesty. Much more does it recall this foolishness than it does the favors it receives, though these favors are as remarkable as the ones mentioned or as those still to be spoken of. These favors are like the waves of a large river in that they come and go; but the memory these souls have of their sins clings like thick mire. It always seems that these sins are alive in the memory, and this is a heavy cross.

3. I know a person[1] who, apart from wanting to die in order to see God, wanted to die so as not to feel the continual pain of how ungrateful she had been to One to whom she ever owed so much and would owe. Thus it didn't seem to her that anyone's wickedness could equal her own, for she understood that there could be no one else from whom God would have had so much to put up with and to whom He had granted so many favors. As for the fear of hell, such persons don't have any. That they might lose God, at times—though seldom—distresses them very much. All their fear is that God might allow them out of His hand to offend Him, and they find themselves in as miserable a state as they were once before. In regard to their own suffering or glory, they don't care. If they don't want to stay long in purgatory, the reason comes from the fact of their not wanting to be away from God—as are those who are in purgatory—rather than from the sufferings undergone there.

4. I wouldn't consider it safe for a soul, however favored by God, to forget that at one time it saw itself in a miserable state. Although recalling this misery is a painful thing, doing so is helpful for many. Perhaps it is because I have been so wretched that I have this opinion and am always mindful of my misery. Those who have been good will not have to feel this pain, although there will always be failures as long as we live in this mortal body. No relief is afforded this suffering by the thought that our Lord has already pardoned and forgotten the sins. Rather, it adds to the suffering to see so much goodness and realize that favors are granted to one who deserves nothing but hell. I think such a realization was a great martyrdom for Saint Peter and the Magdalene. Since their love for God had grown so deep and they had received so many favors and come

to know the grandeur and majesty of God, the remembrance of their misery would have been difficult to suffer, and they would have suffered it with tender sentiments.

5. It will also seem to you that anyone who enjoys such lofty things will no longer meditate on the mysteries of the most sacred humanity of our Lord Jesus Christ. Such a person would now be engaged entirely in loving. This is a matter I wrote about at length elsewhere.[2] They have contradicted me about it and said that I don't understand, because these are paths along which our Lord leads, and that when souls have already passed beyond the beginning stages it is better for them to deal with things concerning the divinity and flee from corporeal things. Nonetheless, they will not make me admit that such a road is a good one. Now it could be that I'm mistaken and that we are all saying the same thing. But I myself see that the devil tried to deceive me in this matter, and thus I have so learned my lesson from experience that I think, although I've spoken on this topic at other times,[3] I will speak of it again here that you will proceed very carefully in this matter. And take notice that I dare say you should not believe anyone who tells you something else. I'll try to explain myself better than I did elsewhere. If anyone perhaps has written what a certain person told me, this would be good if the matter is explained at length, but to speak of it so summarily could do much harm to those of us who are not well informed.[4]

6. It will also seem to some souls that they cannot think about the Passion, or still less about the Blessed Virgin and the lives of the saints; the remembrance of both of these latter is so very helpful and encouraging. I cannot imagine what such souls are thinking of. To be always withdrawn from corporeal things and enkindled in love is the trait of angelic spirits, not of those who live in mortal bodies. It's necessary that we speak to, think about, and become the companions of those who, having had a mortal body, accomplished such great feats for God. How much more is it necessary not to withdraw through one's own efforts from all our good and help, which is the most sacred humanity of our Lord Jesus Christ. I cannot believe that these souls do so, but they just don't understand; and they will do harm to themselves and to others. At least I assure them that they will not enter these last two dwelling places. For if they

lose the guide, who is the good Jesus, they will not hit on the right road. It will be quite an accomplishment if they remain safely in the other dwelling places. The Lord Himself says that He is the way; the Lord says also that He is the light and that no one can go to the Father but through Him, and "anyone who sees me sees my Father."[5] They will say that another meaning is given to these words. I don't know about those other meanings; I have got along very well with this one that my soul always feels to be true.

7. There are some souls—and there are many who have spoken about it to me—who brought by our Lord to perfect contemplation would like to be in that prayer always; but that is impossible. Yet this favor of the Lord remains with them in such a way that afterward they cannot engage as before in discursive thought about the mysteries of the Passion and life of Christ. I don't know the reason, but this inability is very common, for the intellect becomes less capable of meditation. I believe the reason must be that since in meditation the whole effort consists in seeking God and that once God is found the soul becomes used to seeking Him again through the work of the will, the soul doesn't want to tire itself by working with the intellect. Likewise, it seems to me that since this generous faculty, which is the will, is already enkindled, it wants to avoid, if it can, using the other faculty; and it doesn't go wrong. But to avoid this will be impossible, especially before the soul reaches these last two dwelling places; and the soul will lose time, for the will often needs the help of the intellect so as to be enkindled.

8. And note this point, Sisters; it is important, and so I want to explain it further: The soul desires to be completely occupied in love and does not want to be taken up with anything else, but to be so occupied is impossible for it even though it may want to; for although the will is not dead, the fire that usually makes it burn is dying out, and someone must necessarily blow on the fire so that heat will be given off. Would it be good for a soul with this dryness to wait for fire to come down from heaven to burn this sacrifice that it is making of itself to God, as did our Father Elijah?[6] No, certainly not, nor is it right to expect miracles. The Lord works them for this soul when He pleases, as was said and will be said further on.[7]

146

But His Majesty wants us to consider ourselves undeserving of them because of our wretchedness, and desires that we help ourselves in every way possible. I hold for myself that until we die such an attitude is necessary however sublime the prayer may be.

9. It is true that anyone whom the Lord places in the seventh dwelling place rarely, or hardly ever, needs to make this effort. (I will give the reason for this fact when speaking of that dwelling place, if I remember.)[8] But such a person walks continually in an admirable way with Christ, our Lord, in whom the divine and the human are joined and who is always that person's companion. As for the above, when the fire in the will that was mentioned[9] is not enkindled and God's presence is not felt, it is necessary that we seek this presence. This is what His Majesty wants us to do, as the bride did in the Song of Songs,[10] and He wants us to ask creatures who it is who made them—as Saint Augustine says, I believe, in his *Meditations* or *Confessions*[11]—and not be like dunces wasting time waiting for what was given us once before. At the beginning of the life of prayer it may be that the Lord will not give this fire in a year, or even in many years. His Majesty knows why; we must not desire to know nor is there any reason why we should. Since we know the path by which we must please God, which is that of the commandments and counsels, we should follow it very diligently, and think of His life and death and of the many things we owe Him; let the rest come when the Lord desires.

10. At this point, someone may respond that he cannot dwell on these things, and, because of what was said,[12] perhaps he will in a certain way be right. You already know that discursive thinking with the intellect is one thing and representing truths to the intellect by means of the memory is another. You may say, perhaps, that you do not understand me, and indeed it could be that I don't know how to explain the matter; but I shall do the best I can. By meditation I mean much discursive reflection with the intellect in the following way: We begin to think about the favor God granted us in giving us His only Son, and we do not stop there, but go on to the mysteries of His whole glorious life; or we begin to think about the prayer in the garden, but the intellect doesn't stop until He is on the cross; or we take a phase of the Passion like,

let us say, the arrest, and we proceed with this mystery considering in detail the things there are to think of and feel about the betrayal of Judas, the flight of the apostles, and all the rest; this kind of reflection is an admirable and very meritorious prayer.

11. This prayer is the kind that those whom God has brought to supernatural things and to perfect contemplation are right in saying they cannot practice. As I have said,[13] I don't know the reason, but usually they cannot practice discursive reflection. But I say that a person will not be right if he says he does not dwell on these mysteries or often have them in mind, especially when the Catholic Church celebrates them. Nor is it possible for the soul to forget that it has received so much from God, so many precious signs of love, for these are living sparks that will enkindle it more in its love for our Lord. But I say this person doesn't understand himself, because the soul understands these mysteries in a more perfect manner. The intellect represents them in such a way, and they are so stamped on the memory, that the mere sight of the Lord fallen to the ground in the garden with that frightful sweat is enough to last the intellect not only an hour but many days, while it looks with a simple gaze at who He is and how ungrateful we have been for so much suffering. Soon the will responds, even though it may not do so with tender feelings, with the desire to serve somehow for such a great favor and to suffer something for One who suffered so much, and with other similar desires relating to what the memory and intellect are dwelling on. I believe that for this reason a person cannot go on to further discursive reflection on the Passion, and this inability makes him think that he cannot think about it.

12. If he doesn't dwell on these mysteries in the way that was mentioned, it is good that he strive to do so, for I know that doing so will not impede the most sublime prayer. I don't think it's good to fail to dwell often on these mysteries. If as a result the Lord suspends the intellect, well and good; for even though the soul may not so desire He will make it abandon what it was dwelling on. And I am very certain that this procedure is not a hindrance but a very great help toward every good; the hindrance would come from a great deal of work with the discursive reflection I mentioned in the beginning. I hold that one who has advanced further along cannot

practice this discursive reflection. It could be that one can, for God leads souls by many paths. But let not those who can travel by the road of discursive thought condemn those who cannot, or judge them incapable of enjoying the sublime blessings that lie enclosed in the mysteries of our good, Jesus Christ. Nor will anyone make me think, however spiritual he may be, that he will advance by trying to turn away from these mysteries.

13. There are some principles and even means that certain souls use, by which it is thought that when a person begins to experience the prayer of quiet and to relish the enjoyment and spiritual delights given by the Lord, the important thing is to remain always in that state of delight. Well, now, let them believe me and not be so absorbed, as I have said elsewhere.[14] Life is long, and there are in it many trials, and we need to look at Christ our model, how He suffered them, and also at His apostles and saints, so as to bear these trials with perfection. Jesus is too good a companion for us to turn away from Him and His most blessed Mother, and He is very pleased that we grieve over His sufferings even though we sometimes leave aside our own consolation and delight. Moreover, daughters, enjoyment in prayer is not so habitual that there is not time for everything. I would be suspicious of anyone who says this delight is continual; I mean, who can never do what was mentioned. And you should be suspicious too, and strive to free yourselves from this error and avoid such absorption with all your strength. If your efforts aren't enough, tell the prioress so that she might give you some task demanding such care that this danger is removed. For if this absorption continues, it is extremely dangerous, at least for the brain and the head.

14. I believe I've explained that it is fitting for souls, however spiritual, to take care not to flee from corporeal things to the extent of thinking that even the most sacred humanity causes harm. Some quote what the Lord said to His disciples that it was fitting that He go.[15] I can't bear this. I would wager that He didn't say it to His most Blessed Mother, because she was firm in the faith; she knew He was God and man, and even though she loved Him more than they did, she did so with such perfection that His presence was a help rather than a hindrance. The apostles must not have been as firm then in the

faith as they were afterward and as we have reason to be now. I tell you, daughters, that I consider this a dangerous path and think the devil could make one lose devotion for the most Blessed Sacrament.

15. The mistake it seemed to me I was making wasn't so extreme; rather it consisted of not delighting so much in the thought of our Lord Jesus Christ but in going along in that absorption, waiting for that enjoyment. And I realized clearly that I was proceeding badly. Since it wasn't possible for me to experience the absorption always, the mind wandered here and there. My soul, it seems to me, was like a bird flying about that doesn't know where to light; and it was losing a lot of time and not making progress in virtue or improving in prayer. I didn't understand the reason, nor would I have understood it, in my opinion, because it seemed to me that what I was doing was very correct, until a person with whom I was discussing my prayer, who was a servant of God, warned me. Afterward, I saw clearly how wrong I had been, and I never stop regretting that there had been a time in which I failed to understand that I could not gain much through such a great loss. And even if I could gain, I wouldn't want any good save that acquired through Him from whom all blessings come to us. May He be always praised, amen.

CHAPTER EIGHT

Discusses how God communicates Himself to the soul through an intellectual vision; gives some counsels. Tells about the effects such a vision causes if it is genuine. Recommends secrecy concerning these favors.

1. For you to see, Sisters, that what I have told you is true and that the further a soul advances the more it is accompanied by the good Jesus, we will do well to discuss how, when His Majesty desires, we cannot do otherwise than walk always with Him. This is evident in the ways and modes by which His Majesty communicates Himself to us and shows us the love He bears us. He does this through some very wonderful apparitions and visions. That you might not be frightened if He grants you some of these, I want briefly to mention something about these visions—if the Lord be pleased that I succeed—so

that we might praise Him very much even though He may not grant them to us. We would praise Him because being so filled with majesty and power He nonetheless desires to communicate thus with a creature.

2. It will happen while the soul is heedless of any thought about such a favor being granted to it, and though it never had a thought that it deserved this vision, that it will feel Jesus Christ, our Lord, beside it. Yet, it doesn't see Him, neither with the eyes of the body nor with those of the soul. This is called an intellectual vision; I don't know why. I saw the person[1] to whom God granted this favor, along with other favors I shall mention further on, quite worried in the beginning because, since she didn't see anything, she couldn't understand the nature of this vision. However, she knew so certainly that it was Jesus Christ, our Lord, who showed Himself to her in that way that she couldn't doubt; I mean she couldn't doubt the vision was there. As to whether it was from God or not, even though she carried with her great effects to show that it was, she nonetheless was afraid. She had never heard of an intellectual vision, nor had she thought there was such a kind. But she understood very clearly that it was this same Lord who often spoke to her in the way mentioned.[2] For until He granted her this favor I am referring to, she never knew who was speaking to her, although she understood the words.

3. I know that since she was afraid about this vision (for it isn't like the imaginative one that passes quickly, but lasts many days and sometimes even more than a year), she went very worried to her confessor. He asked her how, since she didn't see anything, she knew that it was our Lord—what kind of face He had.[3] She told him she didn't know, that she didn't see any face, and that she couldn't say any more than what she had said, that what she did know was that He was the one who spoke to her and that the vision had not been fancied. And although some persons put many fears in her, she was still frequently unable to doubt, especially when the Lord said to her: "Do not be afraid, it is I."[4] These words had so much power that from then on she could not doubt the vision, and she was left very much strengthened and happy over such good company. She saw clearly that the vision was a great help toward walking with a habitual remembrance of God and a

deep concern about avoiding anything displeasing to Him, for it seemed to her that He was always looking at her. And each time she wanted to speak with His Majesty in prayer, and even outside of it, she felt He was so near that He couldn't fail to hear her. But she didn't hear words spoken whenever she wanted; only unexpectedly when they were necessary. She felt He was walking at her right side, but she didn't experience this with those senses by which we can know that a person is beside us. This vision comes in another unexplainable, more delicate way. But it is so certain and leaves much certitude; even much more than the other visions do because in the visions that come through the senses one can be deceived, but not in the intellectual vision. For this latter brings great interior benefits and effects that couldn't be present if the experience were caused by melancholy; nor would the devil produce so much good; nor would the soul go about with such peace and continual desires to please God, and with so much contempt for everything that does not bring it to Him. Afterward she understood clearly that the vision was not caused by the devil, which became more and more clear as time went on.

4. Nonetheless, I know that at times she went about very much frightened; other times, with the most intense confusion, for she didn't know why so much good had come to her. We were so united, she and I, that nothing took place in her soul of which I was ignorant; so I can be a good witness, and believe me all I have said of this matter is the truth.

It is a favor from the Lord that she bears in herself the most intense confusion and humility. If the vision were from the devil, the effects would be contrary. And since the vision is something definitely understood to be a gift from God and human effort would not be sufficient to produce this experience, the one who receives it can in no way think it is his own good but a good given through the hand of God. And even though, in my opinion, some of those favors that were mentioned are greater, this favor bears with it a particular knowledge of God. This continual companionship gives rise to a most tender love for His Majesty, to some desires even greater than those mentioned[5] to surrender oneself totally to His service, and to a great purity of conscience because the presence at its side makes the soul pay attention to everything. For even though we already know that God is present in all we do, our nature is such that we neglect to think of this. Here the truth cannot be forgotten, for the Lord awakens the soul to His presence beside it. And even the favors that were mentioned[6] became much more common since the soul goes about almost continually with actual love for the One who it sees and understands is at its side.

5. In sum, with respect to the soul's gain, the vision is seen to be a most wonderful and highly valuable favor. The soul thanks the Lord that He gives the vision without any merits on its part and would not exchange that blessing for any earthly treasure or delight. Thus, when the Lord is pleased to take the vision away, the soul feels very much alone. But all the efforts it could possibly make are of little avail in bringing back that companionship. The Lord gives it when He desires, and it cannot be acquired. Sometimes also the vision is of some saint, and this too is most beneficial.

6. You will ask how if nothing is seen one knows that it is Christ, or a saint, or His most glorious Mother. This, the soul will not know how to explain, nor can it understand how it knows, but it does know with the greatest certitude. It seems easier for the soul to know when the Lord speaks; but what is more amazing is that it knows the saint, who doesn't speak but seemingly is placed there by the Lord as a help to it and as its companion. Thus there are other spiritual things that one doesn't know how to explain, but through them one knows how lowly our nature is when there is question of understanding the sublime grandeurs of God, for we are incapable even of understanding these spiritual things. But let the one to whom His Majesty gives these favors receive them with admiration and praise for Him. Thus He grants the soul particular graces through these favors. For since the favors are not granted to all, they should be highly esteemed; and one should strive to perform greater services since God in so many ways helps the soul to perform these services. Hence the soul doesn't consider itself to be any greater because of this, and it thinks that it is the one who serves God the least among all who are in the world. This soul thinks that it is more obligated to Him than anyone, and any fault it commits pierces to the core of its being, and very rightly so.

7. These effects from the vision that were mentioned[7] and that are left in the soul can be recognized by any one of you whom the Lord has brought by this road. Through them you can know that the vision is not an illusion or a fancy. As I have said,[8] I hold that it would be impossible for a vision caused by the devil to last so long and benefit the soul so remarkably, clothing it with so much interior peace. It is not customary for something so evil to do something so good, nor can the devil even though he may want to. If he could, there would at once be some outward show of self-esteem and thought of being better than others. But that the soul goes about always so attached to God and with its thoughts so occupied in Him causes the devil such rage that even though he might try he would not often return. And God is so faithful[9] that He will not allow the devil much leeway with a soul that doesn't aim for anything else than to please His Majesty and spend its life for His honor and glory; He will at once ordain how it may be undeceived.

8. My theme is and will be that since, as a result of these favors from God, the soul walks in the way here mentioned, His Majesty will make it be the one to gain. And if He sometimes permits the devil to tempt the soul, He will so ordain that the evil one will be defeated. As a result, daughters, if someone should walk along this road, as I have said, do not be astonished. It is good that there be fear and that we walk with more care. Nor should you be self-confident, for since you are so favored you could grow more careless. If you do not see in yourselves the effects that were mentioned,[10] it will be a sign that the favor is not from God. It is good that at the beginning you speak about this vision under the seal of confession with a very learned man, for learned men will give us light. Or, with some very spiritual person, if there be one available; if there isn't, it's better to speak with a very learned man. Or with both a spiritual person and a learned man if both are at hand. And should they tell you the vision is fancied, do not be concerned, for the fancy can do little good or evil. Commend yourself to the divine Majesty that He not let you be deceived. If they should tell you that your vision is from the devil, it will be a greater trial, although no one will say this if he is indeed

learned and the effects mentioned are present. But if he says so, I know that the Lord Himself who walks with you will console you, assure you, and give the confessor light that he may give it to you.

9. If the confessor is a person whom, although he practices prayer, the Lord has not led by this path, he will at once be frightened and condemn it. For this reason I advise you to have a confessor who is very learned and, if possible, also spiritual. The prioress should give permission for such consultation. Even though, judging by the good life you live, you may be walking securely, the prioress will be obligated to have you speak with a confessor so that both you and she may walk securely. And once you have spoken with these persons, be quiet and don't try to confer about the matter with others; at times the devil causes some fears so excessive that they force the soul, without its having anything really to fear, not to be satisfied with one consultation. If, especially, the confessor has little experience, and the soul sees that he is fearful, and he himself makes it continue to speak of the matter, that which by rights should have remained very secret is made public, and this soul is persecuted and tormented. For while it thinks the matter is secret, it finds out that the visions are publicly known. As a result many troublesome things happen to it and could happen to its religious order, the way these times are going.[11] Hence a great deal of discretion is necessary in this matter, and I highly recommend it to the prioresses.

10. A prioress should not think that since a Sister has experiences like these she is better than the others. The Lord leads each one as He sees is necessary. This path is a preparation for becoming a very good servant of God, provided that one cooperates. But sometimes God leads the weakest along this path. And so there is nothing in it to approve or condemn. One should consider the virtues and who it is who serves our Lord with greater mortification, humility, and purity of conscience; this is the one who will be the holiest. Yet, little can be known here below with certitude; we must wait until the true Judge gives to each one what is merited. In heaven we will be surprised to see how different His judgment is from what we can understand here below. May He be forever praised, amen.

TERESA OF AVILA

CHAPTER NINE

Treats of how the Lord communicates with the soul through an imaginative vision; gives careful warning against desiring to walk by this path and the reasons for such a warning. The chapter is very beneficial.

1. Now let us come to imaginative visions, for they say the devil meddles more in these than in the ones mentioned,[1] and it must be so. But when these imaginative visions are from our Lord, they in some way seem to me more beneficial because they are in greater conformity with our nature. I'm excluding from that comparison the visions the Lord shows in the last dwelling place; no other visions are comparable to those.

2. Well, now, let us consider what I have told you in the preceding chapter[2] about how this Lord is present. It is as though we had in a gold vessel a precious stone having the highest value and curative powers. We know very certainly that it is there although we have never seen it. But the powers of the stone do not cease to benefit us provided that we carry it with us.[3] Although we have never seen this stone, we do not on that account cease to prize it, because through experience we have seen that it has cured us of some illnesses for which it is suited. But we do not dare look at it or open the reliquary, nor can we, because the manner of opening this reliquary is known solely by the one to whom the jewel belongs. Even though he loaned us the jewel for our own benefit, he has kept the key to the reliquary and will open it, as something belonging to him, when he desires to show us the contents, and he will take the jewel back when he wants to, as he does.

3. Well, let us say now that sometimes he wants to open the reliquary suddenly in order to do good to the one to whom he has loaned it. Clearly, a person will afterward be much happier when he remembers the admirable splendor of the stone, and hence it will remain more deeply engrained in his memory. So it happens here: When our Lord is pleased to give more delight to this soul, He shows it clearly His most sacred humanity in the way He desires; either as He was when He went about in the world or as He is after His resurrection. And even though the vision happens so quickly that we could compare it to a streak of lightning, this most glorious image

156

remains so engraved on the imagination that I think it would be impossible to erase it until it is seen by the soul in that place where it will be enjoyed without end.

4. Although I say "image," let it be understood that, in the opinion of the one who sees it, it is not a painting but truly alive, and sometimes the Lord is speaking to the soul and even revealing great secrets. But you must understand that even though the soul is detained by this vision for some while, it can no more fix its gaze on the vision than it can on the sun. Hence this vision always passes very quickly, but not because its brilliance is painful, like the sun's, to the inner eye. It is the inner eye that sees all of this. I wouldn't know how to say anything about a vision that comes through the exterior sense of sight, because this person mentioned, of whom I can speak so particularly,[4] had not undergone such a vision, and one cannot be sure about what one has not experienced. The brilliance of this inner vision is like an infused light coming from a sun covered by something as sparkling as a properly cut diamond. The garment seems made of a fine Dutch linen. Almost every time God grants this favor the soul is in rapture, for in its lowliness it cannot suffer so frightening a sight.

5. I say "frightening" because although the Lord's presence is the most beautiful and delightful a person could imagine even were he to live and labor a thousand years thinking about it (for it far surpasses the limitations of our imagination or intellect), this presence bears such extraordinary majesty that it causes the soul extreme fright. Certainly it's not necessary here to ask how the soul knows, without having been told, who the Lord is, for it is clearly revealed that He is the Lord of heaven and earth. This is not true of earthly kings, for in themselves they would be held in little account were it not for their retinue, or unless they tell who they are.

6. O Lord, how we Christians fail to know you! What will that day be when You come to judge, for even when You come here with so much friendliness to speak with your bride she experiences such fear when she looks at You? O daughters, what will it be like when He says in so severe a voice, *depart you who are cursed by My Father?*[5]

7. As a result of this favor granted by God, let us keep in mind the above thought, for it will be no small blessing. Even

Saint Jerome, though he was a saint, kept it in mind. And thus all that we suffer here in the strict observance of the religious life will seem to us nothing; for, however long it lasts, it lasts but a moment in comparison with eternity. I tell you truthfully that as wretched as I am I have never had fear of the torments of hell, for they would be nothing if compared to what I recall the condemned will experience on seeing the anger in these eyes of the Lord, so beautiful, meek, and kind. It doesn't seem my heart could suffer such a sight. I've felt this way all my life. How much more will the person fear this sight to whom the Lord has thus represented Himself since the experience is so powerful that it carries that person out of his senses. The reason the soul is suspended must be that the Lord helps its weakness, which is joined to His greatness in this sublime communication.

8. When the soul can remain a long while gazing on this Lord, I don't believe it will be experiencing a vision but some intense reflection in which some likeness is fashioned in the imagination; compared with a vision this likeness is similar to something dead.

9. It happens to some persons (and I know this is true, for they have spoken with me—and not just three or four but many) that their imagination is so weak, or their intellect so effective, or I don't know what the cause is, that they become absorbed in their imagination to the extent that everything they think about seems to be clearly seen. Yet, if they were to see a real vision, they would know without any doubt whatsoever their mistake, for they themselves are composing what they see with their imagination. This imagining doesn't have any effect afterward, but they are left cold—much more than if they were to see a devotional image. It's wise not to pay any attention to this kind of imagining and thus what was seen is forgotten much more than a dream.

10. In the vision we are dealing with the above is not so; rather, while the soul is very far from thinking that anything will be seen, or having the thought even pass through its mind, suddenly the vision is represented to it all at once and stirs all the faculties and senses with a great fear and tumult so as to place them afterward in that happy peace. Just as there was a tempest and tumult that came from heaven when Saint Paul

was hurled to the ground,[6] here in this interior world there is a great stirring; and in a moment, as I have said,[7] all remains calm, and this soul is left so well instructed about so many great truths that it has no need of any other master. For without any effort on the soul's part, true Wisdom has taken away the mind's dullness and leaves a certitude, which lasts for some time, that this favor is from God. However much the soul is told the contrary, others cannot then cause it fear that there could be any deception. Afterward, if the confessor puts fear in it, God allows it to waver and think that because of its sins it could possibly be deceived. But it does not believe this; rather, as I have said concerning those other things,[8] the devil can stir up doubts, as he does with temptations against matters of faith, that do not allow the soul to be firm in its certitude. But the more the devil fights against that certitude, the more certain the soul is that the devil could not have left it with so many blessings, as they really are, for he cannot do so much in the interior of the soul. The devil can present a vision, but not with this truth and majesty and these results.

11. Since the confessors cannot witness this vision—nor, perhaps, can it be explained by the one to whom God grants this favor—they fear and rightly so. Thus it's necessary to proceed with caution, wait for the time when these apparitions will bear fruit, and move along little by little looking for the humility they leave in the soul and the fortitude in virtue. If the vision is from the devil, he will soon show a sign, and will be caught in a thousand lies. If the confessor has experience and has undergone these experiences, he needs little time for discernment; immediately in the account given he will see whether the vision is from God or the imagination or the devil, especially if His Majesty has given him the gift of discernment of spirits. If he has this latter as well as learning, even though he may have no experience, he will recognize the true vision very well.

12. What is necessary, Sisters, is that you proceed very openly and truthfully with your confessor. I don't mean in regard to telling your sins, for that is obvious, but in giving an account of your prayer. If you do not give such an account, I am not sure you are proceeding well, nor that it is God who is teaching you. He is very fond of our speaking as truthfully and

clearly to the one who stands in His place as we would to Him and of our desiring that the confessor understand all our thoughts and even more our deeds, however small they be. If you do this you don't have to go about disturbed or worried. Even if the vision is not from God, it will do you no harm if you have humility and a good conscience. His Majesty knows how to draw good from evil, and the road along which the devil wanted to make you go astray will be to your greater gain. Thinking that God grants you such wonderful favors, you will force yourselves to please Him more and be always remembering His image. As a very learned man said,[9] the devil is a great painter and if the devil were to show him a living image of the Lord, he wouldn't be grieved but allow the image to awaken his devotion, and that he would thereby wage war on the devil with the evil one's own wickedness. Even though a painter may be a very poor one, a person shouldn't on that account fail to reverence the image he makes if it is a painting of our every Good.

13. That learned man was strongly opposed to the advice some gave about making the fig[10] when seeing a vision, for he used to say that wherever we see a painting of our King we must reverence it. And I see that he is right, because even here below a similar action would be regretted: If a person knew that before a portrait of himself another whom he loved manifested such contempt, he would be unhappy about the act. Well how much greater reason there is always to have respect for any crucifix or portrait we see of our Emperor? Although I have written of this elsewhere,[11] I am glad to write of it here, for I saw that a person went about in distress when ordered to use this remedy.[12] I don't know who invented a thing that could so torment a person who wasn't able to do anything else than obey, if the confessor gave her this counsel, because she thought she would go astray if she didn't obey. My counsel is that even though a confessor gives you such advice, you should humbly tell him this reason and not accept his counsel. The good reasons given me by that learned man I found very acceptable.

14. A wonderful benefit the soul draws from this favor of the Lord is that when it thinks of Him or of His life and

Passion it remembers His most meek and beautiful countenance. This remembrance is the greatest consolation, just as
here below it would be far more consoling to see a person who
has done a great deal of good for us than someone we had never
met. I tell you that so delightful a remembrance brings much
consolation and benefit.

Many are the other blessings these visions bring, but since
so much has been said about such effects, and more will be said,
I don't want to tire myself, or tire you, but advise you strongly
that when you learn or hear that God grants these favors to
souls you never beseech Him or desire Him to lead you by this
path.

15. Although this path may seem to you very good, one to
be highly esteemed and reverenced, desiring it is inappropriate
for certain reasons: First, the desire to be given what you have
never deserved shows a lack of humility, and so I believe that
whoever desires this path will not have much humility. Just as
the thoughts of a lowly workman are far from any desire to be
king since such a thing seems impossible to him, and he thinks
he doesn't deserve it, so too with the humble person in similar
matters. I believe that these favors will never be given to those
who desire them, because before granting them God gives a
deep self-knowledge. For how will he who has such desires
understand in truth that he is being granted a very great favor
at not being in hell? Second, such a person will very certainly
be deceived or in great danger because the devil needs nothing
more than to see a little door open before playing a thousand
tricks on us. Third, the imagination itself, when there is a great
desire, makes a person think that he sees what he desires and
hears it, as with those who desiring something during the day
and thinking a great deal about it happen to dream of it at
night. Fourth, it would be extremely bold to want to choose a
path while not knowing what suits me more. Such a matter
should be left to the Lord who knows me—for He leads me
along the path that is fitting—so that in all things I might do
His will. Fifth, do you think the trials suffered by those to
whom the Lord grants these favors are few? No, they are
extraordinary and of many kinds. How do you know you
would be able to bear them? Sixth, by the very way you think

you will gain, you will lose, as Saul did by being king.[13]

16. In sum, Sisters, besides these reasons there are others; believe me, the safest way is to want only what God wants. He knows more than we ourselves do, and He loves us. Let us place ourselves in His hands so that His will may be done in us, and we cannot err if with a determined will we always maintain this attitude. And you must note that greater glory is not merited by receiving a large number of these favors; rather, on the contrary the recipients of these favors are obliged to serve more since they have received more. The Lord doesn't take away from us that which, because it lies within our power, is more meritorious. So there are many holy persons who have never received one of these favors; and others who receive them but are not holy. And do not think the favors are given continually; rather, for each time the Lord grants them there are many trials. Thus, the soul doesn't think about receiving more but about how to serve for what it has received.

17. It is true that this vision must be a powerful help toward possessing the virtues with higher perfection, but the person who has gained them at the cost of his own labors will merit much more. I know a person or two persons—one was a man—to whom the Lord had granted some of these favors, who were so desirous of serving His Majesty at their own cost, without these great delights, and so anxious to suffer that they complained to our Lord because He bestowed the favors on them, and if they could decline receiving these gifts they would do so.[14] I am speaking not of the delights coming from these visions—for in the end these persons see that the visions are very beneficial and to be highly esteemed—but of those the Lord gives in contemplation.

18. It is true that these desires also, in my opinion, are supernatural and characteristic of souls very much inflamed in love. Such souls would want the Lord to see that they do not serve Him for pay. Thus, as I have said,[15] they never, as a motive for making the effort to serve more, think about receiving glory for anything they do. But their desire is to satisfy love, and it is love's nature to serve with deeds in a thousand ways. If it could, love would want to discover ways of consuming the soul within itself. And if it were necessary to be always

annihilated for the greater honor of God, love would do so very eagerly. May He be praised forever, amen. For in lowering Himself to commune with such miserable creatures, He wants to show His greatness.

CHAPTER TEN

Tells about other favors God grants the soul, in a way different from those just mentioned, and of the great profit that comes from them.

1. In many ways does the Lord communicate Himself to the soul with these apparitions. He grants some of them when it is afflicted; others, when a great trial is about to come; others, so that His Majesty might take His delight in the soul and give delight to it. There's no reason to go into further detail about each, since my intention is only to explain the different favors there are on this road, insofar as I understand them. Thus you will know, Sisters, their nature and their effects, lest we fancy that everything imagined is a vision. When what you see is an authentic vision, you won't go about disturbed or afflicted if you understand that such a thing is possible. The devil gains much and is extremely pleased to see a soul afflicted and disquieted, for he knows that disturbance impedes it from being totally occupied in loving and praising God.

His Majesty communicates Himself in other ways that are more sublime and less dangerous because the devil, I believe, will be unable to counterfeit them. Thus, since these latter are something very secret, it is difficult to explain them, whereas the imaginative visions are easier to explain.

2. It will happen, when the Lord is pleased, that while the soul is in prayer and very much in its senses a suspension will suddenly be experienced in which the Lord will reveal deep secrets. It seems the soul sees these secrets in God Himself, for they are not visions of the most sacred humanity. Although I say the soul sees, it doesn't see anything, for the favor is not an imaginative vision but very much an intellectual one. In this vision it is revealed how all things are seen in God and how He has them all in Himself.[1] This favor is most beneficial. Even though it passes in a moment, it remains deeply engraved in

the soul and causes the greatest confusion. The evil of offending God is seen more clearly, because while being in God Himself (I mean being within Him) we commit great evils. I want to draw a comparison—if I succeed—so as to explain this to you. For although what I said is true, and we hear it often, either we do not pay attention to this truth or we do not want to understand it. If the matter were understood, it doesn't seem it would be possible to be so bold.

3. Let's suppose that God is like an immense and beautiful dwelling or palace and that this palace, as I say, is God Himself.[2] Could the sinner, perhaps, so as to engage in his evil deeds leave this palace? No, certainly not; rather, within the palace itself, that is within God Himself, the abominations, indecent actions, and evil deeds committed by us sinners take place. O frightful thought, worthy of deep reflection, and very beneficial for those of us who know little. We don't completely understand these truths, for otherwise it wouldn't be possible to be so foolishly audacious! Let us consider, Sisters, the great mercy and compassion of God in not immediately destroying us there, and be extremely thankful to Him, and let us be ashamed to feel resentment about anything that is said or done against us. The greatest evil of the world is that God, our Creator, suffers so many evil things from His creatures within His very self and that we sometimes resent a word said in our absence and perhaps with no evil intention.

4. O human misery! When, daughters, will we imitate this great God? Oh, let us not think we are doing anything by suffering injuries, but we should very eagerly endure everything, and let us love the one who offends us since this great God has not ceased to love us even though we have offended Him very much. Thus the Lord is right in wanting all to pardon the wrongs done to them.[3]

I tell you, daughters, that even though this vision passes quickly it is a great favor from our Lord if one desires to benefit from it by keeping it habitually present.

5. It also happens very quickly and ineffably that God will show within Himself a truth that seems to leave in obscurity all those there are in creatures, and one understands very clearly that God alone is Truth, unable to lie.[4] What David says in a psalm about every man's being a liar is clearly understood.[5]

However frequently the verse may be heard, it is never understood as it is in this vision. God is everlasting Truth. I am reminded of Pilate, how he was often questioning our Lord when during the Passion he asked Him, "What is truth?"[6] and of the little we understand here below about this supreme Truth.

6. I would like to be able to explain more about this, but it is unexplainable. Let us conclude, Sisters, that in order to live in conformity with our God and Spouse in something, it will be well if we always study diligently how to walk in this truth. I'm not merely saying that we should not tell lies, for in that regard, glory to God, I already notice that you take great care in these houses not to tell a lie for anything. I'm saying that we should walk in truth before God and people in as many ways as possible. Especially, there should be no desire that others consider us better than we are. And in our works we should attribute to God what is His and to ourselves what is ours and strive to draw out the truth in everything. Thus, we shall have little esteem for this world, which is a complete lie and falsehood, and as such will not endure.

7. Once I was pondering why our Lord was so fond of this virtue of humility, and this thought came to me—in my opinion not as a result of reflection but suddenly: It is because God is supreme Truth; and to be humble is to walk in truth, for it is a very deep truth that of ourselves we have nothing good but only misery and nothingness. Whoever does not understand this walks in falsehood. The more anyone understands it the more he pleases the supreme Truth because he is walking in truth. Please God, Sisters, we will be granted the favor never to leave this path of self-knowledge, amen.

8. Our Lord grants these favors to the soul because, as to one to whom He is truly betrothed, one who is already determined to do His will in everything, He desires to give it some knowledge of how to do His will and of His grandeurs. There's no reason to deal with more than these two things I mentioned[7] since they seem to me very beneficial. In similar things there is nothing to fear; rather, the Lord should be praised because He gives them. The devil, in my opinion, and even one's own imagination have little capacity at this level, and so the soul is left with profound satisfaction.

Chapter Eleven

Treats of some desires God gives the soul that are so powerful and vehement they place it in danger of death. Treats also of the benefits caused by this favor the Lord grants.

1. Do you think that all these favors the Spouse has bestowed on the soul will be sufficient to satisfy the little dove or butterfly—don't think I have forgotten it—so that it may come to rest in the place where it will die? No, certainly not; rather this little butterfly is much worse. Even though it may have been receiving these favors for many years, it always moans and goes about sorrowful because they leave it with greater pain. The reason is that since it is getting to know ever more the grandeurs of its God and sees itself so distant and far from enjoying Him, the desire for the Lord increases much more; also, love increases in the measure the soul discovers how much this great God and Lord deserves to be loved. And this desire continues, gradually growing in these years so that it reaches a point of suffering as great as that I shall now speak of. I have said "years" so as to be in line with the experience of that person I've mentioned here,[1] for I well understand that one must not put limits on God; in a moment He can bring a soul to the lofty experience mentioned here. His Majesty has the power to do whatever He wants and is eager to do many things for us.

2. Well, here is what happens sometimes to a soul that experiences these anxious longings, tears, sighs, and great impulses that were mentioned[2] (for all of these seem to proceed from our love with deep feelings, but they are all nothing in comparison with this other experience that I'm going to explain, for they resemble a smoking fire that though painful can be endured). While this soul is going about in this manner, burning up within itself, a blow is felt from elsewhere (the soul doesn't understand from where or how). The blow comes often through a sudden thought or word about death's delay. Or the soul will feel pierced by a fiery arrow.[3] I don't say that there is an arrow, but whatever the experience, the soul realizes clearly that the feeling couldn't come about naturally. Neither is the experience that of a blow, although I said "blow"; but it causes a sharp wound. And, in my opinion, it isn't felt where earthly

sufferings are felt, but in the very deep and intimate part of the soul, where this sudden flash of lightning reduces to dust everything it finds in this earthly nature of ours; for while this experience lasts nothing can be remembered about our being. In an instant the experience so binds the faculties that they have no freedom for anything except those things that will make this pain increase.

3. I wouldn't want what I say to appear to be an exaggeration. Indeed, I see that my words fall short because the experience is unexplainable. It is an enrapturing of the faculties and senses away from everything that is not a help, as I said, to feeling this affliction. For the intellect is very alive to understanding the reason why the soul feels far from God; and His Majesty helps at that time with a vivid knowledge of Himself in such a way that the pain increases to a point that makes the one who experiences it begin to cry aloud. Though she is a person who has suffered and is used to suffering severe pains, she cannot then do otherwise. This feeling is not in the body, as was said,[4] but in the interior part of the soul. As a result, this person understood how much more severe the feelings of the soul are than those of the body, and she reflected that such must be the nature of the sufferings of souls in purgatory, for the fact that these souls have no body doesn't keep them from suffering much more than they do through all the bodily sufferings they endure here on earth.

4. I saw a person in this condition; truly she thought she was dying, and this was not so surprising because certainly there is great danger of death.[5] And thus, even though the experience lasts a short while, it leaves the body very disjointed, and during that time the heart beat is as slow as it would be if a person were about to render his soul to God. This is no exaggeration, for the natural heat fails, and the fire so burns the soul that with a little more intensity God would have fulfilled the soul's desires. This is true not because a person feels little or much pain in the body, although it is disjointed, as I said, in such a way that for three or four days afterward one feels great sufferings and doesn't even have the strength to write. And it even seems to me always that the body is left weaker. The reason one doesn't feel the pain must be that the interior feeling of the soul is so much greater that one doesn't

pay any attention to the body. When one experiences a very sharp bodily pain, other bodily pains are hardly felt even though there may be many. I have indeed experienced this. With the presence of this spiritual pain, I don't believe that physical pain would be felt, little or much, even if the body were cut in pieces.

5. You will tell me that this feeling is an imperfection and ask why the soul doesn't conform to the will of God since it is so surrendered to Him. Until now it could do this, and has spent its life doing so. As for now, the reasoning faculty is in such a condition that the soul is not the master of it, nor can the soul think of anything else than of why it is grieving, of how it is absent from its Good, and of why it should want to live. It feels a strange solitude because no creature in all the earth provides it company, nor do I believe would any heavenly creature, not being the One whom it loves; rather, everything torments it. But the soul sees that it is like a person hanging, who cannot support himself on any earthly thing; nor can it ascend to heaven. On fire with this thirst, it cannot get to the water; and the thirst is not one that is endurable but already at such a point that nothing will take it away. Nor does the soul desire that the thirst be taken away save by that water of which our Lord spoke to the Samaritan woman.[6] Yet no one gives such water to the soul.

6. O God, help me! Lord, how You afflict your lovers! But everything is small in comparison with what You give them afterward. It's natural that what is worth much costs much. Moreover, if the suffering is to purify this soul so that it might enter the seventh dwelling place—just as those who will enter heaven must be cleansed in purgatory—it is as small as a drop of water in the sea. Furthermore, in spite of all this torment and affliction, which cannot be surpassed, I believe, by any earthly afflictions (for this person had suffered many bodily as well as spiritual pains, but they all seemed nothing in comparison with this suffering), the soul feels that the pain is precious; so precious—it understands very well—that one could not deserve it. However, this awareness is not of a kind that alleviates the suffering in any way. But with this knowledge, the soul suffers the pain very willingly and would suffer it all its life, if God were to be thereby served; although the soul would

not then die once but be always dying, for truly the suffering is no less than death.

7. Well, let us consider, Sisters, those who are in hell, who do not have this conformity or this consolation and spiritual delight that is placed by God in the soul; nor do they see that their suffering is beneficial, but they always suffer more and more. The torments of the soul are so much more severe than those of the body, and the torment souls in hell suffer is incomparably greater than the suffering we have here mentioned, and must, it is seen, last forever and ever. What, then, will the suffering of these unfortunate souls be? And what can we do or suffer in so short a life that would amount to anything if we were thereby to free ourselves of those terrible and eternal torments? I tell you it would be impossible to explain how keenly felt is the suffering of the soul, and how different it is from that of the body, if one had not experienced these things. And the Lord Himself desires that we understand this so that we may know the extraordinary debt we owe Him for bringing us to a state in which through His mercy we hope He will free us and pardon our sins.

8. Well, to return to what we were dealing with[7]—for we left this soul with much pain—this pain lasts only a short while in such intensity. At the most it will last three or four hours, in my opinion, because if it were to last a long while natural weakness would not be able to endure it unless by a miracle. It has happened that the experience lasted no more than a quarter of an hour but left the soul in pieces. Truly, that time the person lost her senses completely, and the pain came in its rigor merely from her hearing a word about life's not ending. This happened while she was engaged in conversation during Easter week, the last day of the octave, after she had spent all of Easter in so much dryness she almost didn't know it was Easter. In no way can the soul resist. It can no more do so than it can, if thrown in a fire, stop flames from having heat and burning it. This feeling is not one that can be concealed from others, but those who are present are aware of the great danger in which the person lies, although they cannot be witnesses to what is taking place interiorly. True, they provide some company, as though they were shadows; and so, like shadows, do all earthly things appear to that person.

9. And that you realize, in case you might sometime have this experience, what is due to our weakness, it happens at times that while in that state, as you have seen, the soul dies with the desire to die. For the fire afflicts so much that seemingly hardly anything keeps the soul from leaving the body. The soul truly fears and lest it end up dying would want the pain to abate. The soul indeed understands that this fear is from natural weakness, because on the other hand its desire to die is not taken away. Nor can a remedy be found to remove this pain until the Lord Himself takes it away, usually by means of a great rapture, or with some vision, where the true Comforter consoles and strengthens the soul that it might desire to live as long as God wills.

10. This experience is a painful one, but the soul is left with the most beneficial effects, and fear of the trials that can come its way is lost. When compared to the painful feeling experienced in the soul, the trials don't seem to amount to anything. The benefits are such that one would be pleased to suffer the pain often. But one can in no way do this, nor is there any means for suffering the experience again. The soul must wait until the Lord desires to give this favor, just as there is no way to resist it or remove it when it comes. The soul is left with greater contempt for the world than before because it sees that nothing in the world was any help to it in that torment, and it is much more detached from creatures because it now sees that only the Creator can console and satisfy it. And it has greater fear of offending Him, taking more care not to do so, because it sees that He can also torment as well as console.

11. Two experiences, it seems to me, that lie on this spiritual path put a person in danger of death: The one is this pain, for it truly is a danger, and no small one; the other is overwhelming joy and delight, which reaches so extraordinary a peak that indeed the soul, I think, swoons to the point that it is hardly kept from leaving the body—indeed, its happiness could not be considered small.

Here you will see, Sisters, whether I was right in saying that courage is necessary,[8] and whether when you ask the Lord for these favors He is right in answering as He did the sons of Zebedee, *are you able to drink the chalice?*[9]

12. I believe all of us, Sisters, will answer yes; and very rightly so, for His Majesty gives strength to the one He sees has need of it. He defends these souls in all things; when they are persecuted and criticized He answers for them as He did for the Magdalene[10]—if not through words, through deeds. And in the very end, before they die, He will pay for everything at once, as you will now see. May He be blessed forever, and may all creatures praise Him, amen.

THE SEVENTH DWELLING PLACES

CONTAINS FOUR CHAPTERS

CHAPTER ONE

Treats of the great favors God grants souls that have entered the seventh dwelling places. Tells how in her opinion there is a certain difference between the soul and the spirit, although the soul is all one. The chapter contains noteworthy doctrine.

1. You will think, Sisters, that since so much has been said about this spiritual path it will be impossible for anything more to be said. Such a thought would be very foolish. Since the greatness of God is without limits, His works are too. Who will finish telling of His mercies and grandeurs? To do so is impossible, and thus do not be surprised at what was said, and will be said, because it is but a naught in comparison to what there is to tell of God. He grants us a great favor in having communicated these things to a person through whom we can know about them. Thus the more we know about His communication to creatures the more we will praise His grandeur and make the effort to have esteem for souls in which the Lord delights so much. Each one of us has a soul, but since we do not prize souls as is deserved by creatures made in the image of God we do not understand the deep secrets that lie in them.

May it please His Majesty, if He may thereby be served, to move my pen and give me understanding of how I might say something about the many things to be said that God reveals to the one whom He places in this dwelling place. I have earnestly begged this of His Majesty since He knows that my intention is to make known His mercies that His name may be more praised and glorified.

2. I hope, not for myself but for you, Sisters, that He may grant me this favor. Thus you will understand how important it is for you not to impede your Spouse's celebration of this spiritual marriage with your souls, since this marriage brings so many blessings, as you will see. O great God! It seems that a creature as miserable as I should tremble to deal with a thing so foreign to what I deserve to understand. And, indeed, I have been covered with confusion wondering if it might not be better to conclude my discussion of this dwelling place with just a few words. For it seems to me that others will think I know about it through experience. This makes me extremely ashamed; for, knowing what I am, such a thought is a terrible thing. On the other hand, the thought of neglecting to explain this dwelling place seemed to me to be a temptation and weakness on my part, no matter how many of the above judgments you make about me. May God be praised and understood a little more, and let all the world cry out against me; how much more so in that I will perhaps be dead when what I write is seen. May He be blessed who lives, and will live, forever, amen.

3. When our Lord is pleased to have pity on this soul that He has already taken spiritually as His Spouse because of what it suffers and has suffered through its desires, He brings it, before the spiritual marriage is consummated, into His dwelling place, which is this seventh. For just as in heaven so in the soul His Majesty must have a room where He dwells alone. Let us call it another heaven. It's very important for us, Sisters, not to think the soul is something dark. Since we do not see the soul, it usually seems that there is no such thing as interior light but only the exterior light that we all see, and that a certain darkness is in our soul. As for the soul that is not in grace, I confess this is so, but not through any fault of the Sun of Justice who dwells within it giving it being but because such a soul is incapable of receiving the light, as I believe I have said in the first dwelling place, according to what a certain person understood.[1] For these unfortunate souls are as though in a dark prison, bound hands and feet, in regard to doing anything

good that would enable them to merit, and blind and deaf. We can rightly take pity on them and reflect that at one time we were ourselves in this condition and that the Lord can also have mercy on them.

4. Let us take special care, Sisters, to beg this mercy of Him and not be careless, for it is a most generous alms to pray for those who are in mortal sin. Suppose we were to see a Christian with his hands fastened behind his back by a strong chain, bound to a post, and dying of hunger, not because of lack of food, for there are very choice dishes beside him, but because he cannot take hold of the food and eat, and even has great loathing for it; and suppose he sees that he is about to breathe his last and die, not just an earthly death but an eternal one. Wouldn't it be a terrible cruelty to stand looking at him and not feed him? Well, then, what if through your prayer the chains could be loosed? The answer is obvious. For the love of God I ask you always to remember in your prayers souls in mortal sin.

5. We are not speaking about them now but about those who already by the mercy of God have done penance for their sins and are in the state of grace. Thus we are not reflecting about something restricted to a corner but about an interior world where there is room for so many and such attractive dwelling places, as you have seen; and indeed it is right that the soul be like this since within it there is a dwelling place for God.

Now then, when His Majesty is pleased to grant the soul this divine marriage that was mentioned,[2] He first brings it into His own dwelling place. He desires that the favor be different from what it was at other times when He gave the soul raptures. I really believe that in rapture He unites it with Himself, as well as in the prayer of union that was mentioned.[3] But it doesn't seem to the soul that it is called to enter into its center, as it is here in this dwelling place, but called to the superior part. These things matter little; whether the experience comes in one way or another, the Lord joins the soul to Himself. But He does so by making it blind and deaf, as was Saint Paul in his conversion,[4] and by taking away perception of the nature and kind of favor enjoyed, for the great delight the soul then feels is to see itself near God. Yet when He joins it to Himself, it doesn't understand anything; for all the faculties are lost.

6. In this seventh dwelling place the union comes about in a different way: Our good God now desires to remove the scales from the soul's eyes and let it see and understand, although in a strange way, something of the favor He grants it. When the soul is brought into that dwelling place, the Most Blessed Trinity, all three Persons, through an intellectual vision, is revealed to it through a certain representation of the truth. First there comes an enkindling in the spirit in the manner of a cloud of magnificent splendor; and these Persons are distinct, and through an admirable knowledge the soul understands as a most profound truth that all three Persons are one substance and one power and one knowledge and one God alone. It knows in such a way that what we hold by faith, it understands, we can say, through sight—although the sight is not with the bodily eyes nor with the eyes of the soul, because we are not dealing with an imaginative vision. Here all three Persons communicate themselves to it, speak to it, and explain those words of the Lord in the Gospel: that He and the Father and the Holy Spirit will come to dwell with the soul that loves Him and keeps His commandments.[5]

7. O God help me! How different is hearing and believing these words from understanding their truth in this way! Each day this soul becomes more amazed, for these Persons never seem to leave it any more, but it clearly beholds, in the way that was mentioned,[6] that they are within it. In the extreme interior, in some place very deep within itself, the nature of which it doesn't know how to explain, because of a lack of learning, it perceives this divine company.

8. You may think that as a result the soul will be outside itself and so absorbed that it will be unable to be occupied with anything else. On the contrary, the soul is much more occupied than before with everything pertaining to the service of God, and once its duties are over it remains with that enjoyable company. If the soul does not fail God, He will never fail, in my opinion, to make His presence clearly known to it. It has strong confidence that since God has granted this favor He will

not allow it to lose the favor. Though the soul thinks this, it goes about with greater care than ever not to displease Him in anything.

9. It should be understood that this presence is not felt so fully, I mean so clearly, as when revealed the first time or at other times when God grants the soul this gift. For if the presence were felt so clearly, the soul would find it impossible to be engaged in anything else or even to live among people. But even though the presence is not perceived with this very clear light, the soul finds itself in this company every time it takes notice. Let's say that the experience resembles that of a person who after being in a bright room with others finds himself, once the shutters are closed, in darkness. The light by which he could see them is taken away. Until it returns he doesn't see them, but not for that reason does he stop knowing they are present. It might be asked whether the soul can see them when it so desires and the light returns. To see them does not lie in its power, but depends on when our Lord desires that the window of the intellect be opened. Great is the mercy He shows in never departing from the soul and in desiring that it perceive Him so manifestly.

10. It seems that the divine Majesty desires, through this wonderful company, to prepare the soul for more. Clearly, the soul will be truly helped in every way to advance in perfection and to lose the fear it sometimes had of the other favors He granted it, as was said.[7] Such was the experience of this person,[8] for in everything she found herself improved, and it seemed to her, despite the trials she underwent and the business affairs she had to attend to, that the essential part of her soul never moved from that room. As a result, it seemed to her that there was, in a certain way, a division in her soul. And while suffering some great trials a little after God granted her this favor, she complained of that part of the soul, as Martha complained of Mary,[9] and sometimes pointed out that it was there always enjoying that quietude at its own pleasure while leaving her in the midst of so many trials and occupations that she could not keep it company.

11. This will seem to you, daughters, to be foolishness, but it truly happens in this way. Although we know that the soul is all one, what I say is no mere fancy; the experience is very

common. Wherefore I said[10] that interior things are seen in such a way that one understands with certitude that there is some kind of difference, a difference clearly recognized, between the soul and the spirit, even though they are both one. So delicate a division is perceived that sometimes it seems the one functions differently from the other, and so does the savor the Lord desires to give them seem different. It also seems to me that the soul and the faculties are not one but different. There are so many and such delicate things in the interior that it would be boldness on my part to set out to explain them. In heaven we will see all this, if the Lord in His mercy grants us the favor of bringing us there where we shall understand these secrets.

CHAPTER TWO

Continues on the same subject. Explains the difference between spiritual union and spiritual marriage. Describes this difference through some delicate comparisons.

1. Now then let us deal with the divine and spiritual marriage, although this great favor does not come to its perfect fullness as long as we live; for if we were to withdraw from God, this remarkable blessing would be lost.

The first time the favor is granted, His Majesty desires to show Himself to the soul through an imaginative vision of His most sacred humanity so that the soul will understand and not be ignorant of receiving this sovereign gift; with other persons the favor will be received in another form. With regard to the one of whom we are speaking, the Lord represented Himself to her, just after she had received Communion, in the form of shining splendor, beauty, and majesty, as He was after His resurrection, and told her that now it was time that she consider as her own what belonged to Him and that He would take care of what was hers, and He spoke other words destined more to be heard than to be mentioned.[1]

2. It may seem that this experience was nothing new since at other times the Lord had represented Himself to the soul in such a way. The experience was so different that it left her indeed stupefied and frightened: first, because this vision came with great force; second, because of the words the Lord spoke

to her and also because in the interior of her soul, where He represented Himself to her, she had not seen other visions except the former one.[2] You must understand that there is the greatest difference between all the previous visions and those of this dwelling place. Between the spiritual betrothal and the spiritual marriage the difference is as great as that which exists between two who are betrothed and between two who can no longer be separated.[3]

3. I have already said[4] that even though these comparisons are used, because there are no others better suited to our purpose, it should be understood that in this state there is no more thought of the body than if the soul were not in it, but one's thought is only of the spirit. In the spiritual marriage, there is still much less remembrance of the body because this secret union takes place in the very interior center of the soul, which must be where God Himself is, and in my opinion there is no need of any door for Him to enter. I say there is no need of any door because everything that has been said up until now seems to take place by means of the senses and faculties, and this appearance of the humanity of the Lord must also.[5] But that which comes to pass in the union of the spiritual marriage is very different. The Lord appears in this center of the soul, not in an imaginative vision but in an intellectual one, although more delicate than those mentioned,[6] as He appeared to the apostles without entering through the door when He said to them *pax vobis*.[7] What God communicates here to the soul in an instant is a secret so great and a favor so sublime—and the delight the soul experiences so extreme—that I don't know what to compare it to. I can say only that the Lord wishes to reveal for that moment, in a more sublime manner than through any spiritual vision or taste, the glory of heaven. One can say no more—insofar as can be understood—than that the soul, I mean the spirit, is made one with God. For since His Majesty is also spirit, He has wished to show His love for us by giving some persons understanding of the point to which this love reaches so that we might praise His grandeur. For He has desired to be so joined with the creature that, just as those who are married cannot be separated,[8] He doesn't want to be separated from the soul.

4. The spiritual betrothal is different, for the two often separate. And the union is also different because, even though it is the joining of two things into one, in the end the two can be separated and each remains by itself. We observe this ordinarily, for the favor of union with the Lord passes quickly, and afterward the soul remains without that company; I mean, without awareness of it. In this other favor from the Lord, no. The soul always remains with its God in that center. Let us say that the union is like the joining of two wax candles to such an extent that the flame coming from them is but one, or that the wick, the flame, and the wax are all one. But afterward one candle can be easily separated from the other and there are two candles; the same holds for the wick. In the spiritual marriage the union is like what we have when rain falls from the sky into a river or fount; all is water, for the rain that fell from heaven cannot be divided or separated from the water of the river. Or it is like what we have when a little stream enters the sea, there is no means of separating the two. Or, like the bright light entering a room through two different windows; although the streams of light are separate when entering the room, they become one.

5. Perhaps this is what Saint Paul means in saying *He that is joined or united to the Lord becomes one spirit with him,*[9] and is referring to this sovereign marriage, presupposing that His Majesty has brought the soul to it through union. And he also says: *For me to live is Christ, and to die is gain.*[10] The soul as well, I think, can say these words now because this state is the place where the little butterfly we mentioned[11] dies, and with the greatest joy because its life is now Christ.

6. And that its life is Christ is understood better, with the passing of time, by the effects this life has. Through some secret aspirations the soul understands clearly that it is God who gives life to our soul. These aspirations come very, very often in such a living way that they can in no way be doubted. The soul feels them very clearly even though they are indescribable. But the feeling is so powerful that sometimes the soul cannot avoid the loving expressions they cause, such as: O Life of my life! Sustenance that sustains me! and things of this sort. For from those divine breasts where it seems God is

always sustaining the soul there flow streams of milk bringing comfort to all the people of the castle. It seems the Lord desires that in some manner these others in the castle may enjoy the great deal the soul is enjoying and that from that full-flowing river, where this tiny fount is swallowed up, a spurt of that water will sometimes be directed toward the sustenance of those who in corporeal things must serve these two who are wed. Just as a distracted person would feel this water if he were suddenly bathed in it, and would be unable to avoid feeling it, so are these operations recognized, and even with greater certitude. For just as a great gush of water could not reach us if it didn't have a source, as I have said, so it is understood clearly that there is Someone in the interior depths who shoots these arrows and gives life to this life, and that there is a Sun in the interior of the soul from which a brilliant light proceeds and is sent to the faculties. The soul, as I have said,[12] does not move from that center nor is its peace lost; for the very One who gave peace to the apostles when they were together[13] can give it to the soul.

7. It has occurred to me that this greeting of the Lord must have amounted to much more than is apparent from its sound, as well as our Lord's words to the glorious Magdalene that she go in peace.[14] Since the Lord's words are effected in us as deeds, they must have worked in those souls already disposed in such a manner that everything corporeal in them was taken away and they were left in pure spirit. Thus the soul could be joined in this heavenly union with the uncreated spirit. For it is very certain that in emptying ourselves of all that is creature and detaching ourselves from it for the love of God, the same Lord will fill us with Himself. And thus, while Jesus our Lord was once praying for His apostles—I don't remember where—He said that they were one with the Father and with Him, just as Jesus Christ our Lord is in the Father and the Father is in Him.[15] I don't know what greater love there can be than this. And all of us are included here, for His Majesty said: *I ask not only for them but for all those who also will believe in me*; and He says: *I am in them.*[16]

8. O God help me, how true these words are! And how well they are understood by the soul who is in this prayer and

sees for itself. How well we would all understand them if it were not for our own fault, since the words of Jesus Christ, our King and Lord, cannot fail.[17] But since we fail by not disposing ourselves and turning away from all that can hinder this light, we do not see ourselves in this mirror that we contemplate, where our image is engraved.

9. Well, to return to what we were saying.[18] The Lord puts the soul in this dwelling of His, which is the center of the soul itself. They say that the empyreal heaven where the Lord is does not move as do the other heavens; similarly, it seems, in the soul that enters here there are none of those movements that usually take place in the faculties and the imagination and do harm to the soul, nor do these stirrings take away its peace.

It seems I'm saying that when the soul reaches this state in which God grants it this favor, it is sure of its salvation and safe from falling again. I do not say such a thing, and wherever I so speak that it seems the soul is secure, this should be taken to mean as long as the divine Majesty keeps it in His hand and it does not offend Him. At least I know certainly that the soul doesn't consider itself safe even though it sees itself in this state and the state has lasted for some years. But it goes about with much greater fear than before, guarding itself from any small offense against God and with the strongest desire to serve Him, as will be said further on,[19] and with habitual pain and confusion at seeing the little it can do and the great deal to which it is obliged. This pain is no small cross but a very great penance. For when this soul does penance, the delight will be greater in the measure that the penance is greater. The true penance comes when God takes away the soul's health and strength for doing penance. Even though I have mentioned elsewhere[20] the great pain this lack causes, the pain is much more intense here. All these things must come to the soul from its roots, from where it is planted. The tree that is beside the running water is fresher and gives more fruit. What is there, then, to marvel at in the desires this soul has since its true spirit has become one with the heavenly water we mentioned?[21]

10. Now then, to return to what I was saying,[22] it should not be thought that the faculties, senses, and passions are always in this peace; the soul is, yes. But in those other dwell-

ing places, times of war, trial, and fatigue are never lacking; however, they are such that they do not take the soul from its place and its peace; that is, as a rule.

This center of our soul, or this spirit, is something so difficult to explain, and even believe in, that I think, Sisters, I'll not give you the temptation to disbelieve what I say, for I do not know how to explain this center. That there are trials and sufferings and that at the same time the soul is in peace is a difficult thing to explain. I want to make one or more comparisons for you. Please God, I may be saying something through them; but if not, I know that I'm speaking the truth in what I say.

11. The King is in His palace and there are many wars in his kingdom and many painful things going on, but not on that account does he fail to be at his post. So here, even though in those other dwelling places there is much tumult and there are many poisonous creatures and the noise is heard, no one enters that center dwelling place and makes the soul leave. Nor do the things the soul hears make it leave; even though they cause it some pain, the suffering is not such as to disturb it and take away its peace. The passions are now conquered and have a fear of entering the center because they would go away from there more subdued.

Our entire body may ache; but if the head is sound, the head will not ache just because the body aches.

I am laughing to myself over these comparisons for they do not satisfy me, but I don't know any others. You may think what you want; what I have said is true.

CHAPTER THREE

Deals with the wonderful effects of this prayer that was mentioned. It is necessary to pay attention and heed to these effects, for the difference between them and the previous ones is remarkable.

1. Now, then, we are saying that this little butterfly has already died, with supreme happiness for having found repose and that Christ lives in it. Let us see what life it lives, or how this life differs from the life it was living. For from the effects, we shall see if what was said is true. By what I understand these effects are the following.[1]

2. The first effect is a forgetfulness of self, for truly the soul, seemingly, no longer is, as was said.[2] Everything is such that this soul doesn't know or recall that there will be heaven or life or honor for it, because it employs all it has in procuring the honor of God. It seems the words His Majesty spoke to her produced the deed in her. They were that she look after what is His and that He would look after what is hers.[3] Thus, the soul doesn't worry about all that can happen. It experiences strange forgetfulness, for, as I say, seemingly the soul no longer is or would want to be anything in anything, except when it understands that there can come from itself something by which the glory and honor of God may increase even one degree. For this purpose the soul would very willingly lay down its life.

3. Don't think by this, daughters, that a person fails to remember to eat and sleep—doing so is no small torment—and to do all that he is obliged to in conformity with his state in life. We are speaking of interior matters, for there is little to say about exterior works. Rather, the soul's pain lies in seeing that what it can now do by its own efforts amounts to nothing. For no earthly thing would it fail to do all it can and understands to be for the service of our Lord.

4. The second effect is that the soul has a great desire to suffer, but not the kind of desire that disturbs it as previously. For the desire left in these souls that the will of God be done in them reaches such an extreme that they think everything His Majesty does is good. If He desires the soul to suffer, well and good; if not, it doesn't kill itself as it used to.

5. These souls also have a deep interior joy when they are persecuted, with much more peace than that mentioned, and without any hostile feelings toward those who do, or desire to do, them evil. On the contrary, such a soul gains a particular love for its persecutors, in such a way that if it sees these latter in some trial it feels compassion and would take on any burden to free them from their trial, and eagerly recommends them to God and would rejoice to lose the favors His Majesty grants it if He would bestow these same gifts on those others so that they wouldn't offend our Lord.

6. You have already seen the trials and afflictions these souls have experienced in order to die so as to enjoy our Lord.[4]

What surprises me most of all now is that they have just as great a desire to serve Him and that through them He be praised and that they may benefit some soul if they can. For not only do they not desire to die but they desire to live very many years suffering the greatest trials if through these they can help that the Lord be praised, even though in something very small. If they knew for certain that in leaving the body the soul would enjoy God, they wouldn't pay attention to that; nor do they think of the glory of the saints. They do not desire at that time to be in glory. Their glory lies in being able some way to help the Crucified, especially when they see He is so offended and that few there are who, detached from everything else, really look after His honor.

7. It is true that sometimes these things are forgotten, and the loving desires to enjoy God and leave this exile return, especially when the soul sees how little it serves Him. But soon it turns and looks within itself and at how continually it experiences His presence, and with that it is content and offers His Majesty the desire to live as the most costly offering it can give Him.

It has no more fear of death than it would of a gentle rapture. The fact is that He who gave those desires that were so excessive a torment now gives these others. May He be always blessed and praised.

8. The desires these souls have are no longer for consolations or spiritual delight, since the Lord Himself is present with these souls and it is His Majesty who now lives. Clearly, His life was nothing but a continual torment, and He makes ours the same; at least with the desires, for in other things He leads us as the weak, although souls share much in His fortitude when He sees they have need of it.

There is a great detachment from everything and a desire to be always either alone or occupied in something that will benefit some soul. There are no interior trials or feelings of dryness, but the soul lives with a remembrance and tender love of our Lord. It would never want to go without praising Him. When it becomes distracted the Lord Himself awakens it in the manner mentioned,[5] for one sees most clearly that that impulse, or I don't know what to call the feeling, proceeds from the interior depths of the soul, as was said of the impulses in the previous dwelling place.[6] Here, in this dwelling place, these impulses are experienced most gently, but they do not proceed from the mind or the memory, nor do they come from anything that would make one think the soul did something on its own. This experience is an ordinary and frequent one, for it has been observed carefully. Just as a fire does not shoot its flames downward but upward, however great a fire is enkindled, so one experiences here that this interior movement proceeds from the center of the soul and awakens the faculties.

9. Certainly, if there were no other gain in this way of prayer except to understand the particular care God has in communicating with us and beseeching us to remain with Him—for this experience doesn't seem to be anything else—it seems to me that all the trials endured for the sake of enjoying these touches of His love, so gentle and penetrating, would be well worthwhile.

This you will have experienced, Sisters. For I think that when one has reached the prayer of union the Lord goes about with this concern if we do not grow negligent in keeping His commandments. When this impulse comes to you, remember that it comes from this interior dwelling place where God is in our soul, and praise Him very much. For certainly that note or letter is His, written with intense love and in such a way that He wants you alone to understand it and what He asks of you in it. By no means should you fail to respond to His Majesty, even though you may be externally occupied or in conversation with some persons. For it will often happen that our Lord will want to grant you this secret favor in public, and it is very easy—since the response is interior—to do what I'm saying and make an act of love, or say what Saint Paul said: *Lord, what will You have me do?*[7] In many ways He will teach you there what will be pleasing to Him and the acceptable time. I think it is understood that He hears us, and this touch, which is so delicate, almost always disposes the soul to be able to do what was said with a resolute will.

10. The difference in this dwelling place is the one mentioned:[8] There are almost never any experiences of dryness or interior disturbance of the kind that was present at times in all the other dwelling places, but the soul is almost always in quiet. There is no fear that this sublime favor can be counter-

feited by the devil, but the soul is wholly sure that the favor comes from God; for, as I have said,[9] the faculties and senses have nothing to do with what goes on in this dwelling place. His Majesty reveals Himself to the soul and brings it to Himself in that place where, in my opinion, the devil will not dare enter, nor will the Lord allow him to enter. Nor does the Lord in all the favors He grants the soul here, as I have said,[10] receive any assistance from the soul itself, except what it has already done in surrendering itself totally to God.

11. Every way in which the Lord helps the soul here, and all He teaches it, takes place with such quiet and so noiselessly that, seemingly to me, the work resembles the building of Solomon's temple where no sound was heard.[11] So in this temple of God, in this His dwelling place, He alone and the soul rejoice together in the deepest silence. There is no reason for the intellect to stir or seek anything, for the Lord who created it wishes to give it repose here and that through a small crevice it might observe what is taking place. At times this sight is lost and the other faculties do not allow the intellect to look, but this happens for only a very short time. In my opinion, the faculties are not lost here;[12] they do not work, but remain as though in amazement.

12. I am amazed as well to see that when the soul arrives here all raptures are taken away. Only once in a while are they experienced and then without those transports and that flight of the spirit. They happen very rarely and almost never in public as they very often did before. Nor do the great occasions of devotion cause the soul concern as previously. Nor if souls in this dwelling place see a devout image or hear a sermon—previously it was almost as though they didn't hear it—or music are they worried as was the poor little butterfly that went about so apprehensive that everything frightened it and made it fly. Now the reason could be that in this dwelling place either the soul has found its repose, or has seen so much that nothing frightens it, or that it doesn't feel that solitude it did before since it enjoys such company. In sum, Sisters, I don't know what the cause may be. For when the Lord begins to show what there is in this dwelling place and to bring the soul there, this great weakness is taken away. The weakness was a severe trial for the soul and previously was not taken away.

Perhaps the reason is that the Lord has now fortified, enlarged, and made the soul capable. Or it could be that His Majesty wished to make known publicly that which He did with these souls in secret for certain reasons He knows, for His judgments are beyond all that we can imagine here below.

13. These effects, along with all the other good ones from the degrees of prayer we mentioned, are given by God when He brings the soul to Himself with this kiss sought by the bride,[13] for I think this petition is here granted. Here an abundance of water is given to this deer that was wounded. Here one delights in God's tabernacle. Here the dove Noah sent out to see if the storm was over finds the olive branch as a sign of firm ground discovered amid the floods and tempests of this world. O Jesus! Who would know the many things there must be in Scripture to explain this peace of soul! My God, since You see how important it is for us, grant that Christians will seek it; and in Your mercy do not take it away from those to whom You have given it. For, in the end, people must always live with fear until You give them true peace and bring them there where that peace will be unending. I say "true peace," not because this peace is not true but because the first war could return if we were to withdraw from God.

14. But what will these souls feel on seeing that they could lack so great a blessing? Seeing this makes them proceed more carefully and seek to draw strength from their weakness so as not to abandon through their own fault any opportunity to please God more. The more favored they are by His Majesty the more they are afraid and fearful of themselves. And since through His grandeurs they have come to a greater knowledge of their own miseries, and their sins become more serious to them, they often go about like the publican[14] not daring to raise their eyes. At other times they go about desiring to die so as to be safe; although, with the love they have, soon they again want to live in order to serve Him, as was said.[15] And in everything concerning themselves they trust in His mercy. Sometimes the many favors make them feel more annihilated, for they fear that just as a ship too heavily laden sinks to the bottom they will go down too.

15. I tell you, Sisters, that the cross is not wanting but it doesn't disquiet or make them lose peace. For the storms, like a

wave, pass quickly. And the fair weather returns, because the presence of the Lord they experience makes them soon forget everything. May He be ever blessed and praised by all His creatures, amen.

CHAPTER FOUR

Concludes by explaining what she thinks our Lord's purpose is in granting such great favors to the soul and how it is necessary that Martha and Mary join together. This chapter is very beneficial.

1. You must not think, Sisters, that the effects I mentioned[1] are always present in these souls. Hence, where I remember, I say "ordinarily." For sometimes our Lord leaves these individuals in their natural state, and then it seems that all the poisonous creatures from the outskirts and other dwelling places of this castle band together to take revenge for the time they were unable to have these souls under their control.

2. True, this natural state lasts only a short while, a day at most or a little more. And in this great disturbance, usually occasioned by some event, the soul's gain through the good company it is in becomes manifest. For the Lord gives the soul great stability and good resolutions not to deviate from His service in anything. But it seems this determination increases, and these souls do not deviate through even a very slight first movement. As I say, this disturbance is rare, but our Lord does not want the soul to forget its being, so that, for one thing, it might always be humble; for another, that it might better understand the tremendous favor it receives, what it owes His Majesty, and that it might praise Him.

3. Nor should it pass through your minds that, since these souls have such determination and strong desires not to commit any imperfection for anything on earth, they fail to commit many imperfections, and even sins. Advertently, no; for the Lord must give souls such as these very particular help against such a thing. I mean venial sins, for from what these souls can understand they are free from mortal sins, although not immune. That they might have some sins they don't know about is no small torment to them. They also suffer torment in seeing souls go astray. Even though in some way they have great hope that they themselves will not be among these souls, they cannot

help but fear when they recall some of those persons Scripture mentions who, it seems, were favored by the Lord, like Solomon, who communed so much with His Majesty, as I have said.[2] The one among you who feels safest should fear more, for *blessed is the man who fears the Lord*,[3] says David. May His Majesty protect us always. To beseech Him that we not offend Him is the greatest security we can have. May He be praised forever, amen.

4. It will be good, Sisters, to tell you the reason the Lord grants so many favors in this world. Although, if you have paid attention, you will have understood this in learning of their effects, I want to tell you again here lest someone think that the reason is solely for the sake of giving delight to these souls; that thought would be a serious error. His Majesty couldn't grant us a greater favor than to give us a life that would be an imitation of the life His beloved Son lived. Thus I hold for certain that these favors are meant to fortify our weakness, as I have said here at times,[4] that we may be able to imitate Him in His great sufferings.

5. We have always seen that those who were closest to Christ our Lord were those with the greatest trials. Let us look at what His glorious Mother suffered and the glorious apostles. How do you think Saint Paul could have suffered such very great trials? Through him we can see the effects visions and contemplation produce when from our Lord, and not from the imagination or the devil's deceit. Did Saint Paul by chance hide himself in the enjoyment of these delights and not engage in anything else? You already see that he didn't have a day of rest, from what we can understand, and neither did he have any rest at night since it was then that he earned his livelihood.[5] I like very much the account about Saint Peter's fleeing from prison and how our Lord appeared to him and told him "I am on my way to Rome to be crucified again." We never recite the office of this feast, where this account is, that I don't find particular consolation.[6] How did this favor from the Lord impress Saint Peter or what did he do? He went straight to his death. And it was no small mercy from the Lord that Peter found someone to provide him with death.

6. O my Sisters! How forgetful this soul, in which the Lord dwells in so particular a way, should be of its own rest,

how little it should care for its honor, and how far it should be from wanting esteem in anything! For if it is with Him very much, as is right, it should think little about itself. All its concern is taken up with how to please Him more and how or where it will show Him the love it bears Him. This is the reason for prayer, my daughters, the purpose of this spiritual marriage: the birth always of good works, good works.

7. This is the true sign of a thing, or favor, being from God, as I have already told you.[7] It benefits me little to be alone making acts of devotion to our Lord, proposing and promising to do wonders in His service, if I then go away and when the occasion offers itself do everything the opposite. I was wrong in saying it profits little, for everything having to do with God profits a great deal. And even though we are weak and do not carry out these resolutions afterward, sometimes His Majesty will give us the power to do so, even though, perhaps, doing so is burdensome to us, as is often true. Since He sees that a soul is very fainthearted He gives it a severe trial, truly against its will, and brings this soul out of the trial with profit. Afterward, since the soul understands this, the fear lessens and one can offer oneself more willingly to Him. I meant "it benefits me little" in comparison with how much greater the benefit is when our deeds conform with what we say in prayer; what cannot be done all at once can be done little by little. Let the soul bend its will if it wishes that prayer be beneficial to it, for within the corners of these little monasteries there will not be lacking many occasions for you to do so.[8]

8. Keep in mind that I could not exaggerate the importance of this. Fix your eyes on the Crucified and everything will become small for you. If His Majesty showed us His love by means of such works and frightful torments, how is it that you want to please Him only with words? Do you know what it means to be truly spiritual? It means becoming the slaves of God. Marked with His brand, which is that of the cross, spiritual persons, because now they have given Him their liberty, can be sold by Him as slaves of everyone, as He was. He doesn't thereby do them any harm or grant them a small favor. And if souls aren't determined about becoming His slave, let them be convinced that they are not making much progress, for this whole building, as I have said,[9] has humility

as its foundation. If humility is not genuinely present, for your own sake the Lord will not construct a high building lest that building fall to the ground. Thus, Sisters, that you might build on good foundations, strive to be the least and the slaves of all, looking at how or where you can please and serve them. What you do in this matter you do more for yourself than for them and lay stones so firmly that the castle will not fall.

9. I repeat, it is necessary that your foundation consist of more than prayer and contemplation. If you do not strive for the virtues and practice them, you will always be dwarfs. And, please God, it will be only a matter of not growing, for you already know that whoever does not increase decreases. I hold that love, where present, cannot possibly be content with remaining always the same.

10. It will seem to you that I am speaking with those who are beginning and that after this beginner's stage souls can rest. I have already told you[10] that the calm these souls have interiorly is for the sake of their having much less calm exteriorly and much less desire to have exterior calm. What, do you think, is the reason for those inspirations (or to put it better, aspirations) I mentioned, and those messages the soul sends from the interior center to the people at the top of the castle and to the dwelling places outside the center where it is? Is it so that those outside might fall asleep? No, absolutely not! That the faculties, senses, and all that which is corporeal will not be idle, the soul wages more war from the center than it did when it was outside suffering with them, for then it didn't understand the tremendous gain trials bring. Perhaps they were the means by which God brought it to the center, and the company it has gives it much greater strength than ever. For if here below, as David says, in the company of the saints we will become saints,[11] there is no reason to doubt that, being united with the Strong One through so sovereign a union of spirit with spirit, fortitude will cling to such a soul; and so we shall understand what fortitude the saints had for suffering and dying.

11. It is very certain that from that fortitude which clings to it there the soul assists all those who are in the castle, and even the body itself, which often, seemingly, does not feel the strength. But the soul is fortified by the strength it has from drinking wine in this wine cellar, where its Spouse has brought

it[12] and from where He doesn't allow it to leave; and strength flows back to the weak body, just as food placed in the stomach strengthens the head and the whole body. Thus the soul has its share of misfortune while it lives. However much it does, the interior strength increases and thus, too, the war that is waged; for everything seems like a trifle to it. The great penances that many saints—especially the glorious Magdalene, who had always been surrounded by so much luxury—performed must have come from this center; also that hunger which our Father Elijah had for the honor of his God[13] and which Saint Dominic and Saint Francis had so as to draw souls to praise God. I tell you, though they were forgetful of themselves, their suffering must have been great.

12. This is what I want us to strive for, my Sisters; and let us desire and be occupied in prayer not for the sake of our enjoyment but so as to have this strength to serve. Let's refuse to take an unfamiliar path, for we shall get lost at the most opportune time. It would indeed be novel to think of having these favors from God through a path other than the one He took and the one followed by all His saints. May the thought never enter our minds. Believe me, Martha and Mary must join together in order to show hospitality to the Lord and have Him always present and not host Him badly by failing to give Him something to eat. How would Mary, always seated at His feet, provide Him with food if her sister did not help her? His food is that in every way possible we draw souls that they may be saved and praise Him always.[14]

13. You will make two objections: one, that He said that Mary had chosen the better part. The answer is that she had already performed the task of Martha, pleasing the Lord by washing His feet and drying them with her hair.[15] Do you think it would be a small mortification for a woman of nobility like her to wander through these streets (and perhaps alone because her fervent love made her unaware of what she was doing) and enter a house she had never entered before and afterward suffer the criticism of the Pharisee and the very many other things she must have suffered? The people saw a woman like her change so much—and, as we know, she was among such malicious people—and they saw her friendship with the Lord whom they vehemently abhorred, and that she

wanted to become a saint since obviously she would have changed her manner of dress and everything else. All of that was enough to cause them to comment on the life she had formerly lived. If nowadays there is so much gossip against persons who are not so notorious, what would have been said then? I tell you, Sisters, the better part came after many trials and much mortification, for even if there were no other trial than to see His Majesty abhorred, that would be an intolerable one. Moreover, the many trials that afterward she suffered at the death of the Lord and in the years that she subsequently lived in His absence must have been a terrible torment. You see she wasn't always in the delight of contemplation at the feet of the Lord.

14. The other objection you will make is that you are unable to bring souls to God, that you do not have the means; that you would do it willingly but that not being teachers or preachers, as were the apostles, you do not know how. This objection I have answered at times in writing,[16] but I don't know if I did so in this *Castle*. Yet since the matter is something I believe is passing through your mind on account of the desires God gives you, I will not fail to respond here. I already told you elsewhere[17] that sometimes the devil gives us great desires so that we will avoid setting ourselves to the task at hand, serving our Lord in possible things, and instead be content with having desired the impossible. Apart from the fact that by prayer you will be helping greatly, you need not be desiring to benefit the whole world but must concentrate on those who are in your company, and thus your deed will be greater since you are more obliged toward them. Do you think such deep humility, your mortification, service of all and great charity toward them, and love of the Lord are of little benefit? This fire of love in you enkindles their souls, and with every other virtue you will be always awakening them. Such service will not be small but very great and very pleasing to the Lord. By what you do in deed—that which you can—His Majesty will understand that you would do much more. Thus He will give you the reward He would if you had gained many souls for Him.

15. You will say that such service does not convert souls because all the Sisters you deal with are already good. Who has

appointed you judge in this matter? The better they are the more pleasing their praises will be to our Lord and the more their prayer will profit their neighbor.

In sum, my Sisters, what I conclude with is that we shouldn't build castles in the air. The Lord doesn't look so much at the greatness of our works as at the love with which they are done. And if we do what we can, His Majesty will enable us each day to do more and more, provided that we do not quickly tire. But during the little while this life lasts—and perhaps it will last a shorter time than each one thinks—let us offer the Lord interiorly and exteriorly the sacrifice we can. His Majesty will join it with that which He offered on the cross to the Father for us. Thus even though our works are small they will have the value our love for Him would have merited had they been great.

16. May it please His Majesty, my Sisters and daughters, that we all reach that place where we may ever praise Him. Through the merits of His Son who lives and reigns forever and ever, may He give me the grace to carry out something of what I tell you, amen. For I tell you that my confusion is great, and thus I ask you through the same Lord that in your prayers you do not forget this poor wretch.

EPILOGUE[1]

1. Although when I began writing this book I am sending you I did so with the aversion I mentioned in the beginning,[2] now that I am finished I admit the work has brought me much happiness, and I consider the labor, though I confess it was small, well spent. Considering the strict enclosure and the few things you have for your entertainment, my Sisters, and that your buildings are not always as large as would be fitting for your monasteries, I think it will be a consolation for you to delight in this interior castle since without permission from the prioress you can enter and take a walk through it at any time.

2. True, you will not be able to enter all the dwelling places through your own efforts, even though these efforts may seem to you great, unless the Lord of the castle Himself brings you there. Hence I advise you to use no force if you meet with any resistance, for you will thereby anger Him in such a way that He will never allow you to enter them. He is very fond of humility. By considering that you do not deserve even to enter the third you will more quickly win the favor to reach the fifth. And you will be able to serve Him from there in such a way, continuing to walk through them often, that He will bring you into the very dwelling place He has for Himself. You need never leave this latter dwelling place unless called by the prioress, whose will this great Lord desires that you comply with as much as if it were His own. Even though you are frequently outside through her command, you will always find the door open when you return. Once you get used to enjoying this castle, you will find rest in all things, even those involving much labor, for you will have the hope of returning to the castle, which no one can take from you.

3. Although no more than seven dwelling places were discussed, in each of these there are many others, below and above and to the sides, with lovely gardens and fountains and labyrinths, such delightful things that you would want to be dissolved in praises of the great God who created the soul in His own image and likeness.[3] If you find something good in the way I have explained this to you, believe that indeed His Majesty said it so as to make you happy; the bad that you might find is said by me.

4. Through the strong desire I have to play some part in helping you serve my God and Lord, I ask that each time you read this work you, in my name, praise His Majesty fervently and ask for the increase of His Church and for light for the Lutherans. As for me, ask Him to pardon my sins and deliver me from purgatory, for perhaps by the mercy of God I will be there when this is given you to read—if it may be seen by you after having been examined by learned men. If anything is erroneous it is so because I didn't know otherwise; and I submit in everything to what the holy Roman Catholic Church holds, for in this Church I live, declare my faith, and promise to live and die.

May God our Lord be forever praised and blessed, amen, amen.

5. This writing was finished in the monastery of Saint Joseph of Avila in the year 1577, the eve before the feast of Saint Andrew,[4] for the glory of God who lives and reigns forever and ever, amen.

NOTES

INTRODUCTION

1. Cf. *Dei Verbum*, no. 8.
2. Cf. *Acta Apostolicae Sedis*, Vol. LXII, n. 9, p. 592.
3. See *Life*, chap. 4, no. 1.
4. See *Life*, chap. 6.
5. *Life*, chap. 8, no. 7; chap. 8, no. 5; chap. 19, nos. 4, 10-15.
6. *Life*, chap. 7, 17.
7. *Life*, chap. 7, no. 11.
8. See *Life*, chap. 9.
9. See *Life*, chap. 10, no. 1; chap. 23, nos. 1-2.
10. See *Life*, chap. 23.
11. See *Life*, chap. 32.
12. See *Way of Perfection*, chap. 1; *Foundations*, chap. 1, nos. 7-8.
13. See *Way of Perfection*, chap. 1.
14. Ibid., chap. 41, no. 5.
15. *Letters*, February 10, 1577.
16. *Life*, chap. 10, no. 1.
17. See *Life*, chap. 22; *Interior Castle*, chap. 7, no. 6.
18. See *Life*, chap. 24, no. 5; 25, no. 1.
19. See *Life*, chap. 27.
20. *Life*, chap. 28, no. 3.
21. *Life*, chap. 27, no. 4.
22. See *Interior Castle*, VII, chap. 1, nos. 6-10.
23. In Jn. 14:23.
24. *Spiritual Testimonies*, 14.
25. See *Spiritual Testimonies*, 31; *Interior Castle*, VII, chap. 2, no. 1.
26. *Life*, chap. 26, no. 5.
27. See *Way of Perfection*, chap. 21, no. 4.
28. Cf. the chapter headings in *Life*, chaps. 14, 16, 18, 19, 20, 21, 22, 25.
29. See *Spiritual Testimonies*, 65.
30. *Life*, chap. 8, no. 5.
31. *Life*, chap. 22, no. 7.
32. See *Way of Perfection*, chaps. 26-27.
33. Ibid., chap. 26, no. 3.
34. Ibid., no. 9.

NOTES

35. Ibid., no. 10.

36. Ibid., chap. 29, no. 5.

37. Ibid., chap. 28, no. 4.

38. Ibid., chap. 19, no. 1.

39. Ibid.

40. Ibid., chap. 19, no. 2.

41. Ibid., chap. 29, nos. 6-7.

42. Ibid., chap. 28, no. 7.

43. Ibid., no. 4.

44. Ibid., chap. 29, nos. 6-7.

45. Ibid., chap. 28, no. 5.

46. Antonio de San Joaquin, "Anotaciones al P. Ribera," *Ano Teresiano*, 12 vols. (Madrid, 1733-1769), 8:149-150.

47. *Interior Castle*, I, chap. 2, no. 7; see also IV, chap. 1, no. 1; chap. 2, no. 7.

48. Ibid., Prologue, no. 1.

49. For a detailed treatment of this whole question, cf. Efrén de la Madre De Dios and Otger Steggink, *Tiempo Y Vida De Santa Teresa* (Madrid: BAC, 1977), pp. 701-805; cf. also Ildefonso Moriones, *El Carmelo Teresiano* (Vitoria: Edicones El Carmen, 1978), pp. 97-180. For a treatment of these questions from a different perspective, cf. Joachim Smet, *The Carmelites*, vol. 2: *The Post Tridentine Period* (Darien, Ill.: Carmelite Spiritual Center, 1976), pp. 1-131.

50. See *Letters*, October 22, 1577.

51. *Interior Castle*, IV, chap. 2, no. 1.

52. Ibid., V, chap. 4, no. 1.

53. Ibid., Prologue, no. 1.

54. Ibid.

55. Ibid., Epilogue, no. 1.

56. Ibid., VI, chap. 4, no. 9.

57. Ibid., IV, chap. 1, no. 1; see also V, chap. 4, no. 11.

58. See Silverio de Santa Teresa, *Biblioteca Mística Carmelitana*, vol. 18 (Burgos: El Monte Carmelo, 1934), p. 315.

59. *Interior Castle*, I, chap. 1, no. 1.

60. *Way of Perfection*, chap. 28, no. 9.

61. See *Biblioteca Mística*, vol. 18, pp. 276-278.

62. Ibid., vol. 2 (1915):493.

63. *Life*, chap. 40, no. 5.

64. In no. 10.

65. *Interior Castle*, I, chap. 1, nos. 2-3.

66. Ibid., Epilogue, no. 3.

67. Ibid., I, chap. 1, no. 7.

68. Ibid., I, chap. 1, nos. 6, 8.

69. Ibid., chap. 2, no. 14.

70. Ibid., VII, chap. 4, no. 9.

71. Ibid., III, chap. 1, no. 5.

72. Ibid., chap. 2, nos. 4-5; chap. 2, no. 7; chap. 2, no. 8.

73. Ibid., chap. 2, no. 13; chap. 1, no. 7.

NOTES

74. Ibid., chap. 2, no. 9.
75. Ibid., I, chap. 2, no. 7.
76. Ibid., IV, chap. 1, no. 1.
77. Ibid., chap. 1, no. 4.
78. Ibid., no. 7.
79. Ibid.
80. Ibid., chap. 3, nos. 1-3.
81. Ibid., no. 8.
82. Ibid., chap. 2, nos. 3, 8, 9.
83. Ibid., V, chap. 1, nos. 3-5, 9-10.
84. Ibid., nos. 5, 11.
85. Ibid., chap. 2, nos. 2-5.
86. Ibid., chap. 4, no. 4.
87. Ibid., no. 9.
88. Ibid., VI, chap. 1, no. 1.
89. Ibid., chap. 2, no. 1; chap. 4, no. 1.
90. Ibid., chap. 4, no. 1.
91. Ibid., chap. 1, nos. 3, 4, 6, 7, 8, 9.
92. Ibid., chap. 2.
93. Ibid., chap. 4, no. 2.
94. Ibid., nos. 3-4.
95. Ibid., nos. 5, 8.
96. Ibid., chap. 5, no. 10.
97. Ibid., chap. 6, nos. 10-13.
98. Ibid., chap. 7, nos. 6, 7, 11, 12.
99. Ibid., chap. 11, nos. 1, 6.
100. Ibid., nos. 2, 4, 11.
101. Ibid., chap. 4, no. 4.
102. Ibid., VII, chap. 1, no. 5.
103. Ibid., no. 6.
104. Ibid., no. 8
105. Ibid., nos. 8-9.
106. Ibid., chap. 2, no. 1.
107. Ibid., no. 3.
108. Ibid., no. 4.
109. Ibid., no. 5.
110. Ibid., chap. 4, nos. 4, 6, 9, 12.
111. Ibid., nos. 14-15.
112. For a complete introduction to the writings of Saint Teresa, cf. Alberto Barrientos, ed., *Introdución a la Lectura de Santa Teresa* (Madrid: Editorial De Espiritualidad, 1978).

THE INTERIOR CASTLE

Prologue
1. An allusion to her *Life* and *The Way of Perfection.*

NOTES

2. This is a veiled reference to her *Life*. The autograph of this work was requested by the Inquisition in 1576 and kept in its archives until 1588.

3. It was June 2, 1577. She completed the work in Avila on November 29 of the same year.

4. These were Fr. Jerome Gratian and her confessor Dr. Alonso Valázquez, future bishop of Osma and later archbishop of Santiago de Compostela.

The First Dwelling Places

Chapter 1

1. Allusion to Jn. 14:2. Teresa uses the Spanish words *moradas, aposentos,* and *piezas* in approximately the same sense; they refer to rooms or dwelling places within the castle. The fundamental text of Jn. 14:2 has led previous translators to speak of these rooms as mansions. Most people today think of a mansion as a large stately house, not what Teresa had in mind with the term *moradas*. New versions of Scripture render Jn. 14:2 as "in my Father's house there are many dwelling places." "Dwelling places" turns out to be a more precise translation of Teresa's *moradas* than is the classic "mansions," and more biblical and theological in tone.

2. Pr. 8:31.

3. Gn. 1:26–27.

4. In no. 1.

5. Jn. 9:2–3.

6. She is probably alluding to Osuna's *Third Spiritual Alphabet* and Laredo's *Ascent of Mount Sion*, favorite books of hers. See *Life*, chap. 4, no. 7; chap. 23, no. 12.

7. She also received in an intellectual vision mystical understanding of this truth. See *Spir. Test.*, 20.

8. Gn. 19:26.

9. Fr. Gratian added "and eight" after "thirty years," in accordance with Jn. 5:5.

10. Allusion to Mt. 6:21.

Chapter 2

1. Ps. 1:3.

2. The person is Teresa herself. See *Spir. Test.*, 20.

3. For similar comparisons see *Life*, chap. 40, no. 5; *Spir. Test.*, 52.

4. Ps. 127:1.

5. In no. 2.

6. See her *Constitutions*, nos. 2, 7.

7. Teresa laments the fact there are few books that explain mystical (supernatural) prayer in depth. In no. 1 of the following chapter she asserts that there are many books dealing with ascetical matters. Thus her orientation in this book is toward the mystical.

8. She is referring to the *Life* and the *Way of Perfection*, and alludes to a divine influence in the composition of her mystical writings. See *Life*, chap.

39, no. 8: "... many of the things I write about here do not come from my own head, but my heavenly Master told them to me."

    9. In no. 7.

    10. A plant about elbow-length, which grows in Andalusia and Valencia, resembling the palm tree. Only the center or heart, the tender part, is eaten.

    11. In no. 10.

    12. See no. 8. Teresa avoids any arrangement of these dwelling places into neatly structured rows with set numbers. She thereby in her allegory makes it easy for us to imagine a marvelous depth and abundance of inner riches.

    13. In *The Way of Perfection*, chap. 39, no. 5. See also *Life*, chap. 13, no. 15.

    14. In chap. 1, no. 8.

    15. In nos. 4, 12.

    16. Allusion to 2 Co. 11:14.

    17. In *The Way of Perfection*, chap. 38, no. 2; chap. 39 passim.

    18. See *Life*, chap. 13, nos. 8, 10; *Way of Perfection*, chap. 4; *Method for the Visitation of Monasteries*, nos. 17, 20, 21.

THE SECOND DWELLING PLACES

Chapter 1

    1. See *Life*, chaps. 11–13; *Way of Perfection*, passim.

    2. In VI, chap. 3.

    3. Lk. 15:16.

    4. Allusion to Jn. 15:5.

    5. Allusion to Jg. 7:5.

    6. See *Life*, chap. 4, no. 2; chap. 11, nos. 10–15; *Way of Perfection*, chap. 20, no. 2; chap. 21, no. 2; chaps. 23, 36, 41.

    7. Allusion to Ws. 16:20.

    8. Allusion to Mt. 20:22.

    9. In V, chap. 3, nos. 3–12.

    10. Jn. 20:19–21.

    11. In no. 1.

    12. Allusion to Si. 3:25.

    13. Jn. 14:6.

    14. Jn. 14:9.

    15. Allusion to Mt. 10:24.

    16. Allusion to Mt. 26:41.

THE THIRD DWELLING PLACES

Chapter 1

    1. Ps. 112:1.

    2. Teresa commissioned Fr. Jerome Gratian to review her work. Gratian did so scrupulously and made corrections here and there throughout the manuscript. For example, in this passage he crossed out the word "secure"

and substituted "right." In fact this whole chapter has a number of corrections by Gratian who was fearful lest the Saint affirm any certitude about the state of grace, or security about one's own salvation, that would have gone contrary to the teaching of the Council of Trent or have been similar to certain theories of the *Alumbrados*. Fortunately, Gratian made the deletion marks so as to leave the original completely legible. The Jesuit Ribera, in turn, corrected Gratian's corrections with marginal comments such as the following: "One doesn't have to cross out any of the holy Mother's words." A further example of the skirmish that went on in the margins of Teresa's manuscript can be found in no. 8 of this chapter. In that delicate passage Teresa wrote: "Shouldn't we consider ourselves lucky to be able to repay something of what we owe Him for His service toward us? I say these words 'His service toward us' unwillingly; but the fact is that He did nothing else but serve us all the time He lived in this world." Gratian changed "His service toward us" to "having died for us" and crossed out what followed. Ribera again noted: "Nothing should be deleted; what the Saint said has been very well said." All of this led to Ribera's written admonition on the first page of the autograph of *The Interior Castle*: "What the holy Mother wrote in this book is frequently crossed out, and other words are added or a gloss is made in the margin. Usually the cancellation is poorly conceived and the text is better the way it was first written.... And since I have read and looked over this work with a certain amount of care, I think I should advise anyone reading it to read it as the holy Mother wrote it, for she understood and said things better, and to pay no attention to what was added or changed unless the correction was made by the Saint herself in her own hand, which is seldom. And I ask out of charity anyone who reads this book to reverence the words and letters formed by so holy a hand and try to understand her correctly; and you will see that there is nothing to correct. Even if you do not understand, believe that she who wrote it knew better and that the words cannot be corrected well unless their meaning is fully understood. If their meaning is not grasped, what is very appropriately said will seem inappropriate. Such is the way books are ruined and lost."

3. Jn. 11:16.
4. In no. 2.
5. Ps. 112:1.,
6. In no. 1.
7. Mt. 19:16–22.
8. In no. 6.
9. Mt. 19:22.
10. Mt. 19:27.
11. Teresa first wrote "as Saint Paul says," then added between the lines "or Christ." Gratian crossed out both and wrote: "Saint Luke says it in chapter 17." See Lk. 17:10.
12. Allusion to Lk. 12:48.
13. This is a vague reference, perhaps to *The Way of Perfection*, chap. 17, nos. 2, 7.

NOTES

Chapter 2

1. Allusion to the young man in the gospel. See III, chap. 1, no. 6.
2. In no. 1. See III, chap. 1, no. 5.
3. Allusion to Lk. 22:42.
4. In no. 4, see III, chap. 1, no. 7.
5. Allusion to Ps. 119:137. For a similar use of this text see *Life*, chap. 19:9. On the following theme about God's different ways with souls, see *Way of Perfection*, chaps. 16–18, especially chap. 17, no. 7.
6. In III, chap. 1., nos. 1, 5, 8.
7. Words from the Carmelite rule (*The Rule of Saint Albert*) and taken from Is. 30:15.

THE FOURTH DWELLING PLACES

Chapter 1

1. Teresa used the Spanish word *contentos* (here rendered in English as consolations) to denote experiences (such as joy, peace, satisfaction) that are not infused; that is, experiences perceived as a result of prayer and virtue but similar to those derived from everyday events. On the other hand, she uses the Spanish word *gustos* (here rendered in English as spiritual delights) to denote infused experiences. Infused, "supernatural," or mystical prayer begins in these fourth dwelling places with the prayer of infused recollection (chap. 3) and quiet, or spiritual delight (chap. 2). Actually Teresa presents the fourth dwelling places as a stage of transition in which the natural and the supernatural (or the acquired and the infused) are intermingled.
2. In her *Life*. She is alluding to the many chapters there that deal with mystical experiences. See chaps. 14–32 and 37–40. When Teresa wrote the *Life* she had not yet come to the stage she describes in the seventh dwelling places. What she explains in her *Life* under the symbol of the fourth water corresponds to the sixth dwelling places. As a result, she points out that she has a better understanding of some matters concerning the spiritual life than she did in that book. See I, chap. 2, no. 7; IV, chap. 2, no. 5.
3. Allusion to Mt. 20:13. The absolute divine freedom in the granting or denying of mystical favors is frequently insisted on in Teresa's writings. In this work see IV, chap. 2, no. 9; V, chap. 1, no. 12; VI, chap. 4, no. 12; chap. 7, no. 9; chap. 8, no. 5.
4. In III, chap. 2, no. 10.
5. Allusion to Jn. 15:5.
6. Ps. 119:32.
7. In no. 4.
8. In *Life*, chap. 12; *Way of Perfection*, chaps. 16–20.
9. One of Teresa's cherished maxims. See the *Foundations*, chap. 5, no. 2.
10. We do not know who the learned man was. Some suggest that it may have been Saint John of the Cross, who was Teresa's director and confessor from 1572–1575. But Teresa's ignorance of the difference between the imagination (*pensamiento*, or mind, as she often refers to it) and the intellect was not total ignorance. See *Life*, chap. 17, no. 5.

11. For many years this wandering of the mind deeply troubled the Saint. See *Life*, chap. 17, no. 7; *Way of Perfection*, chap. 31, no. 8. In this work she has come to a definite doctrinal position on the matter. The instability and rebellion of the imagination is a consequence of the disorder produced in us through original sin. See no. 11 of this chapter.

12. In the prologue, no. 1.

13. Sg. 8:1.

14. In II, no. 9.

15. See VII, chap. 2, no. 11.

Chapter 2

1. In chap. 1, nos. 4–6.

2. See chap. 1, no. 5.

3. See *Life*, chaps. 14–15.

4. In III, chap. 2, nos. 9–10; IV, chap. 1, nos. 4–6.

5. In chap. 1, nos. 5, 6, 10.

6. In chap. 1, no. 4.

7. Ps. 119:32. See chap. 1, no. 5.

8. In VII, chap. 1, nos. 3, 7, 10; chap. 2, nos. 3, 9.

9. In no. 4.

10. In chap. 1, no. 1, she says fourteen years. She finished the first redaction of her *Life* in 1562 and is writing these pages in the latter part of 1577.

11. In no. 5.

Chapter 3

1. She spoke of the prayer of recollection in various places: *Life*, chaps. 14–15; *Way of Perfection*, chaps. 28–29; *Spiritual Testimonies*, 59, no. 3. But Teresa is not consistent in her terminology. Sometimes she speaks of a recollection that is not infused (in the *Way of Perf.*): at other times of a recollection that is infused: in the *Life*, using the term indiscriminately with "quiet" to designate the first degree of infused prayer, and in the *Spiritual Testimonies* to designate the first faint experience of mystical prayer that prepares the way for the prayer of quiet. See no. 8 of this chapter.

2. She is alluding to works such as Osuna's *Third Spiritual Alphabet*, IX, chap. 7; and Laredo's *Ascent of Mount Sion*, III, chap. 41. See *Life*, chap. 12, nos. 1, 4, 5, 7; chap. 22, nos. 13, 18.

3. In I, chap. 2, nos. 4, 12, 15.

4. In *Confessions*, X, chap. 27; or in the pseudo-Augustine's *Soliloquies*, chap. 31. See *Life*, chap. 40, no. 6; *Way of Perfection*, chap. 28, no. 2.

5. In Osuna's *Third Spiritual Alphabet*, VI, chap. 4.

6. See Loredo's *Ascent of Mount Sion*, III, chap. 27.

7. Treatise on *Prayer and Meditation* by Granada and at that time attributed to Saint Peter of Alcantara.

8. In nos. 4–6; see chap. 2, no. 9.

9. Perhaps she is referring to a parallel passage in *Way of Perfection*, chap. 31, nos. 3, 7.

10. Allusion to Ph. 4:13.

11. In the book of *Foundations*, chap. 6. She will insist on this again in VI, chap. 7, no. 13.

12. See *Life*, chaps. 16–17, where Teresa dwells at greater length on this *sleep of the faculties* as though dealing with a special stage in the degrees of mystical prayer.

13. Teresa makes a pun here with the Spanish words *arrobamiento* (rapture) and *abobamiento* (foolishness).

14. In nos. 11–12.

THE FIFTH DWELLING PLACES

Chapter 1

1. Allusion to 2 Co. 11:14.
2. Allusion to Mt. 22:14.
3. Allusion to Mt. 13:44.
4. In IV, chap. 3, no. 11.
5. In no. 3.
6. Another allusion to 2 Co. 11:14.
7. In IV, chap. 3, nos. 11–14.
8. In IV, chap. 1. nos. 8–12.
9. She made a similar observation in the *Way of Perfection*, chap. 31, no. 10.
10. See Life, chap. 5, no. 3; chap. 13, no. 19; chap. 25, no. 22.
11. In IV, chap. 1, no. 2; chap. 2, no. 9.
12. See no. 6.
13. She speaks of them in the next chapter, nos. 7–14.
14. In no. 8.
15. See *Life*, chap. 18, no. 15; *Spir. Test.*, 49.
16. Sg. 2:4.
17. Sg. 3:2.
18. Jn. 20:19.
19. See VII, chap. 2, no. 3.

Chapter 2

1. In chap. 1, no. 2.
2. In the Dwelling Places I–IV.
3. See Col. 3:3–4.
4. In chap. 1, nos. 10–11.
5. In VI, chap. 6, no. 1; chap. 11 passim.
6. In chap. 1, nos. 2, 3, 13.
7. In chap. 1, no. 12; IV, chap. 2, no. 9.
8. In VI, chap. 10, no 8; VII, chap. 3, no. 4.
9. In chap. 1, no. 12.
10. Allusion to Sg. 2:4.
11. Lk. 22:15.
12. She is referring to herself. See *Life*, chap. 38, no. 18.

NOTES

Chapter 3

1. For Teresa the little dove is equivalent to the little butterfly; she uses these images interchangeably. See chap. 4, no. 1; VI, chap. 2, no. 1; chap. 4, no. 1; chap. 6, no. 1; chap. 11, no. 1; VII, chap. 3, no. 1.

2. She is referring to herself. See *Life*, chap. 7, no. 10.

3. In chap. 2, nos. 6–7.

4. See Jn. 11:33–36.

5. In chap. 1, no. 6; IV, chap. 1, nos. 4–5; chap. 2, nos. 3–5.

6. In chap. 1, nos. 3–4.

7. The delightful union is the infused prayer of union.

8. The union that arises from conformity of wills.

9. Jon. 4:6–7.

10. Jn. 17:22.

11. Allusion to 1 Jn. 4:20.

12. In the *Way of Perfection*, chap. 7, *Foundations*, chap. 5.

Chapter 4

1. The prayer of union.

2. Having begun this work in Toledo, June 2, 1577, Teresa in less than a month and a half had got as far as chapter three of the fifth dwelling place. About the middle of July she moved to Avila where she probably wrote chapter three. She then abandoned all work on her book until the beginning of November. And by November 29, 1577, her task was completed.

3. In her comparison, Teresa makes use of the stages that were followed in her day for the arrangement of a marriage: (1) meetings between the young man and woman; (2) exchanging of gifts; (3) falling in love; (4) the joining of hands; (5) betrothal; (6) marriage.

4. See, e.g., IV, chap. 3, nos. 9–10.

5. In no. 4.

6. In chap. 3, no. 2.

THE SIXTH DWELLING PLACES

Chapter 1

1. Allusion to the meeting referred to in V, chap. 4, no. 4.

2. See V, chap. 1, nos. 9–11; V, chap. 4, nos. 3–4.

3. See VII, chap. 3, nos. 4–5.

4. She is referring to herself. See *Life*, chap. 28, no. 14.

5. The "favor that was mentioned" is the prayer of union or the "meetings" between the two who will be betrothed, the prayer characteristic of the fifth dwelling place. The person Teresa refers to is herself. "Forty years ago" would have been 1537. For an account of these sufferings and trials see *Life*, chaps. 4–6; for her first experiences of union, see *Life*, chap. 4, no. 7.

6. The person here is Teresa, and the confessor is Father Baltasar Alvarez, S.J. See *Life*, chap. 30, no. 13.

7. See *Life*, chap. 30, no. 12.

8. In nos. 9–10.

9. She does so in VI, chap. 11.

Chapter 2

1. In the fourth dwelling places.

2. See IV, chap. 3, nos. 11–14.

3. For a parallel passage from her personal experience see her *Life*, chap. 29, no. 10; in no. 13 of that same chapter she describes her experience of the transverberation.

4. She is alluding to herself. See *Spir. Test.*, 59, no. 13.

5. In *Spir. Test.*, 59, no. 15 she speaks of how even the learned men she consulted were free of fears about this prayer. Saint John of Avila wrote to her assuring her that the prayer was good. For a description of her personal experience of this grace see also her *Life*, chaps. 29 and 20.

6. See nos. 1, 3, and 5. These favors proceed "from very deep within the interior part of the soul," from "The Spouse, who is in the seventh dwelling place," there, "where the Lord who is unchanging dwells."

7. In no. 6.

Chapter 3

1. This chapter restates what was said in chap. 25 of the *Life*. In both places the prevailing effort is to distinguish between genuine locutions (coming from God or His saints) and false ones (from the imagination or the devil). In this chapter Teresa deals first with locutions in general (nos. 1–11); then she goes on to treat of a more subtle kind of mystical locution accompanied by "a certain intellectual vision" (nos. 12–18).

2. In chap. 2, nos. 1–4, 8.

3. In no. 1.

4. In chap. 1, nos. 7–15.

5. In a veiled way she is alluding to her own experience described in her *Life*, chap. 25, nos. 14–19.

6. In no. 7.

7. See Jon. chaps. 1 and 4. Though Teresa refers to Jonah about six times in her writings and could be referring to herself, she might, on the other hand, be thinking of Teresa Layz, the benefactress from Alba about whom she speaks in the *Foundations*, chap. 20, and especially in no. 12.

8. In nos. 5–7.

9. Allusion to Lk. 10:16.

10. She speaks of intellectual visions in chaps. 8 and 10; see also chap. 5, nos. 8–9.

11. In chap. 10; also in chap. 4.

12. A reference to herself. See *Life*, chap. 25, nos. 14–19.

13. In nos. 12–16.

14. In no. 11.

15. Allusion to 1 Co. 10:13.

16. Jos. 10:12–13. See *Life*, chap. 25, no. 1.

NOTES

Chapter 4

1. In regard to this terminology see *Life*, chap. 20, no. 1; *Spir. Test.*, 59, no. 9.

2. The need for great courage in order to receive these mystical graces is often stated by Teresa. See *Life*, chap. 13, no. 2; chap. 20, no. 4; chap. 39, no. 21; *Spir. Test.*, 59, no. 9; *Way of Perfection*, chap. 18; and in these sixth dwelling places, chap. 5, nos. 1, 5, 12; chap. 11, no. 11.

3. In IV, chap. 3, nos. 11–12; VI, chap. 3, no. 10.

4. In *Life*, chap. 20, *Spir. Test.*, 59, no. 9.

5. In chap. 2, no. 4.

6. In chap. 8 she will deal with intellectual visions and in chap. 9, with imaginative ones.

7. Fr. Gratian; see Introduction.

8. See Gn. 28:12.

9. See Ex. 3:1–16.

10. This happened sometime during the first months of 1574. See *Foundations*, chap. 21, nos. 1–2.

11. In IV, chap. 3, nos. 11–13.

12. See Sg. 3:2.

13. Allusion to Jn. 9:6–7.

14. In no. 9.

15. See *Life*, chap. 20, no. 5.

16. See is alluding to herself. See *Life*, chap. 31, no. 13.

17. In nos. 4–5.

Chapter 5

1. On the difference between rapture and flight of the spirit see *Life*, chap. 18, no. 7; chap. 20, no. 1; *Spir. Test.*, 59, nos. 9–10.

2. In chap. 4, no. 1.

3. See the account of her personal experience in *Life*, chap. 20, nos. 3–7.

4. She is speaking of herself; see *Life*, chap. 20, nos. 5–6.

5. For parallel passages see *Life*, chap. 22, no. 13; chap. 20, no. 4.

6. In IV, chap. 2, nos. 2–5.

7. Allusion to Pr. 8:29.

8. Allusion to Lk. 12:48.

9. She is speaking of herself. See *Spir. Test.*, 46.

10. She returns to the theme taken up in no. 1.

11. Allusion to 2 Co. 12:2–4.

12. Concerning the distinction between the soul and the spirit, see VII, chap. 1, no. 11; *Spir. Test.*, 59, no. 11; 25, no. 1; *Life*, chap. 20, no. 14.

13. Nb. 13:18–27.

14. She continues to use the symbolic language (jewels and meetings) introduced in V, chap. 4, no. 3.

15. See nos. 1–5; chap. 4, nos. 1–2.

Chapter 6

1. Ex. 14:21–22; Jos. 3:13–17.

2. Allusion to Gn. 8:8–9, used again in VII, chap. 3. no. 13.

NOTES

3. In chap. 11.

4. "Lord, if I am still necessary to your people I don't refuse to live; may Your will be done." See the liturgical office for Saint Martin in the Roman Breviary.

5. Lk. 15:22–32.

6. She tells about Saint Peter of Alcántara's manner of life in *Life*, chap. 27, nos. 16–20; chap. 30, nos. 2–7.

Chapter 7

1. She is referring to herself. See *Life*, chap. 26, no. 2; chap. 34, no. 10; *Spir. Test.*, 1, no. 26; 48, no. 1; 59, no. 12.

2. In *Life*, chap. 22.

3. In *Life*, chap. 22, nos. 2–3.

4. The person to whom Teresa refers is unknown. The passage is intentionally somewhat enigmatic.

5. See Jn. 8:12; 14:6, 9.

6. 1 K. 18:30–39.

7. In VI, chap. 11, no. 8.

8. In VII, chap. 2, nos. 3, 9, 10; chap. 3, nos. 8, 10, 11; chap. 4, nos. 1–2.

9. At the end of no. 7.

10. Sg. 3:1–3.

11. See *The Confessions of St. Augustine*, X, chap. 6, nos. 9–10.

12. In no. 7.

13. In nos. 9–10.

14. In chap. 4, nos. 2, 9; *Life*, chap. 22, no. 10.

15. Jn. 16:7.

Chapter 8

1. This person is Teresa herself. See *Life*, chap. 27, nos. 2–5.

2. In chap. 3.

3. See *Life*, chap. 27, no. 3.

4. See *Life*, chap. 25, no. 18; *Spir. Test.*, 22, no. 1; 31; 48; 58, no. 16; *Int. Castle*, VI, chap. 3, no. 5.

5. In chap. 6, nos. 1–6.

6. The series of favors mentioned in the preceding chapters.

7. In nos. 3–5.

8. In no. 3.

9. Allusion to 1 Co. 10:13. See chap. 3, no. 17. She also refers to this statement of Saint Paul in her *Life*, chap. 23, no. 15.

10. In no. 1.

11. She is alluding probably to interventions of the Spanish Inquisition.

Chapter 9

1. In chap. 8; the intellectual visions.

2. In nos. 2–3.

3. A popular belief in Teresa's time was that certain stones had curative powers; for example, the bezoar.

4. Teresa is referring to herself. See *Life*, chap. 28, especially no. 4; *Spir.

Test., 58, no. 15, in which she states that "she never saw anything with her bodily eyes."

5. Mt. 25:41.

6. Ac. 9:3–4.

7. In chap. 8, no. 3.

8. In chap. 8, nos. 4, 8.

9. She is referring to Fr. Domingo Bañez, O.P. See her *Book of Foundations*, chap. 8, no. 3.

10. See *Life*, chap. 25, nos. 5–6.

11. In *Foundations*, chap. 8, no. 3.

12. This person is herself. See *Life*, chap. 29, nos. 5–6.

13. See 1 S. 15:10–11.

14. She is speaking of herself. The man could have been Saint John of the Cross, who was confessor at the monastery of the Incarnation in Avila when Saint Teresa was prioress there from 1571–1574.

15. In no. 16; IV, chap. 2, no. 9.

Chapter 10

1. See *Life*, chap. 40, no. 9.

2. For the origin of this comparison see *Life*, chap. 40, no. 10.

3. Allusion to Mt. 6:12, 15; Lk. 6:37.

4. Teresa gives a personal account of this experience in *Life*, chap. 40, nos. 1–4.

5. Ps. 116:11.

6. Jn. 18:36–38.

7. In nos. 2 and 5.

Chapter 11

1. The person is herself. See chap. 10, nos. 2–5.

2. In chap. 2, no. 1; chap. 6, no. 6; chap. 8, no. 4.

3. Teresa describes an equivalent experience of hers that took place at Salamanca in 1571. See *Spir. Test.*, 12, nos. 1–5.

4. In no. 2.

5. She is speaking of herself. See *Spir. Test.*, 59, no. 14; *Life*, chap. 20, nos. 12–13.

6. Jn. 4:7–14.

7. In nos. 2 and 4.

8. See chap. 4.

9. Mt. 20:22.

10. Lk. 7:40–48.

THE SEVENTH DWELLING PLACES

Chapter 1

1. In I, chap. 2, nos. 1–3.

2. In no. 3.

3. In the fifth dwelling place.

4. Ac. 9:8.

NOTES

5. Jn. 14:23. For another description of this grace see *Spir. Test.*, 13.

6. Through an intellectual vision; see no. 6.

7. In VI, chap. 3, nos. 3 and 17; chap. 6, no. 6; chap. 7, no. 3; chap. 8, nos. 3–4.

8. Teresa is referring to herself.

9. Lk. 10:40.

10. In VI, chap. 5, nos. 1 and 9.

Chapter 2

1. See her corresponding account in *Spir. Test.*, 31.

2. The one referred to in chap. 1, nos. 6–7.

3. Teresa first wrote "between two who have consummated marriage." She then changed it to the present reading.

4. In V, chap. 4, no. 3.

5. See no. 1; *Spir. Test.*, 31.

6. See VI, chap. 8.

7. Jn. 20:19–21. See V, chap. 1, no. 12.

8. Again she changed what she had previously written, "those who have consummated marriage," to the present reading.

9. 1 Co. 6:17. This text from Saint Paul and the application were written between the lines. Teresa first wrote and then crossed out: ". . . we are made one spirit with God if we love Him; he doesn't say that we are joined with Him . . . but are made one spirit with Him."

10. Ph. 1:21. Teresa cited the passage in her own form of Latin: *Mi bivere Cristus es mori lucrum.*

11. See V, chap. 3, note 1.

12. In no. 4.

13. Jn. 20:19–21.

14. Lk. 7:50.

15. Jn. 17:21.

16. Jn. 17:20, 23.

17. Allusion to Lk. 21:33.

18. In no. 3.

19. In chap. 3, nos. 3 and 6; chap. 4, no. 2.

20. Probably in V, chap. 2, nos. 7–11.

21. In no. 4; see also IV, chap. 2.

22. In no. 9.

Chapter 3

1. Teresa numbers only the first two effects; the others are present in the midst of a series of digressions and commentary. Here is a list of these effects: (1) forgetfulness of self (in no. 2); (2) desire to suffer (no. 4); (3) deep interior joy in persecution (no. 5); (4) desire to serve (no. 6); (5) great detachment (no. 8); (6) no fear of the devil's deceits (no. 10); and finally a recapitulation in no. 13.

2. In chap. 2, nos. 4–5.

3. An allusion to the grace of spiritual marriage. See chap. 2, no. 1; *Spir. Test.*, 31.

4. She is referring to the experiences spoken of in the sixth dwelling place; see particularly chap. 11.

5. In VI, chap. 2.

6. In VI, chap. 2, no. 1; chap. 11, no. 2.

7. Ac. 9:6.

8. In no. 8.

9. In chap. 2, nos. 3 and 10.

10. In chap. 2, nos. 5–6 and 9.

11. 1 K. 6:7.

12. In Teresa's terminology "not lost" is the equivalent of not being enraptured. In this dwelling place the faculties remain in amazement but not ecstatically suspended.

13. Allusion to Sg. 1:2; there follows a series of biblical allusions to: Ps. 42:2; Rv. 21:3; Gn. 8:8–12.

14. Allusion to Lk. 18:13.

15. In no. 6.

Chapter 4

1. In chap. 3, nos. 2–10;

2. 1 K. 11. See III, chap. 1, nos. 1–4.

3. Ps. 112:1.

4. In VI, chap. 9, nos. 16–17; see also chap. 1, no. 7.

5. Allusion to 1 Th. 2:9.

6. This *quo vadis* legend appeared in the Carmelite breviary, used in the time of Saint Teresa, on the feast of Saint Peter (June 29).

7. In V, chap. 3, no. 11.

8. There is a Teresian proverb that reads in Spanish: *La virtud se ha de ver no en los rincones sino en medio de las ocasiones.* It might go like this in English: "Look for virtue not in corners away from the din but right amidst the occasions of sin." See *Foundations*, chap. 5, no. 15.

9. In I, chap. 2, nos. 8–9, 11, and 13.

10. In chap. 3, nos. 3, 5–8.

11. Ps. 18:26.

12. Allusion to Sg. 2:4.

13. Allusion to 1 K. 19:10. The shield of the Carmelite order takes as its motto the prophet Elijah's words: *Zelo zelatus sum pro Domino Deo exercituum.*

14. Lk. 10:38–42.

15. Allusion to Lk. 7:37–38.

16. See *Way of Perfection*, chaps. 1–3; *Meditations*, chap. 7.

17. In III, chap. 2, no. 13.

EPILOGUE

1. This epilogue was sent in the form of a letter along with the original manuscript to the Discalced Carmelite nuns in Seville.

2. In Prologue, no. 1.

3. Allusion to Gn. 1:26. See I, chap. 1, no. 1.

NOTES

4. That is, November 29, 1577, close to six months after she had begun writing on June 2 of that same year. See Prologue, no. 3.

SELECTED BIBLIOGRAPHY

BIBLIOGRAPHIES

Curzon, Henri de. *Bibliographie Thérèsienne. Ouvrages Français et Étrangers sur Sainte Thérèse et sur Ses Oeuvres.* Bibliographie critique. Paris: Librarie des S-P., 1902.
Obras Completas de Santa Teresa de Jesús. Edited by Efrén De La Madre De Dios, Otilio Del Niño Jesús, and Otger Steggink. 3 vols. Madrid: Biblioteca De Autores Cristianos, 1951–1959. Vol. 1: "Bibliografiá Teresiana," by Otilio Del Niño Jesús (Rodriguez), 1951, pp. 25–127.
Ramge, Sebastian. "A Teresian Bibliography." *An Introduction to the Writings of St. Teresa.* Chicago: Henry Regnery Co., 1963, pp. 124–135.
Simeón de La Sgda Familia. *Bibliographia Operum S. Teresiae A Jesus Typis Editorum* (1583–1967). Rome: Edizione Del *Teresianum,* 1969. "Bibliographia Carmeli Teresiani." *Archivum Bibliographicum Carmelitanum.* Rome: Edizioni Del Teresianum, 1956– . This bibliography, which includes all recent Teresian publications, appears annually.
Tomás de la Cruz and Castellano, Jesús. "Santa Teresa De Jesús. Actualidad. Panorama Editorial. Estudios Biográficos. Estudios Doctrinales." *Ephemerides Carmeliticae* 19 (1968): 9–44.

CRITICAL EDITIONS AND ENGLISH TRANSLATIONS

Obras de Santa Teresa de Jesús. Edited and annotated by Silverio De Santa Teresa. Vols. 1–9: *Biblioteca Mística Carmelitana.* Burgos: El Monte Carmelo, 1915–1924.
Obras Completas de Santa Teresa de Jesús. New revision of the original text with critical notes by Efrén de la Madre De Dios, Otilio Del Niño Jesús, and Otger Steggink. 3 vols. Madrid: Biblioteca De Autores Cristianos, 1951–1959.
Obras de Santa Teresa de Jesús. Text revised and annotated by Tomás de la Cruz. Burgos: El Monte Carmelo, 1971.
The Complete Works of St. Teresa of Jesus. Translated and edited by E. Allison Peers. New York: Sheed and Ward, 1946.
The Collected Works of St. Teresa of Avila. Translated by Kieran Kavanaugh and Otilio Rodriguez. Vol. 1: *The Book of Her Life, Spiritual Testimonies, Solilo-*

BIBLIOGRAPHY

quies. Washington, D.C.: ICS Publications, 1976. Vol. 2: *The Way of Perfection, Meditations on The Song of Songs, The Interior Castle*. Washington, D.C.: ICS Publications, in press.

BIOGRAPHICAL STUDIES

Auclair, M. *Teresa of Avila*. Translated by Kathleen Pond. New York: Pantheon Books, Inc., 1953.

Efrén de la Madre De Dios and Otger Steggink. *Tiempo Y Vida De Santa Teresa*. Madrid: Biblioteca De Autores Cristianos, 1977.

Papasogli, Giorgio. *St. Teresa of Avila*. Translated by G. Anzilotti. New York: Society of St. Paul, 1958.

Silverio De Santa Teresa, ed. *Biblioteca Mística Carmelitana*. 20 vols. Burgos: El Monte Carmelo, 1915–1935. Volumes 18–20: *Procesos De Beatificación Y Canonización De Santa Teresa De Jesús*, 1934–1935.

_____. *Vida de Santa Teresa de Jesús*. 5 vols. Burgos: El Monte Carmelo, 1935–1937.

Walsh, William T. *Saint Teresa of Avila*. Milwaukee: Bruce, 1943.

STUDIES

Barrientos, Alberto, ed. *Introducción a la Lectura de Santa Teresa*. Madrid: Editorial De Espiritualidad, 1978.

Blas De Jesús. *Ascética Teresiana: Estudio Positivo de la Doctrina Ascética en Santa Teresa de Jesús*. Burgos: El Monte Carmelo, 1960.

Castro, Secundino. *Cristología Teresiana*. Madrid: Editorial De Espiritualidad, 1978.

Deneuville, Dominique. *Sainte Thérèse d'Avila et la femme*. Preface de P. Blanchard. Lyon-Paris: Éditions du Chalet, 1964.

Di Rienzo, Cirilo. *La Direzione Spirituale Negli Scritti Di St. Teresa d'Avila*. Rome: Teresianum, 1965.

Efrén De La Madre De Dios. *Santa Teresa Por Dentro*. Madrid: Editorial De Espiritualidad, 1973.

_____. *Beas Y Santa Teresa*. Madrid: Editorial De Espiritualidad, 1975.

_____. *La Herencia Teresiana*. Madrid: Editorial De Espiritualidad, 1975.

Etchegoyen, Gaston. *L'Amour Divin. Essai sur les Sources de Sainte Thérèse*. Bordeaux-Paris: Féret et Fils, 1923.

Gabriel De Santa Maria Magdalena. *Saint Teresa of Jesus: Mistress of the Spiritual Life*. Translated by a Benedictine of Stanbrook Abbey. Cork: The Mercier Press, 1949.

García Ordás, Angel María. *La Persona Divina en la Espiritualidad de Santa Teresa*. Rome: Teresianum, 1967.

Hoornaert, Rodolphe. *Sainte Thérèse, Écrivain: Son Milieu, Ses Facultés, Son Oeuvre*. Paris: Desclée de Brouwer, 1922.

Istituto Di Spiritualitá. *Santa Teresa Maestra di Orazione*. Rome: Teresianum, 1963.

BIBLIOGRAPHY

Instituto Di Spiritualitá. *Santa Teresa Maestra di Orazione*. Rome: Teresianum, 1963.

Lepee, Marcel. *Sainte Thérèse d'Avila: Le Réalisme Chrétien*. Paris: Desclée de Brouwer, 1947.

———. *Sainte Thérèse Mystique: Une Divine Amitié*. Brussels: Desclée de Brouwer, 1951.

Llamas Martínez, Enrique. *Santa Teresa de Jesús y la Inquisición Española*. Madrid: C.S.I.C., 1972.

Luis De S. José. *Concordancias de las Obras y Escritos de Santa Teresa de Jesús*. Burgos: El Monte Carmelo, 1965.

Marie-Eugène de l'Enfant Jésus. *I Want To See God*. Translated by Sister M. Verda Clare. Chicago: Fides, 1953.

———. *I Am a Daughter of the Church*. Translated by Sister M. Verda Clare. Chicago: Fides, 1955.

Nazario De Santa Teresa. *La Psicología De Santa Teresa: Posturas-Feminismo-Elegancia*. Madrid: Gráficas Sebastián, 1950.

Pablo Maroto, Daniel de. *Dinámica De La Oración: Acercamiento del Orante Moderno a Santa Teresa de Jesús*. Madrid: Editorial De Espiritualidad, 1973.

Peers, E. Allison. *Handbook to the Life and Times of St. Teresa and St. John of the Cross*. London: Burns Oates, 1954.

Ramge, Sebastian. *An Introduction to the Writings of St. Teresa*. Chicago: Henry Regnery Company, 1963.

Renault, Emmanuel. *Ste. Thérèse d'Avila Et L'Expérience Mystique*. Paris: Seuil, 1970.

———. "La Manière D'Oraison Thérèsienne." In *(Revue d'Histoire de la Spirituallité (Revue D'Ascétique et de Mystique)* 51 (1975): 43–72.

Rodriguez, Otilio. *The Teresian Gospel. An Introduction to a Fruitful Reading of the Way of Perfection*. Darlington, England: Darlington Carmel, 1974.

———. *Leyenda Aurea Teresiana*. Madrid: Editorial De Espiritualidad, 1970.

Sancta Theresia a Jesus, Doctor Ecclesiae: Historia, Doctrina, Documenta. Rome: Teresianum, 1970.

Steggink, Otger. *Experiencia y Realismo en Santa Teresa y San Juan de la Cruz*. Madrid: Editorial De Espiritualidad, 1974.

Teresa's Doctorate. Spiritual Life 16 (Winter 1970): 210–263.

Thomas, Fr., and Gabriel, Fr. *St. Teresa of Avila. Studies in Her Life, Doctrine and Times*. Westminster, Md.: The Newman Press, 1963.

Tomás De La Cruz (Alvarez). "Santa Teresa De Jesús Contemplativa." *Ephemerides Carmelitica* 13 (1962): 9–62. "La Oración Camino A Dios: El Pensamiento De Santa Teresa." *Ephemerides Carmeliticae* 21 (1970): 115–168.

Trueman Dicken, E. W., *The Crucible of Love*. New York: Sheed and Ward, 1963.

Index to Introduction

Ahumada, Doña Beatriz de, 1.
Alba, Duchess of, 6.
Alba, Duke of, 5.
Alonso de Madrid, 9.
Andalusia, 17.
Antonio de Jesus, Father, 6.
Arevalo, 20.
Asceticism, 13, 22.
Augustine, St., *Confessions of*, 3, 8.
Augustine, pseudo-*Meditationes*, 8;
  Soliloquys, 8.
Avila, 1, 2, 4, 12, 18, 29; Bishop of, 3.
Ayala, Doña Constancia de, 29.

Báñez, Domingo, 9.
Barrón, Fr. Vicente, 7.
Becedas, 2.
Bernabé de Palma, 9.
Bernardino de Laredo, 9.
Bible, 9.
Borgia, Francis, 9.
Burgos, 6.

Capeda, Don Alonso Sanchez de, 1,
  2.
Capeda, Lorenzo de, 5.
Carmelites, 2, 15, 29; general of, 4,
  17; and reform, 17; rule of, 4, 9,
  11.
Cassian, *Collationes of*, 8.
Castile, 17.
Christ, as Bridegroom, 13, 25, 26; di-
  vinity of, 26, 27; faith of, 4; and
  Father, 13; and friendship, 13;

grace of, 22; humanity of, 7, 8, 26,
  27, 28; imitation of, 8, 29; life in,
  28; new life in, 25; person of, 14,
  27; and prayer, 11, 15; presence
  of, 7; Risen, 7; trust in, 3; union
  with, 28; vision of, 7, 8; as Word,
  28.
Church, contemplative life in, 4;
  Doctor of, 1, 9; Fathers of, 8; and
  mission, 4; and mysticism, 1; service to, 4, 11.
Contemplation, life of, 4, 12; and
  prayer, 11.
Conversion, 3, 13, 27.

David, 13.
Divinity, mysteries of, 26, 27; and
  prayer, 7; and soul, 8.
Dominicians, 3, 7, 9.

Flos Sanctorum, 8.
Franciscans, 2.

God, desire for, 25; dwelling in, 8,
  25; favors of, 11; friendship of, 13;
  as King of Glory, 20, 22; knowledge of, 25, 26; mercy of, 12, 13,
  18; offending of, 22, 24; omnipresence of, 6; pleasing of, 24;
  presence of, 6, 7, 14, 21, 24; return to, 13; service of, 13, 26; and
  soul, 1, 8, 11, 13, 14, 15; suffering
  for, 6; union with, 12, 13, 14, 21,

217

Index to Text

210; 119:32, 203, 204; 119:137, 203; 127:1, 200.

120, 173, 176, 180, 181; pain in, 116, 132, 138, 168, 169, 181, 183; peace of, 47, 53, 59, 61, 71, 72, 74, 88, 94, 98, 103, 117, 120, 121, 125, 137, 140, 141, 142, 152, 158, 159, 180–187; persecuted, 110, 111, 138, 155, 171, 183; returns to itself, 130, 132; and sin, 39, 40, 45; and spirit, 172–177, 182; strength of, 45, 46, 86, 87, 110, 170, 171, 191, 192; superior part of, 71, 119, 120, 136, 174; suspended, 126–133, 139, 158, 163; testing of, 59, 83, 107, 120; trials of, 108–115, 117, 118, 126, 129, 137, 139, 149, 161, 163, 170, 176, 182–186, 190, 193; transformation of, 93, 94; ungratefulness of, 143, 144, 148.

Spirit, of light, 125; of truth, 125.

Suffering, of Christ, 93, 96, 135, 148, 149, 184, 189; and favors of God, 114; for God, 60, 72, 97, 106, 118, 139; in hell, 112; interior, 111; of soul, 112, 113, 114, 115, 116, 120, 121, 126, 127, 131, 132, 135, 138, 140, 143–150, 161, 166, 167, 168, 169, 173, 182, 183, 184, 188, 191, 192; testing by, 65.

Supernatural, experience, 67, 162; favors, 74, 98, 130; and prayer, 77, 84, 142, 148.

Temptations, 47, 51, 54, 58, 68, 110, 120, 154, 159, 173, 182.

1 Thessalonians, 2:9, 212.

Thomas, Saint, 56.

Trinity, 175.

Union, cf. also Will; effects of, 98; nature of, 91; prayer of, 85–97, 99, 101, 102–107, 174, 185; of soul and God, 36, 71, 85, 87, 88, 89, 90, 92, 93, 96, 97, 98, 100, 101, 102, 103, 109, 121, 129, 138, 174, 175, 177–182, 185, 186, 191; of soul and Lord, 127; of spiritual marriage, 177–182, 190.

Usrula, Saint, 104.

Vanity, 50, 51.

Virtue, acknowledgment of, 61; false, 101; growth in, 51, 82, 150, 162; practice of, 43, 44, 60, 62, 64, 86, 97, 106, 141, 191; source of, 40.

Visions, 89; discernment of, 158, 159, 163; effects of, 150–155, 158, 159, 161, 162, 163–165, 189; imaginative, 128, 130, 136, 151, 156–163, 175, 177, 178; intellectual, 123, 128, 130, 136, 150–155, 163, 175, 178; nature of, 128; and seventh dwelling, 178; spiritual, 178.

Will, awakened, 70, 146, 147; determination of, 59, 72, 125, 162, 165, 185, 191; divine, 61; of God, 52, 56, 62, 72, 77, 80, 95, 96, 97, 98, 100, 103, 105, 131, 162, 165, 168, 183; good, 78; and love, 50, 132; of man united to God's, 76, 82, 98, 99, 102, 140, 161; and recollection, 81; and self, 43, 52, 62, 93, 98; surrender of, 62, 90, 95, 96.

Wisdom, 75, 89, 92, 159.

Wisdom, 16:20, 201.

Works, of charity, 114, 194; in Christ's service, 54, 101, 107; good, 40, 45, 68, 80, 107, 190; in grace, 40, 41; of the intellect, 81, 146; interior, 80; of man, 59, 135; practice of, 64, 141; of the spirit, 79; of will, 146.

World, absorption in, 44, 45, 50; and castle, 38, 49, 50; detachment from, 57, 59, 82, 86, 93, 95, 105, 142; died to, 86, 93; malice of, 132.

Zebedee, sons of, 170.